MISSING BOUNDARIES

Refugees, Migrants, Stateless and Internally Displaced Persons in South Asia

MISSING BOUNDARIES

Refugees, Migrants, Stateless and Internally Displaced Persons in South Asia

Edited by

P.R. CHARI
MALLIKA JOSEPH
SUBA CHANDRAN

MANOHAR
2003

First published 2003

ISBN 81-7304-503-8

Published by
Ajay Kumar Jain for
Manohar Publishers & Distributors
4753/23 Ansari Road, Daryaganj
New Delhi 110002

Printed at
Lordson Publishers Pvt Ltd
Delhi 110007

Contents

Introduction

Barring the Maldives, all other countries in South Asia have suffered the ravages from movements, both between and within states, of population over the last five and a half decades. These population flows include refugees, economic migrants, Stateless persons and Internally Displaced Persons (IDPs). South Asia has also witnessed some of the largest population flows in the post World War period. The partition of British India in 1947 resulted in the brutal uprooting of nearly 15 million people in the subcontinent. During the liberation war of Bangladesh, some 10 million refugees from the erstwhile East Pakistan fled to India. In truth, the countries of South Asia have often been both the principal recipients and the originating sources for refugees. According to the UN High Commissioner for Refugees (UNHCR), the refugees in South Asia constitute roughly 14 per cent of the total world refugee population. No accurate figures are available to estimate the number of IDPs in the region, but it is evident that an incessant movement of the rural population to urban centres in search of employment is proceeding, exacerbating the problems of unplanned urbanization.

Within the subcontinent, Pakistan hosts the largest number of 1.2 million refugees, mainly Afghans, escaping from the unsettled conditions in neighbouring Afghanistan, but including some 900 from Somalia, 500 from Iran and 500 from Iraq. This estimate was made before the September 11 attacks and its cascading effects that led to the War on Terrorism being launched against Afghanistan. A further uprooting of the local population took place, and it is difficult to estimate the number of people who might have returned to Afghanistan after these operations ceased, and to discover how many might have dispersed throughout Pakistan.

In the aggregate, however, India remains the principal country hosting refugees from all over South Asia and its adjoining regions. According to UNHCR figures, at the beginning of 2000, there were

2,92,000 refugees in India of whom 1,10,000 were from Tibet; 42,000 from Myanmar; 14,500 from Afghanistan; 15,000 from Bhutan and 1,10,000 from Sri Lanka. Besides, India had an estimated 5,07,000 internally displaced persons, which included 3, 50,000 Kashmiris, and more than 1,57,000 belonging to the states of Northeast India. In Nepal, there are more than 1,30,000 refugees, of whom 1,10,000 are Bhutanese and 20,000 are Tibetans. Bangladesh has 53,000 refugees, mostly from Myanmar. It also has 2,38,000 'Biharis', who are 'stateless' persons. In Sri Lanka, there is no population classifiable as refugees, but there are 6,89,000 internally displaced persons who are victims of the two-decade long ethnic strife in that country.

Three factors are responsible for the refugee influx in the region: Firstly, the breakdown of colonial rule leading to adverse repercussions, but resulting in the continuance of colonial legacies in the new nations formed; the end of colonial rule and the partition of British India, for instance, led to large scale migration which has continued from East Bengal/ Bangladesh into India to the present day. Secondly, the problems of nation and state building resulted in political, ethnic, religious and economic conditions being engendered that forced people to migrate outside their countries of origin as apparent from the movement of Bangladeshi and Sri Lankan refugees to India, Bhutanese refugees to Nepal and Nepalese/ Bangladeshi economic migrants to India. Thirdly, political developments in neighboring regions have resulted in large numbers of refugees entering the South Asian countries; the movement of Afghan refugees into Pakistan and Rohingyas into Bangladesh are the direct consequence of continuing political instability in countries adjoining South Asia.

Despite their huge influx, large numbers of these refugees, including those from Myanmar and Afghanistan, have been absorbed within the region. Three reasons can be ascribed for this infinite capacity of the region to absorb refugees and migrants: Firstly, cultural and linguistic affinities that cut across national frontiers in South Asia and have traditionally integrated the region. The Nepali speaking Lhotsampa refugees from Bhutan, Pathan refugees from Afghanistan, and Tamil refugees from Sri Lanka have been easily absorbed in other countries within the region due to these factors. Secondly, the political and material support provided by the host countries to struggles by ethnic groups within their neighbours for various historical, cultural and real politik reasons, creates the milieu for refugees from these countries to settle within the region, as in the case of India-supported Sri Lankan refugees in South India and Afghan refugees within Pakistan. Thirdly, the physical proximity of the host countries to their erstwhile homes in Myanmar, Afghanistan, Tibet, Bhutan, Bangladesh or Sri Lanka facilitates the movement of refugees into the South Asian region.

Should they be absorbed, but not assimilated, refugees are seen to constitute a threat to the social, economic and political fabric of the host country, simultaneously jeopardizing its security. The pervasiveness and seriousness of this internal threat naturally depends on the numbers of these refugees and their demands on the one hand, and the size, nature and capabilities of the host country on the other. These are general propositions. More specifically, the question of migration assumes importance in the South Asian region for various related reasons. Firstly, the causes underlying the displacement – political instability, armed conflict, lack of resources and so on in the region and its immediate neighborhood have not declined but are, in fact, increasing. Secondly, none of the countries in South Asia has signed any major international convention or treaty relating to refugees; nor have they enacted any national legislation or established a regional framework to deal with these issues of displacement. Hence, a refugee regime, either at the national or regional level, is not available to regulate this phenomenon, nor does one seem likely in the foreseeable future. Thirdly, the security threats posed by refugees and internally displaced persons seem destined to enlarge in future taking into account the lack of resources, environmental decay in parts of South Asia and poor governance prevalent in the region.

A comprehensive study focusing on the several dimensions of displacement in South Asia including refugees, migrants, stateless persons and Internally Displaced Persons (IDPs) was decided to be undertaken by the Institute of Peace and Conflict Studies (IPCS) by inviting scholars to bring under focus various aspects of these problems and issues. A two-day conference was organized with participation from India, Bangladesh, Sri Lanka and Nepal in March 2002. Eleven papers were presented in this conference and discussed in separate seminars. The paper writers were requested to review their papers in the light of these presentations; thereafter they were collated and have been published in this volume. We hope, thereby, to illumine an important subject that has been ignored for too long, more largely out of neglect rather than a phasing of priorities.

This study was possible by a grant generously made available by the Japan Foundation, Asia Centre. We are grateful to them for their support to this effort that has implications for region security but also, at one remove, for peace and stability in the international system.

The conference was inaugurated by Justice Verma, Chairman of the National Human Rights Commission. His keynote address highlighted the legitimate concerns of refugees and other classes of displaced people in South Asia; it set the scene for the deliberations in the conference. The keynote address has been included in this publication in the place of a foreword to contextualize the debate on displaced populations by highlighting the plight of the refugees, and identifying the strands of domestic law that can be interpreted to fill the lacunae created by the absence of appropriate refugee laws.

The first chapter by P.R. Chari flags the pertinent issues encompassing the debate on refugees in the South Asian context. In broad strokes, he has sought to answer some of the key questions that frame the relevant issues involved: Who are refugees? How are migrants different from internally displaced persons? What are the sources for the originating of refugee flows within and into the region? Why are the statistics in regard to their numbers inaccurate? What are the laws governing this displaced population? Do migrants constitute a threat to security? The overview provided defines the contours of this debate, which are then dwelt upon in detail in the succeeding chapters.

V. Suryanarayanan, in the second chapter, focuses on Sri Lankan refugees and traces the origins of this problem, which has resulted in Sri Lanka becoming an "Island of Refugees." Replete with statistics and details of the continuous refugee flows of Sri Lankan Tamils into India, this chapter analyses the different categories of Sri Lankan Tamil refugees who enter India but also addresses the larger issues relating to their repatriation.

The next chapter by Tapan Bose offers useful insights into the deplorable living conditions of the Bhutanese refugees who are stranded in Nepal. An irritant in Nepal-Bhutan relations, the refugee issue remains immobile and stuck in a political quagmire. The author, after providing an overview of the problem and highlighting the humanitarian concerns embedded in this situation, makes a strong case for third party intervention to persuade Bhutan to take back these Lhotsampa refugees.

The paper presented by C.R. Abrar provides a broad overview of the complexities of the decade-old Rohingya refugee problem. Apart from tracing the history of these refugee flows into Bangladesh, he also highlights the measures adopted by the government to manage the refugee problem. Like the others, Abrar highlights the need for Bangladesh to enact national refugee legislation to remove current ambiguities about their rights and relief entitlements.

T. Ananthachari addresses the concerns raised by all the authors—the absence of national legislation for refugees. After passing under review the various migrant groups that have sought refuge in India over the last five decades, he balances the refugee-related security challenges with their claims to humanitarian assistance and argues for enacting unambiguous national refugee legislation.

In chapter six, D.R. Kaarthikeyan assesses the role of various human rights organizations in India, particularly the National Human Rights Commission (NHRC) for addressing the concerns of refugees. In the absence of appropriate legislation, Kaarthikeyan highlights the challenges faced by the NHRC for assuring basic minimum living standards to the refugees and, in this regard, highlights the role played by the judiciary to protect refugees.

Incessant clashes along the India-Bangladesh border; rise of militancy in India's north-east; Bangladesh's constant denial that its nationals have found refuge in India are issues that are part of the informed debates that proceed on the situation relating to migration from Bangladesh into India. In his paper, Wasbir Hussain takes the debate forward by providing relevant statistics and analyzing the suggestions made for ameliorating this situation.

Suba Chandran addresses a central question that underlies most debates on this subject: do refugees truly constitute a security threat? He examines the threat perceived at three levels – social, economic and political, and comes to the conclusion that refugees do impinge on the security of the state. But, to what extent does this happen and under what conditions can the situation be exacerbated? Can refugees alone be blamed for the parlous state of affairs in the undeveloped pockets of the country in which they take refuge?

In the next chapter, Zarin Ahmad explores the vexed issue of Bihari Muslims in Bangladesh and addresses the difficulty in categorizing them as refugees. With their recognition in dispute, no solution to their problems is regrettably in sight, as concluded in this narrative.

Senanayake, in chapter ten, portrays the predicament of those who could not settle and therefore get displaced from one settlement to another due to the ongoing conflict in Sri Lanka. She highlights the challenges that have attended the resettlement and rehabilitation programs undertaken by various national and international institutions.

What role does the UN body mandated to handle this issue—the UNHCR—play in meeting the aspirations of the various categories of migrants discussed in this volume? The last chapter by Sumbul Rizvi provides an insight into UNHCR's role in the region, making specific references to the refugee groups detailed in the previous chapters, and analyses the solutions available to South Asian countries at the national and regional levels.

The IPCS has been seeking to provide an alternate discourse on security. Urging that the non-traditional sources of insecurity are the cornerstone of human insecurity, the IPCS has sought to focus attention on the non-military threats to security including Drug Trafficking, Terrorism, Refugees, Organized Crime, Governance and Environmental Issues. The current volume highlighting the issues of migration and displacement is a small step in that direction.

May 2003 EDITORS

Keynote Address

JUSTICE J.S. VERMA

Thank you Air Chief Marshal Mehra, Mr Chari, Lt Gen Vohra, Maj Gen Krishna, Mr Kaarthikeyan and distinguished ladies and gentlemen.

I have been recently involved in something that is a matter of direct concern to the theme of this exercise which you are performing, and in that sense, I would say it is very timely. Refugees and all other displaced persons, though not strictly falling within the definition of 'refugees', face similar problems. However, the problems in a particular category might be more acute and pressing than those in other categories. And, that is because of the changing dynamics of displacement, particularly forced displacement, which brings catastrophe upon certain individuals or groups. This changing dynamics of displacement is also the result of the changing nature of conflict.

Earlier, armed conflicts between nations and serious political situations within nations triggered displacement and forced people to seek refugee elsewhere. Now, the force may not always be direct; it may even be invidious or indirect. However, the result is the same: certain persons, because of certain compulsions, are forced to leave their hearths and homes and are displaced.

In India, we face a problem not merely because of large numbers of refugees coming from our neighbouring countries through long porous borders, but also because the distinction between those who have come from across the border and those living within is getting obliterated. This has caused several hardships, not only to those displaced, but also to our country, and has been an issue of concern to the National Human Rights Commission and the Supreme Court.

The track record of our country, comparatively, is much better, if I may say so, as we are more liberal in accepting displaced persons from even across borders. The Supreme Court of India has gone to the extent of holding that Article 14 (Right to Equality) and Article 21 (Right to Life and Dignity) apply equally to every one—to citizens and non-citizens—residing within the territory of India. It has further held that they can even resort to constitutional remedies under Article 32 and approach the Supreme Court directly for grant of relief. Within the ambit of these two Articles, you can bring in everything that is necessary for the maintenance of full dignity for an individual and ensure non-discrimination; Right to Life and Dignity and non-discrimination are sacrosanct and universally acknowledged human rights. These are guaranteed in India even without India being a party to the 1951 Covenant or 1967 Protocol. None of the South Asian countries, probably with the exception of Bangladesh, is signatory to these international instruments.

Another thing that has happened (because of which I am tempted to say that India is more liberal when compared to others) is that the Supreme Court has held in a decision known as the *Visaka* judgement (and I was privileged to write that judgement) that, to the extent that provisions of any international covenant or instrument is not inconsistent with the domestic law, then those provisions can be read into the fundamental guarantees which we have in the Constitution for filling in the gap therein or expanding the scope thereof. This is a step ahead of the Banglaore declaration of more than a decade back, which had said that attempt should be made to interpret domestic legislations consistent with the provisions of international instruments.

Name any provision in any international instrument and I will tell you how it is already within the guarantees of the Constitution of India, and it can be interpreted as such by virtue of the *Visaka* judgement. Through a canon of construction, principles of international covenants that do not become part of domestic law until passed by Parliament as legislation, can now become a part of existing laws; everything that is needed can be read into existing laws by this judicial creativity. This is how, many provisions like Article 3 of the Convention Against Torture, which is significant in the context of refugees, can be read into our existing Article 21.

The net result is, though there is a need for uniform refugee law and right to make that law is only in the hands of the Parliament, existing laws can continue to be interpreted to fill the lacunae; the absence of any refugee law should not thwart efforts of doing all that is necessary to give succor to the refugees. Thus, we not only need to realize that we are far ahead of other countries in this regard, but also highlight it.

The need for a uniform refugee law exists because everyone, particularly those who need the benefit of this law, need to know that such a law exists and thereby there is certainty. When the problems of refugees and those forcibly displaced are similar everywhere, why should there not be a uniform law applicable everywhere, especially when we talk about the world as a global village.

Today, internal displacement in our country as well as others is considerable and the conditions of those displaced are similar. As you are aware, I recently visited Gujarat. I asked to be taken to the camp with the largest number of refugees and was taken to one that had 9,000 people. They were strewn around like goods all over the place. I think, practically everyone I saw had only those clothes that they were wearing and some of them were not even fully clad. After listening to the incidents and their personal experiences that they narrated, I do not think they had suffered any less than those ravaged by a war. Internally displaced persons need immediate attentions and care and the voice of the community must be mobilized and raised for that purpose.

You must be aware of the plight of the Kashmiri Pandits who have suffered for many years. Forget the few affluent ones who might have even benefited (I might sound harsh) benefited by the displacement; but, that is only a handful—most others continue to face a situation that is shocking. The NHRC is monitoring their camps in Jammu even today and the conditions of those who are there, and many others who are not there, is shocking.

The condition of those who have become refugees in their own country is something that should trouble us much more. Unfortunately, people are not even conscious of the extent or magnitude of the problem. If some suffer because of armed conflict then public attention is focused there; and, when they suffer because of invidious ways and are forcibly displaced, people may not even know about it. That is where we need to address ourselves with greater vigour as social sanction is more effective than legal sanction. Public opinion has to be built to deter people who cause internal displacement from doing anything to trigger that process, and if it has already started, prevent them from accelerating it.

These are serious issues and every time I talk of anything in this context, I am reminded of what I saw in those camps. I went to Godhra on 21 March, nearly three weeks after the incident. The town presented a deserted look. A young man, not affiliated to any particular group, said, 'Sir, forget that we are not able to sleep. I have a four-year-old son. With the best of our efforts, we try to put him to sleep. But, he hardly sleeps for a few minutes and then starts shouting, suffering from nightmares and hallucinations.' This only indicates the level of hurt caused, which is not merely physical or externally manifested; it is psychological hurt. If I, an outsider, am unable to forget what I saw, which is only a fringe of what these people had actually experienced, how long will this child, of only four years, take to forget it. Time has come when the trauma experienced by people in these situations needs greater care and attention. When you deal with the refugee problem, please also address measures needed for tackling these issues, which most often go unnoticed and have a long-range effect on not only the person directly affected but also his milieu.

Let me end by thanking you very much for giving me an opportunity to talk to you on an issue, which in the present context is a very important one. I hope that in your deliberations you will address all these issues. At the end of it, if you come out with recommendations that might be helpful in the present context, please let me know, as it would be of great help to us; I hope to be engaged in this exercise and try to do whatever I can. Thank you very much.

1. *Refugees, Migrants and Internally Displaced Persons in South Asia: An Overview*

P.R. CHARI

Recognizing the Problematique

The history of mankind is the history of human movement, mostly voluntary, but as the world became more populated and as open spaces began to shrink, these movements have increasingly become involuntary. People subjected to different forms of insecurity, whether stemming from violence or from lack of freedom or from lack of access to a decent life or as the result of economic deprivation, are leaving their hearths and homes in search of safety and greater opportunities elsewhere. Masses are everywhere in flight. The reasons compelling their movements are various. But this population in transit conforms to the dictionary meaning of refugees, viz., persons seeking shelter from danger or trouble, especially in a foreign country; from religious or political persecution; or from war, earthquakes, and so on.

These population movements can be broadly categorized into those arising as a result of violence, whether incipient or overt, and those arising as a result of environmental causes which encourage migration; this latter category includes factors such as natural calamities, land erosion, ecological degradation, and development processes leading to displacement such as the construction of large dams, industrial facilities, and power installations. Other factors leading to migration are economic motivations such as the desire to seek gainful employment and a better quality of life.

Moreover, the movement of populations need not occur across borders; they are equally traumatic for emigrants if they take place within the borders of a country for all the reasons cited above. Internal displacement ensuing from involuntary movements mimics those movements arising from the compulsion to seek refuge in foreign lands. The complex nature of the issues underlying human displacement has led the United Nations High Commissioner for Refugees (UNHCR), which is chiefly concerned with their problems, to extend its mandate over the years; this now includes 'those displaced within the borders of their own countries, returnees (refugees or internally displaced persons who have returned), asylum seekers (whose formal status has not yet been assessed), stateless persons, war-affected populations and others'.[1] This comprehensive approach has permitted equal emphasis to be placed on the obligations of the homeland countries, from where refugees have fled, and their host nations.

The point that the refugee experience embodies a sense of deep personal loss hardly needs belabouring; this experience has its concomitant influence on the psychology and character of the individuals affected by it. The refugee suffers from the trauma of being uprooted from familiar surroundings, from the pain of being forced to abandon basic worldly possessions such as land and residence, and from the stress caused by the loss or diminution of social and economic status previously enjoyed in the homeland. None of these conditions from the refugee's old life is likely to be available in the different and unfamiliar surroundings of his or her new environment in the place of refuge. Adding to these travails is a sense of anxiety about the uncertain future, since most displaced persons hope to return to the place of their original habitation, if that is at all possible. The empirical evidence also reveals that:

> The experience of exile falls heavily on the most vulnerable members of a population: disabled people, children, the elderly, widows and other refugee women who are attempting to bring up their children without the support of a partner . . . Once they arrive in a country of asylum, men, women and children may all have to assume unfamiliar (and unwelcome) roles and responsibilities.[2]

A gender sensitivity in treating the problems caused by population movements at the operational and academic levels, therefore, is wholly appropriate.

Internally displaced persons (IDPs) often need to relocate temporarily in dangerous places; they have to suffer through this experience since they might have been living in conflict zones. Unlike refugees, for whom international assistance can become available, there is some reluctance among the international humanitarian agencies to provide relief for assisting IDPs. Indeed, the corrective processes to address the causes of displacement lie in the spheres of domestic strife or governance or economic reform, wherein the international community can only play a marginal role to ameliorate the underlying problems. Consequently, there is fair agreement that the plight of IDPs is likely to be much worse than that of refugees. Despite the destabilizing potential of large-scale movements of IDPs, however, there is little international capacity to avert the situations generating this phenomenon. An unusual degree of interest shown by the international community in IDPs could also raise knotty questions regarding national sovereignty, the ethics of humanitarian intervention, and the possible realization that civilian populations which remain in their homes could be suffering from disabilities even worse than those suffered by the IDPs.

At the conceptual level, it is possible to make a distinction between involuntary and forced displacement of people and the voluntary movement of people arising from their own volition; this differentiates the 'refugees' from the 'migrants'. The state and/or powerful communities within a state are generally responsible for creating conditions which compel people to seek refuge across borders. These conditions include internal conflicts arising from a variety of reasons generically reflecting the failure of governance by the state. These conditions may be distinguished from population movements caused by natural calamities and environmental degradation, or those arising as the result of developmental policies pursued by the state, or those population movements motivated by the understandably human desire of people to pursue a better quality of life. Such involuntary and voluntary movements may take place within states as well as between states.

A major part of the migration from rural to urban areas within developing countries and from the developing world to the developed world is driven by the search for gainful employment and a better quality of life. It is difficult to describe such migrants as refugees or internally displaced persons needing state or societal support. States have an understandable desire to distinguish between involuntary and voluntary population movements in their national policies. For their part, developed countries are increasingly making this distinction to prevent the entry of persons seeking gainful employment in the guise of 'asylum seekers'. Over time, practical experience has revealed that all these distinctions are eroding, and it is becoming difficult for states to distinguish between immigrants seeking asylum due to their well-founded fears of persecution in their home countries and those people motivated by economic reasons. According to an idealistic position, 'the emphasis should shift from the factors that created the refugees to defining a refugee by the circumstances that they live in [*sic*], i.e. as stateless and vulnerable to abuse'.[3] This humane formulation must be weighed against the basic principle guiding the international refugee regime, which envisages the temporary protection of the immigrants, although the issue of their permanent residence could also be addressed while appreciating the difficulties that refugees may encounter in returning to their original homes. The immensity of the problem can be gauged by the fact that the UNHCR estimates that 'at the end of the 20th century some 150 million people were living outside the country of their birth, amounting to about 2.5 per cent of the world's population, or one out of every 40 people'.[4]

RESPONSES TO THE REFUGEE/ IDP PROBLEM

According to the UNHCR, the total population with which the organization is concerned was 22.3 million on 31 December1999, of whom 52.4 per cent were refugees and 18.3 per cent were IDPs, in addition to asylum seekers and other categories of people.[5] Asia hosts the largest number of refugees among the continents (41 per cent of the world total), and South Asia has the fourth largest number of this Asian population.[6] It should be emphasized that all statistics relating to refugees, migrants, and IDPs are approximations; accurate estimates are difficult to arrive at due to the obvious difficulty in counting people in transit, especially if, as occurs in South Asia, populations of similar ethnicity inhabit both sides of an international frontier, leading refugees to merge into their extended families across the border. Further, the governments have a widespread tendency to either under- or over-estimate the figures or to keep the numbers of refugees confidential for political reasons. More often than not, such estimates are based on the population living in camps since it is difficult to enumerate people living elsewhere. Consequently, a fair assumption could be made that the number of persons displaced from their normal place of residence is much higher than the figures mentioned in the official statistics. As the former Secretary General of the United Nations, Boutros Boutros-Ghali, observed, 'Refugees and other uprooted people are the products of failure—the failure to resolve conflict and its underlying causes: intolerance, antagonism and poverty. Radical economic and social changes have, in many cases, added to an already volatile mix—providing a fertile breeding ground for the violence and human rights abuses which provoke large-scale population displacements.'[7] The post-Cold War world is distinguished by a general weakening of central authority in developing countries and a rapid growth in conflicts associated with identity crises, fuelled by the easy availability of small arms and funds generated from local resources ranging from diamonds to opium. The profits of war are propelling conflict, which is difficult to constrain or reverse. Hence, the factors conducive to refugee generation are not under control.

What has been the international response to this problem? Recent developments within the international system reveal contradictory trends. Forms of authoritarian governance are on the retreat with the diffusion of egalitarianism throughout the international system and the spread of the democratic idea within nations. The need for good governance is universally recognized. There is also a greater appreciation of the dangers to national security posed by transnational threats such as international terrorism, the proliferation of small arms, landmines, and explosives, although these issues are being addressed in a feeble manner. In the current geopolitical climate, there is greater hostility to the presence of migrating populations, leading to the closure of national borders, the containing of migrant peoples within limited spaces in the host country, and their repatriation at the earliest available opportunity. The reasons for this rising intolerance are largely occasioned by the growing global population and the limitations of space and employment opportunities; this leads to competition between the migrant population and the host population, and the growth of resentments within the local people in the host country.

The problem in defining terms such as 'refugees' and 'internally displaced persons' becomes germane here. The basic international covenant governing refugees is the UN Convention on the Status of Refugees (1951) and its 1967 Protocol. Article 1 of this Convention defines a refugee as:

> Any person who as a result of events occurring before 1 January 1951 and owing to [a] well-founded fear of being persecuted for reasons of race, religion, nationality, membership of a particular social group or political opinion, is outside the country of his nationality and is unable or owing to such fear, is unwilling to avail himself of the protection of the country; or who, not having a nationality and being outside the country of his formal habitual residence as a result of such events, is unable or owing to such fear, is unwilling to return to it.

This definition was expressly designed to identify the refugees in the post-World War II period, but it needed to be extended to deal with continuing refugee movements. This need led to the addition of the 1967 Protocol, which defines refugees as persons:

> . . . who owing to [a] well-founded fear of being persecuted for reasons of race, religion, nationality or political opinion is outside the country of his nationality and is unable or, owing to such fears *or for reasons other than personal convenience,* is unwilling to avail himself of the protection of that country; or who, not having a nationality and being outside the country of his former habitual residence, is unable, or owing to such fear *or for reasons other than personal convenience,* is unwilling to return to it. [The words in italics were added by the 1967 Protocol to the original definition in the 1951 Convention.]

The restricted nature of this formulation militates against conferring refugee status upon a broader section of migrants to reflect current realities. Developed countries, however, have sought to further dilute their international obligations under the Refugee Convention on the plea that most asylum seekers are, in truth, economic migrants wishing to gain entry into their territories.

The position regarding IDPs, whose numbers have greatly increased in the post-Cold War era due to the proliferation of internal conflicts, is even more anomalous. There is no satisfactory definition available to identify them. A working definition evolved by the UN Secretary General in 1992 describes IDPs as 'persons who have been forced to flee their homes suddenly or unexpectedly in large numbers as a result of armed conflict, internal strife, systematic violation of human rights or natural or man-made disasters, and who are within the territory of their own country'.[8] The Brookings Institution and the Global IDP Survey recognize IDPs, more broadly, to be:

> persons or groups of persons who have been forced to flee or to leave their homes or places of habitual residence as a result of, or in order to avoid, in particular the effects of armed conflict, in situations of generalized violence, violations of human rights or natural or human-made disasters, and who have not crossed an internationally recognized state border.[9]

For establishing definitional clarity, two possibilities exist: first, to designate only those migrants as IDPs if they are forced to leave their normal place of residence under circumstances resembling those leading to the creation of refugees; and second, by extending this definition to include those forced to re-locate themselves due to environmental or industrial disasters. The difficulty in treating IDPs as a distinct group arises from the problem of differentiating them from migrants who are compelled to shift their residence as a result of economic compulsions. The adoption of a maximalist position here raises delicate problems impinging on the sensitive issue of state sovereignty. However, it has been argued that: 'What distinguishes the internally displaced and makes them of concern to the international community is the coercion that impels their movement, the human rights abuse they suffer as a result of their displacement, and the lack of protection for them within their own countries.'[10] In reality, the situation of IDPs is far worse than that of refugees since they are not eligible for receipt of international aid, and may not be recognized by national governments as qualifying for any assistance either.

The Situation in South Asia

South Asia is generally recognized to comprise the seven SAARC nations which are attempting to establish economic cooperation among themselves; it is hoped that this regional cooperation would, in time, ameliorate the political and security concerns of the member nations. In the post-Cold War period, the salience of transnational threats to the national security of the South Asian nations has been greatly exacerbated; these now constitute the more important and significant dangers to the national security of the SAARC countries. It would be difficult to exclude Afghanistan and Myanmar from consideration in this perspective; instability in these countries spills over into the South Asian region and leads to the accentuation of the threat from drugs and arms smuggling and terrorism. It is likewise difficult to exclude Afghanistan and Myanmar from considerations of cross-border migration problems in South Asia; there is a two-way population movement from Afghanistan and Myanmar into Pakistan, India, and Bangladesh, which adds a significant dimension to the national security concerns of these countries.

South Asia demands international attention since it hosts some 14 per cent of the total population of direct concern to the mandate of the UNHCR.[11] Except for the Maldives, all the other countries in the region are either the source of refugees in the region or have become their hosts. Migration within South Asia has generally been provoked or initiated by a sense of persecution or by the lack of economic opportunities in the originating countries; sometimes the host country has exacerbated its own problems by creating situations conducive to emigration from outside its borders. Two such instances which come readily to mind are Pakistan's support to the Afghan *mujahideen* during their struggle against the Soviet occupation of Afghanistan, and India's covert assistance to the Tamil militants in Sri Lanka in the 1980s. These situations, in turn, produced a climate propitious for the Afghans and the Jaffna Tamils to migrate into Pakistan and India respectively in search of sanctuary, local support, hospitality, and funding for their activities.

Another phenomenon which merits attention is the accompaniment of migration with violence in South Asia, both in the originating country and in the host country. This is evident from a review of twelve important population movements in the region since the partition of the subcontinent in 1947. These twelve movements are:

(i) India-Pakistan refugee flows, 1947-48, involving nearly 15,000,000 Hindus and Muslims; (ii) exodus of Burmese Indians numbering about 1,000,000 during 1948-65; (iii) exodus of Sri Lankan Indians and Tamils to the tune of about 1,000,000 from 1954 which is still continuing; (iv) flight of about 10,000,000 Bangladeshis [*sic*] to India in 1971; (v) 'stranded Pakistanis' in Bangladesh numbering nearly 300,000; (vi) flight of some 200,000 Burmese Muslims to Bangladesh in 1978; (vii) flight of about 100,000 Chakmas to India in 1981; (viii) nearly 3,000,000 Afghans fled from Afghanistan to Pakistan during 1978-93, of whom an estimated 2,000,000 have returned; (ix) flight of Tibetans to India from 1958 to 1963 numbering about 100,000; (x) exodus of nearly 60,000 Bhutanese of Nepali origin to Nepal in 1990-1; and the two controversial and unwanted population flows, (xi) from Bangladesh to Assam in India and (xii) the two-way flow between Nepal and India. Certainly these cases are different and distinct but violence remains their common denominator.[12]

Further, the inter-state tensions arising from these population movements have led to conflicts in the past between the host and the originating countries. The best-known example here is the Indo-Pakistan war in 1971, triggered by the eviction of some 10 million East Bengalis by Pakistan's military regime, which resulted in the creation of Bangladesh; this conflict raised delicate issues pertaining to the ethics of humanitarian intervention and the basis of waging just wars.[13] Similar situations are possible in the future.

Causes of Refugee Movements in South Asia

Migration movements within the South Asian region have primarily occurred for several reasons largely deriving from the geographical proximity of its member nations, strengthened by the familial, ethnic, religious, and linguistic affinities of their populations. Tamil, Bengali, Nepalese, and Pathan populations live on both sides of dividing borders; this encourages their cross-border migration and permits their absorption within the host country, often within separated families that provide both the economic and emotional anchor to survive and the means to avoid detection by the authorities. Matrimonial links assist in this process of absorption, as may be observed in Tamil Nadu between the Sri Lankan refugees and the local people. The geographical configuration of the region is also unique. India shares maritime or land borders with all the South Asian countries; this encourages emigration to India from all directions. Indeed, India has become the natural destination for refugees from all over the region.

Proceeding further, the Partition of British India in 1947 witnessed the creation of two new states, which led large populations to abandon their homes and move across the newly drawn borders. Approximately 14 million people (no accurate estimates exist) moved across the Indo-Pak border. Around 10 million people (again numbers are guesstimates) fled to India from East Pakistan following the crackdown by the military regime in Pakistan in March 1971; most of them returned to Bangladesh after the birth of this country at the end of 1971. These instances of mass migration in South Asia triggered by major geopolitical changes have also occurred elsewhere in the post-Cold War world, which is witnessing a marked increase in forced cross-border migrations due to national and international crises.

There are several other factors which determine population movements in South Asia.[14] These include:

- The crumbling of states following the withdrawal of support by their powerful benefactors. The prime example here would be Afghanistan, which embodies the features distinguishing a failing state;
- The proliferation of internal conflicts within countries arising from ethnic, communal, and sectarian violence. Sri Lanka provides the obvious example here;
- The use of coercive state authority against minority groups, dissidents, and opposition groups. This is illustrated by the intimidatory tactics employed by Bhutan to expel its ethnic Nepalese population;
- The easy availability of small arms, landmines, and explosives to fuel armed struggles by militants. This is happening all over South

Asia due to the region bordering zones of long-enduring conflicts such as those in Afghanistan and Myanmar.

- The growth of egalitarianism and the spread of the democratic idea in the global polity has also had repercussions in South Asia. The indifferent workings of democracy during the last two decades of the twentieth century in South Asia has encouraged the emergence of dissent and resurgent sub-nationalisms within its multi-ethnic and multicultural societies. The failure of Bhutan to absorb its Nepalese immigrants is a case in point; this has driven them to seek refuge in India and Nepal. Similarly, the failure of the Sinhala elite to resolve the ethnic crisis in Sri Lanka has promoted the episodic migration of its Tamils into Tamil Nadu. The causes underlying these crises and the resulting population displacements in South Asia have their roots in the predicaments facing the task of nation building, as well as in the failures of governance. Hence, it has been argued that 'states which are not sufficiently nations must develop into nations to gain legitimacy. Such states, therefore, go on producing, of necessity, majorities and minorities, for they can survive only on the basis of a continuing and permanent agenda of building an "ethnic core" and thereby marginalizing the others.'[15]
- Environmental degradation—resulting from desertification, salinization of soil, dwindling water resources, deforestation leading to floods and famines—has added to the causes of forced migration. Environmental factors such as the deforestation of the Himalayas in Nepal and the land erosion due to floods and the loss of the coastline in Bangladesh have propelled out-migration from these countries into India.
- Historically, population flows occurred within the South Asian region; the obvious examples here are the traditional movements of hill populations to the plains in search of land and employment opportunities. Besides, the open borders existing between India and Nepal envisaged under the Treaty of Peace and Friendship (1951) encourage an untrammeled two-way migration. Similarly, the Bengali population in Bangladesh (formerly East Pakistan) has customarily moved into the north-eastern states of India (formerly Assam) and the Arakans area of Myanmar (formerly Burma) in search of employment. In an alarming note, the Governor of Assam has forecast: 'This silent and invidious [Bangladeshi] demographic invasion of Assam may result in [the]

> loss of the geo-strategically vital districts of Lower Assam. The influx of these illegal migrants is turning these districts into a Muslim majority region. It will then only be a matter of time when a demand for their merger with Bangladesh may be made.'[16] It is worth noting that the diversities persisting in South Asia predicate the continuing of such population movements in the region. Hence, it would be optimistic to hope that these population movements would abate in the foreseeable future.

None of these causes underlying migration and, by extension, the internal displacements of population within South Asia, incidentally, are mutually exclusive. Several such reasons could occur simultaneously. Afghanistan offers a prime example of this reality. Apart from extensive internal displacements within the country itself, out-migrations from Afghanistan have occurred into Pakistan and Iran. Indeed, instances of multiple uprooting have taken place as a result of the continuing strife in Afghanistan since 1979. This has been exacerbated in the last few years by the prevailing drought and famine conditions in that country.

The Indian Constitution, incidentally, makes no distinction between the fundamental rights of citizens and non-citizens; it also recognizes the non-citizen's right 'to move freely throughout the territory of India and to reside and settle in any part of the territory of India', subject, however, to 'reasonable restrictions' being imposed 'either in the interests of the general public or for the protection of the interests of any Scheduled Tribe' [Article 19]. Visa restrictions can regulate the entry of non-citizens, but the empirical evidence reveals that borders are permeable and that once initial entry is gained, non-citizens easily merge into the local population and are very difficult to detect.

Particularities of Population Movements in South Asia

Do refugee and IDP movements in South Asia exhibit any particularities? Some features that are typical to the region are identified below:

- It is noteworthy that the displaced people in the region have generally found migration outside the region neither possible nor congenial. Hence, this is a contained phenomenon in the sense that the region is the principal source for both originating and hosting its refugees and migrants. Two instances of extra-regional movement are the flight of Afghan refugees to Iran mainly due to its proximity to Afghanistan and the ethnic similarities of the population on the Iran-Afghanistan border, and the Sri Lankan Tamil Diaspora, which is scattered across the globe. Often the same country is both the source for originating and hosting refugees. For instance, the Chakmas from Bangladesh fled to the Arakans area of Myanmar, but the Rohingyas from Myanmar came into Bangladesh.

- South Asia boasts of several instances of the successful rehabilitation and resettlement of refugees, as well as their successful repatriation. Some 100,000 Tibetans escaped from Chinese persecution into India, mostly in the late 1950s and the early 1960s, and have assimilated within the country. On the other hand, East Pakistanis and Chakmas returned to Bangladesh from India in 1971 and 1998. South Asia has also seen mass migrations which occurred at the time of Partition, as well as witnessing instances of trickle migration, notably of Bangladeshis into India, Afghans into Pakistan, and Tamils into Tamil Nadu that continued over extended periods of time. This trickle migration has fluctuated with the internal situation in the originating countries, displaying a hemorrhaging phenomenon.
- It is a cause for some surprise that India absorbs refugees but has not generated refugees from its own territory since the time of the Partition despite the several ethno-political and communal-religious problems afflicting its body politic. Several reasons can be adduced to explain this phenomenon: the large size of the country, its multicultural and multi-ethnic society, the federal structure of its polity, and so on. This is not true in the case of IDPs who have had to move to different parts of India for security and economic reasons; they notably include the Kashmiri Hindus displaced from the Valley into Jammu and scattered over several parts of India due to a prevailing sense of insecurity. Furthermore, the drift of the rural population to urban areas in search of employment, where they survive in sub-human conditions in slum clusters, is a phenomenon common to the entire region.
- All the countries of South Asia are multicultural and multi-ethnic in character to varying degrees; this lack of social homogeneity contains the seeds of internecine strife between the diverse segments of their societies, leading to the generation of both refugees and IDPs. Only the Maldives has no such problems;

nor does it suffer from internal strife, which is largely due to the noteworthy social and religious homogeneity of the nation.

- A recent trend in population movements within South Asia is the temporary use of host countries to facilitate the further migration of these people to other preferred destinations. A flourishing industry in preparing fake travel documents and procuring refugee status has sprung up in Tamil Nadu to assist the entry of Sri Lankan Tamil 'refugees' into India, en route to Europe and North America.[17] Similarly, Bangladeshi Muslims are transiting through India to smuggle themselves into Pakistan and then seek entry into the Gulf states.[18]

Security Dimensions of Population Displacements in South Asia

Population movements need not be negative in their impact. It is universally acknowledged that migrants provide a source of cheap labour to the host country and offer useful skills to invigorate the developmental process. Migrants have provided the plantation labour that led to the development of the tea industry in Assam and the opening up of the Terai region in the Himalayan foothills. Besides, migrants can easily integrate into the host population, especially if they belong to common cross-border ethnic and linguistic groups.

However, the negative aspects of population movements in South Asia are also well recognized. Some of these disadvantages are described below.

- These include cultural, political, socio-economic, and security aspects as immigrants cause irretrievable damage to the environment by settling down on marginal lands or by undertaking wide-scale deforestation. Their competition with the local population for limited arable lands and employment opportunities is a universal cause of friction between the emigrating and the host populations, since desperate immigrants are willing to work harder and for lower wages. Access to limited resources such as fodder and fuel-wood can also become sources of tension in marginal economies. *The Report of the Group of Ministers on National Security* duly recognizes the national security implications of unchecked migration into India. The *Report* notes:

> Today, we have about 15 million Bangladeshis, 2.2 million Nepalese, 70,000 Sri Lankan Tamils and about one lakh Tibetan migrants living in India. Demographic changes have been brought about in the border belts . . . There is an all-round failure in India to come to grips with the problem of illegal immigration. Unfortunately, action on this subject invariably assumes communal over-tones with political parties taking positions to suit the interest of their vote banks. The massive illegal immigration poses a grave danger to our security, social harmony and economic well being.

This maximalist viewpoint encapsulates both the risks and the problems involved in dealing with migration in South Asia.

- The receipt of assistance in the form of doles and goods by the refugees, which is unavailable to the local population, is a further cause of discontent among the people of the host country; inadvertently this creates an unintended gap between the living conditions of the refugees and the living standards of the indigenous population. This dissatisfaction can deteriorate with the passage of time into open hostility; this is occurring in the case of Tibetan refugees in some parts of India, since they have successfully established themselves in business and other avocations, making them the easy targets of jealousy and frustration on the part of the local people.

- The influx of alien people in large numbers can disrupt the domestic polity in the host country, which happened when millions of East Bengalis fled from persecution by the Pakistan military regime in 1971 and escaped to the adjoining states in India. Over the longer time frame, such refugee movements raise fears of demographic submergence; this is happening in the north-eastern states of India due to the unceasing flow of migrants from Bangladesh. The influx of immigrants strengthens the assertion of ethnic identity among the local people; this occurred in Tamil Nadu during the 1980s, with its rival Tamil parties vying with each other to promote the cause of the Sri Lankan Tamils by pressuring the central government to take up the Tamil cause with the Sinhala government. Competing political parties in the host country have also manipulated the migrants as part of vote-bank politics to derive political mileage by supporting rival refugee groups and being influenced, in turn, by them. Tamil Nadu politics has been deeply riven by the linkages of its political parties with rival militant Tamil groups from Sri Lanka. Currently, some political parties in Tamil Nadu are actively supporting the officially banned LTTE, which has been held responsible for the assassination of the former Prime Minister of India, Rajiv Gandhi. Similarly, the internal politics of West Bengal and the north-eastern states in India have also been profoundly affected by vote-bank politics in defining their policy responses to migrants from Bangladesh, adding to the vicissitudes of state politics in this part of India. It is recognized that the Illegal Migrants' (Determination by Tribunal) Act 1983, designed to detect and deport aliens from Assam, has been ineffective, but it has succeeded in weakening the Foreigners Act 1946 that was available earlier, and has thereby highlighted the hypocrisy of the political parties in Assam.[19]

- It is widely suspected that migrants can become available to criminal organizations due to their vulnerability to expulsion from the host country; hence, a general increase in criminality results from these population movements. The involvement of Afghan refugees in drugs and arms smuggling on a major scale has cast a shadow over the socio-political stability of Pakistan, and a nexus between Pakistan's political leaders and the drug lords in Afghanistan has been established; even the higher echelons of Pakistan's military leadership are known to have been infiltrated. The emergence of a 'Kalashnikov culture' in Pakistan, having close links with its 'jihadist' culture, reveals the further ramifications of the refugee problem and the security threat it constitutes for the host country.

- Migrants who belong to rival social and political groups in their country of origin can transfer their rivalries to the host country, leading to a deterioration of the local law and order situation. This occurred when the Sri Lankan Tamil militant organizations fought pitched battles against each other in Tamil Nadu during the 1980s, greatly worsening the internal security situation within that state. A further threat to national security is posed when refugees fear their ouster and turn against their host country; this situation occurred between the Chakmas and the locally resident Bengalis and the tribal population in Tripura. Regarding this situation, it has been commented: 'There are fears of collusion between unhappy Chakmas and the TNV (Tripura National Volunteers), which has, according to reports from Indian intelligence sources, contributed to the build up of arms with the militant TNV. The Chakmas are believed to be a conduit for arms to not only the TNV but [also to] other secessionist movements and groups in the North East.'[20]

• Migration across borders invariably creates friction between the originating country and the host country. Often the conditions compelling refugees to flee their country of origin persist for years, which makes their return problematic, despite the fact that they might have long outlived their initial welcome in the host country. This is apparent in the case of the Afghan refugees in Pakistan who were, until recently, unable to return to their homes due to the unsettled conditions in their home country. A similar sense of insecurity persists among the Jaffna Tamils in Tamil Nadu, and the oustees from Bhutan, who are living in camps in Nepal and India. The inability of the refugees to return to their countries of origin despite the fact that they have become unwelcome burdens to their hosts is a prescription for generating inter-state tensions and regional instabilities. In theory, 'national security is compromised when one or more of the three dimensions viz. the strategic dimension, regime dimension and structural dimension is threatened or eroded . . . in South Asia there are "dramatic examples" not of the familiar story of wars producing refugees, but rather of refugees producing wars.'[21] The Indo-Pakistan war in 1971 caused by the large-scale eviction of the Bengali population into India is often cited as the classic illustration of this assertion.

• Finally, South Asia also reveals the phenomenon of the 'refugee warrior'. The UNHCR noted that very often, 'States had clear strategic interests in granting asylum, but they showed little interest in finding long-term, durable solutions for the refugees; on the contrary, the refugees were used as pawns in geopolitical games to destabilize regimes and to encourage insurgency in their countries of origin.'[22] Some instances that come readily to mind include India training the Mukti Bahini for use against the erstwhile East Pakistan in 1971; Pakistan using the Afghan *mujahideen*—with active US assistance and encouragement—against the Soviets in Afghanistan during the 1980s and later in the 1990s to establish Taliban hegemony over that country; and India using the LTTE against Sri Lanka during the mid-1980s. Refugees are thus co-opted into the broader pattern of conflicts in South Asia by serving as the instruments to achieve the strategic objectives of regional states. Two further conclusions based on empirical evidence can be drawn from the readiness of South Asian states to use 'refugee warriors' against their regional neighbours. First, refugees can become a security threat to their countries of origin by providing motivated recruits to their host countries for instigating dissidence and mounting insurgent action against their home states. Second, the use of these 'refugee warriors' has almost invariably recoiled on the host country; ultimately, the host country which uses them to further its own designs suffers as much as the countries of origin. Thus, India exacerbated the law and order situation in its own turbulent north-eastern states by arming the Mukti Bahini. The LTTE's depredations in Tamil Nadu are well known, where they had been trained and armed by India. Similarly, Pakistan has greatly complicated its internal security problems by creating the *mujahideen* and the 'Jihadists' for intended use in Afghanistan and Kashmir; they are now a threat to the internal security of Pakistan itself. Incidentally, it has been argued that: 'It may be useful to draw a comparison here between the roles of Iran and Pakistan in relation to the Afghan refugees. Iran did not use the Afghan refugees as an instrument in its policy towards the Soviet presence in Afghanistan and consequently it has not suffered many of the adverse internal and external security implications [*sic*] that Pakistan has had to confront . . . '[23]

The general observation is, therefore, possible that refugee movements in South Asia have had an adverse impact on regional security, requiring both a greater dialogue and a greater degree of cooperation between these countries to mitigate the ensuing problems. This general observation could be extended to cover both inter-state and intra-state migration as well as the internal displacements of population in the region, unless these are planned and regulated to the extent possible.

CONCLUSIONS

Both experience and wisdom suggest that the underlying causes promoting migration in South Asia need to be addressed quickly and effectively. The causes are complex and are linked with difficult political, social, and economic questions. Consequently, it is unlikely that population movements within the region will ever be halted, especially now that the international system is deeply influenced by the process of globalization, which encourages the mobility of both capital and labour. Moreover, the political borders between the South Asian states are porous; the administrative barriers erected between them cannot keep out migrants, even if the political will existed to prevent it. But it is increasingly being recognized that unless the fundamental and generic problems underlying population movements are addressed in a proactive manner, it would not be possible to stem them or to mitigate their adverse impact. At the global level, the UNHCR observes that, 'Greater efforts are now being made to avert refugee movements before they begin, to contain armed conflicts and the population movements which they provoke, and to create the conditions which will enable displaced people to return to their homes.'[24] Further, the UNHCR also notes that 'the international community has concluded that lasting solutions to the problem of human displacement will only be found if a concerted effort is made to protect human rights, to keep the peace within and between states, to promote sustainable development and to manage international migration'.[25] In other words, a holistic approach to the migration issue is necessary, suggesting that it is important to secure the cooperation of international organizations like the United Nations, security alliances like the Organization for Security and Cooperation in Europe (OSCE), financial institutions like the World Bank, and regional bodies like SAARC.

A role for SAARC is, therefore, conceivable, despite its well-known frailties. No doubt, SAARC is a weak reed to lean upon in these difficult times; the continuing standoff between its two largest constituents—India and Pakistan—ensures that constructive regional initiatives have neither gained acceptance nor have they been fully implemented. The obvious solution—to negotiate a SAARC Convention and regulate migration within the region—is unlikely to fructify; even if negotiated, it might suffer the same fate as the Terrorism Convention, finalized in 1987, which has yet to be implemented. An alternative suggestion could be that the countries affected by refugee and migration movements might initiate mediatory efforts at the bilateral level. The difficulty here, as seen in the case of Bengali economic migrants into India, is that Bangladesh refuses to acknowledge their existence in India. This denial of reality is also seen in the case of Bhutan's refusal to recognize its primary responsibility towards the Lhotsampas (Bhutanese Hindus of Nepalese origin) who were expelled to India and Nepal. Fortunately, in the latter case, Nepal and Bhutan have constituted a Joint Verification Team to classify the refugees for deciding their nationality, which has held several meetings to narrow down the differences between the two countries. Still, cases of successful bilateral negotiations yielding answers to these complex human problems are not unknown. This was possible when India and Sri Lanka jointly resolved the problem of the stateless 'Indian Tamils,' emigrants working for generations as plantation labour in eastern and central Sri Lanka. A pragmatic policy is, therefore, required; it would be dogmatic to suggest that only a regional or bilateral or unilateral approach should be pursued. Clearly, a bilateral approach should be pursued in the first instance before contemplating regional or international modalities.

In truth, the solution offered by repatriation, though ideal, is not easy to execute, particularly if the conditions that led to population displacements in the first place—internecine conflict, environmental degradation, natural disaster, or lack of gainful employment—persist in the country of origin. Moreover, refugees are often opposed to the ruling regime in their own country, which makes their return difficult, as in the case of the repatriation of the anti-Taliban, non-Pashtun tribes comprising a major segment of the Afghan refugees in Pakistan. The prominent refugee-generating countries in South Asia—Afghanistan and Sri Lanka—continue to exist in semi-permanent crises, which greatly complicates the regional refugee situation. The economic and environmental conditions forcing the affected migrants to move elsewhere do not admit either to any easy quick-fix solutions. Host countries are, therefore, faced with a Hobson's choice: of either undertaking a long-term resettlement of the migrants within their own territory or seeking their transfer and rehabilitation in a third country; both these options are clearly limited and highly problematic. The same is true of IDPs within the region.

Recognition of the multifaceted aspects of these problems has led the UNHCR to proceed beyond its refugee-centric focus on migration to explore permanent solutions and to 'address the situation of people who have been displaced within their own country, exiled populations who have returned to their homeland, and those communities which are at risk of being uprooted'.[26] The originating countries must be helped to create conditions conducive for the return of their own people who have sought refuge elsewhere; this is a role that could be performed by regional organizations such as SAARC. An area of non-controversial regional cooperation that brooks no further delay is the de-mining of former conflict zones. The absence of mine clearance in Afghanistan, in parts of Sri Lanka, and in some areas in Kashmir has proved a strong disincentive to the return of civilian populations to their former places of residence. Similarly, it is possible to pursue cooperation in the identification of potential militants seeking to escape in the guise of refugees, provided the modalities could be agreed upon.

The situation in South Asia is that SAARC has not envisaged any role for itself in addressing the refugee issue, and there is considerable reluctance in the countries of the region to join the international covenants available for this purpose. The result is a policy of drift with ad hocism being the leitmotif of the national approaches to the refugees' problem, which extends to migrants and IDPs. That the issue of refugees has a low priority in the national agendas of the South Asian countries is evident from the fact that none of them has acceded to the UN Convention Relating to the Status of Refugees (1951) and its Protocol (1967). Several reasons explain their reluctance and hesitation,[27] but the most plausible is their fear of the economic burden involved in implementing the provisions of the Convention, such as the prohibition by the contracting states on expelling or returning the refugees against their consent (*refoulement*), the right of refugees to work and education, and the provision of housing. Similarly, the maximalist positions adopted by the left liberals (on behalf of migrants) and by nationalists (on behalf of states) on meeting these provisions of the Convention are not helpful. The argument that it would be anomalous to provide better conditions of living to the refugees that are unavailable to the local population has considerable persuasion. But it should be pointed out that the Indian Constitution makes no distinction between aliens and citizens in the matter of their fundamental rights. And it is a moot point whether a body of law to regulate the status and rights of refugees, migrants, and IDPs would not be infinitely better than a situation where there are no laws on the statute book.

Meanwhile, the problem of refugees persists in South Asia and could be further aggravated in the future; it is compounded by the allied problems of migrants and IDPs, which is also likely to worsen in the years ahead. The need for a body of law to regulate the rights of refugees and IDPs is essential, assuming that the rule of law generally prevails and is respected in the region. Otherwise, national approaches to refugees and IDPs would remain *ad hoc* and arbitrary. In essence, a balance must be struck between respecting the human rights of the refugees and respecting the sovereign rights of the host country. In addition, a balance must be struck between the rights of the refugees and the rights of the indigenous population. How these balances should be struck is the intellectual challenge before all theoretical and practical approaches to the problems of refugees, migrants, and IDPs in South Asia.

NOTES

1. UNHCR, *The State of the World's Refugees, 2000: Fifty Years of Humanitarian Action*, Oxford: Oxford University Press, 2000, p. 3.
2. UNHCR, *The State of the World's Refugees, 1995: In Search of Solutions*, Oxford: Oxford University Press, 1995, pp. 26-7.
3. Tapan K. Bose, 'Protection of Refugees in South Asia: Need for a Legal Framework', *South Asia Forum for Human Rights (SAFHR) Paper Series 6*, January 2000, Kathmandu, p. 12.
4. UNHCR, *The State of the World's Refugees, 2000*, p. 280, citing J. Harding, *The Uninvited: Refugees at the Rich Man's Gate*, London: Profile Books, 2000, p. 7.
5. Ibid., p. 10, Figure 0.1.
6. Ibid., Annexes 3 and 4, pp. 310-13. *SAFHR Paper Series 6*, op. cit., p. 12.
7. UNHCR, *The State of the World's Refugees, 1995*, p. 7.
8. Quoted in Roberta Cohen and Francis M. Deng, *Masses in Flight: The Global Crisis of Internal Displacement,* Washington, D.C.: Brookings Institution Press, 1998, p. 16.
9. Mahendra P. Lama, *Managing Refugees in South Asia: Protection, Aid, State Behaviour and Regional Approach,* Occasional Paper 4, Refugee and Migratory Movements Research Unit, University of Dhaka, Dhaka, April 2000, p. 47, f.n. 8.
10. Roberta Cohen and Francis M. Deng, *Masses in Flight,* p. 17.
11. UNHCR, *The State of the World's Refugees, 2000,* op. cit.
12. Ranabir Samaddar, *The Marginal Nation, Transborder Migration from Bangladesh to West Bengal,* New Delhi: Sage Publications, 1999, pp. 29-30, citing Myron Wiener, 'Rejected Peoples and Unwanted Migrants in South Asia', *Economic and Political Weekly,* 21 August 1993, pp. 1737-46.
13. Michael Walzer, *Just and Unjust Wars: A Moral Argument with Historical Illustrations,* New York: Basic Books Inc. Publishers, 1977, pp. 105-7. Walzer cites the Indian invasion of East Pakistan (later Bangladesh) as a good example of humanitarian intervention.
14. For a useful compilation of the causes underlying mass movements across borders in South Asia, see S.D. Muni and Lok Raj Baral, eds., *Refugees and Regional Security in South Asia,* Delhi: Konark Publishers Pvt. Ltd., 1996, pp. 7-24; and Mahendra P. Lama, *Managing Refugees in South Asia,* pp. 6-14.
15. Ranabir Samaddar, *The Marginal Nation,* p. 41.
16. Wasbir Hussain, 'Demographic Invasion, Anxiety and Anger in India's Northeast', *Faultlines,* vol. 7, November 2000, pp. 114-15, citing 'Report on Illegal Migration into Assam', submitted by Lt. Gen. (retd.) S.K. Sinha, Governor of Assam, to the President of India, November 1998.
17. Suresh Nambath, 'Their homeland beckons but . . . ', *Hindu,* 17 March 2002.
18. A startling revelation made in this regard is that these Bangladeshi illegal migrants were assisted to reach Pakistan by India's Border Security Force and that 'several thousand Bangladeshis were shepherded across the Punjab border.' This was designed as retaliation against the infiltration of terrorists by Pakistan into the Punjab during the Sikh militancy movement in the 1980s. Cf. Prakash Singh, 'Bangladeshi Immigration: Are We Heading for Another Partition', *Dialogue Quarterly,* vol. 3, no. 2, October-December 2001 (Astha Bharati, Delhi), p. 42.
19. Ibid., p. 39.
20. Shikha Bose, 'Victims of a Security Dilemma: Chakmas and Refugees from

Bangladesh', in S.D. Muni and Lok Raj Baral, eds., *Refugees and Regional Security in South Asia*, p. 112.

21. Mahendra P. Lama, *Managing Refugees in South Asia*, p. 20.
22. UNHCR, *The State of the World's Refugees, 2000*, p. 7.
23. S.D. Muni and Lok Raj Baral, *Refugees and Regional Security in South Asia*, p. 32.
24. UNHCR, *The State of the World's Refugees, 1995*, op. cit., p. 15.
25. Ibid.
26. UNHCR, *The State of the World's Refugees, 1995*, op. cit., p. 49.
27. These are documented in Mahendra P. Lama, *Managing Refugees in South Asia*, pp. 39-42. Lama also argues that a regional convention, even if it were possible to negotiate this, would probably be as ineffective as the other conventions established by SAARC, for example the Convention on Terrorism finalized in 1987.

2. *Humanitarian Concerns and Security Needs: Sri Lankan Refugees in Tamil Nadu*

V. SURYANARAYAN

> It is vital that the international community continue to seek lasting solutions to problems of human displacement. Those who would ignore them do so at their peril. History has shown that displacement is not only a consequence of conflict; it can also cause conflict. Without human security, there can be no peace and stability.
>
> SADAKO OGATA[1]

Sri Lanka is a small country with a population of less than 19 million, yet it is one of the world's principal sources of refugees and displaced persons. In an Issue Paper published in October 1991, the United States Committee for Refugees (USCR) rightly characterized Sri Lanka as an 'Island of Refugees'.[2]

An important consequence of the long-standing ethnic conflict in the island is the voluntary and involuntary migration of Sri Lankan Tamils overseas. Exact statistics are not available, but according to perceptive observers, 25 per cent of the Sri Lankan Tamil population lives abroad. This includes 220,000 in North America; 220,000 in Europe; 150,000 in India; 10,000 in Africa and the Middle East; and 60,000 in Australasia.[3] Because of geographical proximity and ethnic affinity, Tamil Nadu, from the very beginning, was a safe haven for Sri Lankan Tamil refugees. Historically, the narrow and shallow Palk Strait which divides Sri Lanka from India had never been a barrier; rather it was a bridge which united the two countries. In fact, Tamil Nadu and the northern part of Sri Lanka are like Siamese twins; what afflicts one will affect the other.

INDIAN TRADITIONS OF TOLERANCE

Before analysing the complex problems relating to the Sri Lankan Tamil refugees, it is necessary to underscore certain basic realities. First, it is important to acknowledge India's abiding traditions of tolerance, hospitality, and goodwill towards foreigners, in general, and towards those who seek asylum within its territory, in particular. Here, it is worth recalling Gandhiji's famous remarks addressed to the Indian community in Ceylon, made during the course of his visit to the island in November 1927:

> I would leave one or two thoughts with you before I leave Colombo. Since you are earning your bread in this beautiful island, I would ask you to live as sugar in milk. Even as a cup of milk which is full to the brim does not overflow when sugar is gently added to it, the sugar accommodating itself in the milk and enriching its taste, in the same way I would like you to live in the island so as not to become interlopers and so as to enrich the lives of the people in whose midst you are living.[4]

The analogy of sugar and milk is also quoted with reference to the arrival of the Parsis in the western part of India centuries ago. There are many variations of this historical incident, but the following may be the most appropriate account. When the Parsis, fleeing religious persecution in Iran, arrived at the Gujarat coast, they struck fear among the Gujaratis because the foreigners were armed with spears. The king sent the Parsis an overfull milk jug signifying that his kingdom was already overpopulated and that there was no place for the newcomers in the land. The Parsi religious leader mixed some sugar in the milk and sent it back to the king, conveying the subtle message that the Parsis would live in Gujarat as sugar lives in the midst of milk, but without spilling over from the jug, and at the same time sweetening the drink. It must be stated to the credit of the Parsis—today a miniscule community in India, numbering around 100,000—that they have contributed much to the economic, educational, cultural, and industrial advancement of the country. What is more, they are proud to be regarded as an integral part of the Indian nation.

The Indian traditions of tolerance and goodwill made the country from very early times a haven for refugees from many corners of the world. India had been the home of all religions in the world. It is worth mentioning that St. Thomas brought Christianity to India, specifically to Kerala, in the first century AD, long before the Vatican was Christianized. Jews fleeing from Roman persecution found refuge in Cranganore in Kerala in AD 68 and from there they moved to different parts of the country. There was a flourishing Jewish community in Cochin until after World War II, when the Jews migrated to Israel.

In the Indian tradition, a stranger who comes as a guest is an *atithi* and the host is expected to treat him as God, next only to mother, father, and the preceptor. In the *Yuddhakanda* of the *Valmiki Ramayana*, when Vibhishana approached Rama seeking asylum, Rama told Sugriva, 'O Sugriva, Chief of the Monkeys, please bring him here; I have granted him fearlessness, whether he is Vibhishana or even Ravana.' *Periya-puranam*, the Tamil classic, recounts the story of the Chola king, Meyyaporul Nayanar, who was not only a temporal leader but was also a 'realized soul'. One of his enemies wanted to kill him and came disguised as a devotee of Siva. He greeted the king with folded hands in which he had concealed a knife. When the king responded in the same way, his enemy killed him, inflicting stab injuries. The dying saint-king intoned: 'The holy garb—form—itself is the Truth Supreme (*Meypporul*)—and thus proved himself [a] real victor in spirit.' Dattan, the king's *aide*, wanted to catch the culprit, but the dying king dissuaded him, saying the killer was a devotee of Siva and should be treated as God himself. The king implored in soft tones, 'Just ensure that this devotee of our Lord goes back safe to his place, unmolested by any one.' In other words, the king saw divinity in every human being, particularly in a guest.[5]

Thirukkural, which has influenced the lives of the people of Tamil Nadu for several centuries down to the present day, specifically enumerates the ways in which those who come in search of food and succour should be treated. A few quotations from *Thirukkural* are given below:

(1) All the household articles that one possesses at home are only for the sake of pleasing and making the guests happy.
(2) Even if it is the nectar of the Gods, it should not be eaten alone by the householder, but should be shared by the guests.
(3) The life of the householder will not be spoiled by poverty, nor his health go to waste, if he receives and feasts his guests.
(4) Lakshmi, the Goddess of Wealth, will live in the home of a person who treats his guests with a smiling face.
(5) A person who waits on his guests at home and looks forward to the unexpected guests is a guest to the Gods.
(6) The quality of hospitality cannot be measured. It depends upon the worth of the feast that is given.
(7) Just as the *anchikam* flower fades when it is smelt, so also the

guest is displeased when the host has an expression of displeasure on his face.[6]

Shilappadikaram (The Ankle Bracelet), the great Tamil classic, written by Ilango Adigal, describes in vivid detail how a person entrusted to another's care should be treated. Kuvundi tells Madari how Kannaki should be taken care of:

> When the merchants of this city discover who is the father-in-law of this girl, they will invite her and her husband into their well-guarded homes, considering it a privilege. Until we can bring her to these wealthy mansions, keep Kannaki under your protection. Give her a good cool bath and put black collyrium on her long, reddened eyes. Rearrange her hair with fresh flowers. Dress her in a well-washed garment, as is proper for people of her rank. Be her servant, for she is of high birth, but be also her mother and guardian. Take care of her.[7]

Keeping aloft the noble traditions of Tamil culture, it must be pointed out that the government and people of Tamil Nadu have been generous in their dealings with the Sri Lankan Tamils, a record that could be the envy of many developing countries. Not even one Sri Lankan Tamil was harmed following the dastardly assassination of Rajiv Gandhi in May 1991 by the suicide squad of the LTTE. This is in striking contrast to what happened to innocent Sikh minority families in New Delhi—all Indian citizens—in the tumultuous days that followed the tragic killing of Indira Gandhi. The Sri Lankan Tamils and their leaders, in turn, should ask the question: have they been fair to the host country which spontaneously extended the hand of friendship and trust to them in the time of their distress?

India's Sri Lanka Policy

The flow of Sri Lankan Tamil refugees into Tamil Nadu is closely linked with the violence unleashed in Sri Lanka against the civilian population. The twists and turns in India's Sri Lanka policy also had their inevitable impact on the refugees. It should be noted that the Sri Lankan Tamils are highly politicized and that the refugees 'were the warm waters in which the militant fishes thrived.' The competitive nature of Tamil Nadu politics, with the two Dravidian parties vying with each other in championing the Sri Lankan Tamil cause, and New Delhi's policy of arming the Tamil militants paved the way for the setting up of a large number of militant camps in different parts of Tamil Nadu. As time went on, for a variety of reasons, the Liberation Tigers of Tamil Eelam (LTTE) emerged as a close-knit, disciplined, and ruthless organization. The Tigers had twelve units in Tamil Nadu to fuel their war machine. These dozen units were:

(1) Procurement of explosives—Dharmapuri
(2) Arms and ammunition manufacturing—Coimbatore
(3) Manufacturing of explosives—Salem
(4) Military uniforms—Erode
(5) Coastal area from where supplies were sent to Jaffna—Vedaranyam
(6) Transit area—Madurai
(7) Landing area for supplies from abroad—Nagapattinam
(8) Area where refugees arrived and where militants were recruited—Rameshwaram
(9) Communication centre—Thanjavur
(10) Trade in silver, gold, and narcotics—Tuticorin
(11) Liaison with political parties—Chennai
(12) Treatment of wounded guerrillas—Trichy.[8]

What was tragic-comic about the whole situation was the fact that New Delhi was trying to conceal the presence of militant camps in India. As time went on, the militants became a law unto themselves and the peace and tranquility of Tamil Nadu were vitiated by gun-toting Tamil militants. As Narayan Swamy has described: 'All Tamil groups had their own camps, which were virtually prohibited zones for outsiders. One could do anything in these secluded fortresses, no question asked. Even when some one was tortured to death, the screams would reach nowhere. If the victim died, he would be simply buried there or in the barren vicinity.'[9]

The assassination of Rajiv Gandhi by the LTTE guerrillas swung the pendulum to the other extreme. The people and political parties of Tamil Nadu have yet to recover from the trauma. A report of the Jesuit Research Service, which visited Tamil Nadu in March 1994, accurately mirrored the feelings of the people. 'Many of the locals, including the church people, now view their Tamil brothers and sisters no longer as refugees, but as militants and terrorists.'[10] Presumably spurred by security considerations, the Government of Tamil Nadu persuaded the Government of India to ban the LTTE. The ban continues to this day. What is more. Jayalalithaa, then Chief Minister of Tamil Nadu, demanded immediate action so that all Sri Lankan Tamils could be sent back: 'I appeal, rather demand, that the Centre should take immediate action so that all Sri Lankan Tamils are sent back. . . . It should take place immediately.'[11] The Government of India imposed restrictions on the facilities for higher education available to Sri Lankan students and also started repatriating the refugees. The controversy relating to the repatriation will be discussed in a subsequent section.

The Sri Lankan Tamil refugees are the creation of a particular political process and to expect them to be apolitical is asking for the impossible. After the assassination of Rajiv Gandhi, the refugees were very guarded in their statements, but a discerning observer could easily discover their sympathy and admiration for the Tigers. After the Tigers captured the strategically important Elephant Pass, gateway to Jaffna town, from the Sri Lankan Army, NDTV, a private television channel, visited the refugee camps located near Chennai. They have graphically described the jubilant scenes which celebrated this LTTE victory, with refugee children dancing and singing in chorus.

Flow of Refugees

Refugees, as Sadako Ogata, UN High Commissioner for Refugees rightly puts it, 'tend to evoke images of sprawling camps housing large number[s] of distressed and impoverished people who have had to escape from their own country at short notice and with nothing but the clothes on their back.'[12] This description captures the reality which affects the lives of a majority of the Sri Lankan Tamil refugees who live in 111 camps spread across Tamil Nadu. Geographical contiguity, the easy availability of boats, and ethnic affinity made Tamil Nadu a natural destination when large sections of Sri Lankan Tamils were forced to leave their country. New Delhi and Chennai alike recognized the need to provide asylum and admitted them with understanding and sympathy. Unlike many European countries, India did not demand that the refugees be subjected to any time-consuming bureaucratic procedures; nor were any restrictions placed on the movements of the incoming Tamils.

The Sri Lankan Tamils came to Tamil Nadu in three waves. The first exodus of refugees began on 24 July 1983, soon after the communal riots in Sri Lanka and continued till 29 July 1987, when the India-Sri

Lanka Accord was signed. During this period, 134,053 Sri Lankan Tamils arrived in India. Following the India-Sri Lanka Accord of 1987, refugees began to return to Sri Lanka. Between 24 December 1987 and 31 August 1989, 25,585 refugees and non-camp Sri Lankan nationals returned to Sri Lanka by chartered ships.[13] The remaining Tamils either returned to Sri Lanka without government assistance or continued to stay in Tamil Nadu either with their relatives or on their own.[14] According to Sri Lanka watchers, the period witnessed large-scale voluntary movements of Sri Lankan Tamils to different parts of Europe and Canada.

The Second Eelam War between Colombo and the Tigers commenced in June 1990 and resulted in the second wave of refugees. After 25 August 1989, 122,000 Sri Lankan Tamils came to Tamil Nadu. Of these 115,680 were destitutes and were accommodated in refugee camps.[15] The repatriation of refugees commenced on 20 January 1992. According to the UNHCR, 54,188 refugees were voluntarily repatriated to Sri Lanka by chartered ships and flights from 20 January 1992 to 20 March 1995.[16]

The Third Eelam War commenced in April 1995 and once again the refugees started coming to Tamil Nadu.[17] As of 2 February 2002, 22,331 refugees had come to India. They comprised 7,968 families, consisting of 9,705 adult males, 8,110 adult females, 2,281 male children, and 2,235 female children.[18]

The flow of refugees was a consequence of the Sri Lankan Army's operations in the LTTE-controlled areas. Most refugees took the Talaimannar-Rameshwaram route, while a few came via the Nacheguda-Rameshwaram route. The refugees trekked long distances, assembled in Talaimannar, paid huge amounts to boat operators, and reached Rameshwaram.[19] The sufferings of the Tamil refugees became evident when a boat capsized and 165 Sri Lankan Tamils were drowned in February 1997. This was the second such incident. In October 1996, another tragedy took place near the Mannar island, which took a toll of 14 lives.[20]

The flow of refugees to Tamil Nadu has now become a trickle. The following statistics are self-evident. The number of refugees who came to Tamil Nadu in September 2001 was 26; in October 2001 the figure was 78; in November 2001 the figure dropped to 11; in December 2001 it was only 6; and in January 2002 the number of refugees was 10. It should be emphasized that most Sri Lankan Tamils who wanted to leave the island and who had the financial means to do so have left for greener pastures in Europe, the United States, and Canada. Equally important, the Sri Lankan Navy controls the outer islands in the Tamil areas and it is extremely difficult for the boat operators to bring the Sri Lankan Tamils to India. What is more, the Indian Navy and the Coast Guard have stepped up their vigil in the Palk Strait. According to a Sri Lankan Tamil journalist, a few mechanized boats from Tamil Nadu smuggle scarce commodities and, on some occasions, bring back refugees with them for a good fee. They drop anchor at Nachiguda, Vallaipadu, and other safe spots between Pooneryn and Mannar.[21] It is Sri Lankan fishermen who ferry most of the refugees to India. The Government of Tamil Nadu has impounded a few boats owned by the Sri Lankan fishermen that were used to transport the refugees. This preventive measure has failed to deter the organized gangs of operators; in fact, every journey has given them more money than the cost of the boat. In 1997-8, the transport fee became exorbitant and ranged from Rs. 15,000 to Rs. 30,000 depending upon the need of the refugees and the size of the boat. The boat operators also exploit the shallowness of the Palk Strait; they drop the refugees in the sea (very near the coast) and ask them to wade through the water and report to the Mandapam camp.

Four Categories

The Sri Lankan Tamils in Tamil Nadu can be divided into four categories: (1) Refugees in camps; (2) Recognized refugees outside camps; (3) Sri Lankan nationals; and (4) Tamil militants detained in Special Camps.

It is essential to keep in mind the differences among the four categories and also their different legal status. Unfortunately, the government, political leaders, and the NGOs use the term 'refugee' very loosely and interchangeably. This has created not only semantic confusion, but also administrative and legal bottlenecks. For example, in an interview with the *City Express,* Chandrahasan, founder of the Organization for Eelam Refugee Rehabilitation (OFERR), clubs the four categories together and refers to all of them as refugees.[22]

1. REFUGEES

At the end of January 2002, there were 63,941 refugees, belonging to 16,955 families accommodated in 111 camps spread throughout Tamil Nadu. This aspect is covered in detail in a later section.

2. RECOGNIZED REFUGEES OUTSIDE CAMPS

Some Sri Lankan Tamils come by boat to Rameshwaram and inform the officials of the Rehabilitation Department that they do not want to stay in the refugee camps, as they can fend for themselves economically. They were asked to register themselves in the police station, which is adjacent to their place of residence and also to get a refugee certificate from the office of the District Collector. They are not eligible for financial doles from the Government of Tamil Nadu nor are they eligible to receive subsidized rations. These people are categorized as non-camp refugees. However, they can avail of the educational facilities earmarked for refugees, especially admission to professional colleges and institutions of higher learning. According to the officials of the Rehabilitation Department, the non-camp refugees number approximately 20,184.

3. SRI LANKAN NATIONALS

They obviously belong to the well-to-do sections of the Sri Lankan society. Their exact number in Tamil Nadu is not known, but according to informed sources the Sri Lankan nationals are estimated to be around 80,000. Approximately 25,000 entered India with valid travel documents issued by the Indian High Commission in Colombo. Some of them continue to stay in India even after the expiry of the visa period. A few others make use of India as a transit point for migrating to other countries. According to informed travel agents, they pose as Indian nationals, proceed to Kathmandu (Indian nationals do not require travel documents to go to Nepal), and from Kathmandu they fly to Bangkok, Singapore, or Hong Kong (Sri Lankan passport holders are issued visas on entry in Bangkok, Singapore, and Hong Kong), and from there they travel to the capitals of the Western world.

Following Rajiv Gandhi's assassination, the Government of India asked Sri Lankan nationals to register themselves at the nearest police station. The police began to apprehend those who had not registered themselves; this resulted in the detention of 1,800 Sri Lankans under the Foreigners Act 1946. In 1999, the Government of India asked all Sri Lankan nationals in Chennai who had arrived between 1 January 1983 and 31 December 1992 to register themselves with the Immigration Office before 31 August 1999. According to informed sources, only 1,500 Sri Lankans have registered in Chennai so far, a figure far below the actual population.

According to Government of India sources, the Sri Lankan nationals outside the camps have become a law unto themselves. A few own apartments and business houses without obtaining the required clearance from the Reserve Bank of India. A few others have taken out ration cards, a privilege to which only Indian citizens are entitled. What is more, some have got their names included in the records as Indian nationals during the census enumeration.

Another point which has not yet attracted the attention of the authorities deserves mention. According to the Sri Lankan Citizenship Act, children born to Sri Lankan nationals outside the island will have to apply for Sri Lankan citizenship by registration through the nearest Sri Lankan Embassy/Consulate/High Commission. According to the Sri Lankan Deputy High Commission in Chennai, the number of applications received from Sri Lankan nationals for citizenship by registration are very few. As far as Indian citizenship rules are concerned, originally Section 3 of the Citizenship Act of 1955 fully followed the principle of *Jus Soli* and all children born in India, irrespective of the nationality of their parents, became citizens of India by birth. The only exceptions were children whose fathers claimed diplomatic immunity or whose fathers were enemy aliens and those children whose birth had taken place in a territory occupied by the enemy. Thus, the children born in India to illegal immigrants from Bangladesh became Indian citizens. Hence, Section 5 was amended as a consequence of the Assam Accord by the Citizenship Amendment Act, 1986 (Central Act 51 of 1986) with effect from 1 July 1987. Thereafter, a child born in India after 1 July 1987 would acquire Indian citizenship by birth only if one of its parents was a citizen of India at the time of its birth. Thus, the legal position is that children born to Sri Lankan parents cannot claim Indian citizenship by birth. But in actual practice, if a birth certificate is obtained, the child can claim Indian citizenship since the nationality of the parents is not mentioned in the certificate. The Government of India should immediately take up this matter with the Government of Sri Lanka and ensure that the children born to Sri Lankan nationals in India are compelled to apply for Sri Lankan citizenship.

4. TAMIL MILITANTS DETAINED IN SPECIAL CAMPS

Sri Lankan nationals and refugees who are suspected to have militant leanings or those who have criminal cases registered against them are accommodated in Special Camps. In 1992, 1,629 militants were stationed in five Special Camps in Vellore, Pudukkottai, Salem, Chengalpattu, and Chennai. Militants against whom there were no specific charges were permitted to leave the country. At present, there are 128 Sri Lankans in three Special Camps: Vellore – 22 males; Chengalpattu – 72 males, 14 females, and 6 children; and Melur – 13 males and 1 female. According to a Peoples Union of Civil Liberties (PUCL) team which visited the Special Camp in Vellore in July 1999, security arrangements in Special Camps are 'unprecedented and surpass the security arrangements in any of the central prisons in the State'. Although the inmates are not 'technically and legally prisoners, their plight is even worse than those prisoners who are convicted and sentenced to specific terms of imprisonment'.[23] Following the recommendations of the National Human Rights Commission (NHRC), the Government of Tamil Nadu has enhanced the feeding charges for the inmates of the Special Camps to Rs. 35 per adult per day and Rs. 20 per child per day.

Life in the Refugee Camps

While analysing the living conditions of the Sri Lankan Tamil refugees, it is necessary to highlight the fact that they have come from a poor country to a poorer country. The government provides free housing, free medical care, and free education. Clothing, materials required for simple living, and utensils are also provided free of cost. Rice priced at 57 paise per kilo and sugar and kerosene at subsidized rates from the public distribution system are also made available to the refugees. Every fortnight the cash dole given out amounts to Rs. 200 for one member, Rs. 144 for each additional adult member, Rs. 90 per child below 12 years for the first child, and Rs. 45 for each additional child. The Government of Tamil Nadu has permitted the refugees to take up work outside the camps, a gesture not extended to the Chakma refugees from Bangladesh. The refugees are included among the weaker sections of society and they are entitled to a free supply of sarees and dhoties during the Pongal festival. From the academic year 1996-7, the DMK government has removed the restrictions on higher education imposed by the earlier AIADMK government. In some cases, the family income is supplemented by remittances from relatives abroad.

These facts are highlighted not to deny the refugees their due. In fact, it is my contention that living conditions in the camps could be easily improved if the lower rungs of the bureaucracy become more sensitive to the aspirations and feelings of the refugees, but to set the record straight in the context of misguided criticisms levelled by certain human rights organizations. The local people, for example, have to pay Rs. 3.50 per kg. of rice from the public distribution system. According to the *Tamil Nadu Social Development Report 2000*, only 15.6 per cent of the Tamil Nadu households enjoy all the three basic needs of electricity, drinking water, and sanitation. What is more, 32.48 per cent of the rural population and 39.77 per cent of the urban population live below the poverty line. According to the Planning Commission, the dividing line of the poverty level is Rs. 264 per capita per month in urban areas and Rs. 229 per capita per month in the rural areas. The literacy rate in Tamil Nadu is 62.66 per cent, 73.75 per cent for the males, and 51.33 per cent for the females.[24] The US Committee for Refugees (USCR), in its 1991 Report, notes that 'India has accorded a welcome to the Tamil asylum seekers that is as generous as any refugee group in Asia.'[25] The expenditure per year on the refugees works out to Rs. 25 crores. The expenditure is initially incurred by the Government of Tamil Nadu and subsequently reimbursed by the Government of India.

India's Refugee Policy

The basic principle underlying New Delhi's refugee policy is to view the problem strictly in a bilateral perspective. The refugees should return to their homeland once the situation there has improved. Referring specifically to the Tibetan refugees, Jawaharlal Nehru declared that India's policy on the subject was governed by three factors: (1) India's desire to maintain friendly relations with the Peoples Republic of China; (2) Protection of the security and territorial integrity of India; and (3) India's deep sympathy for the people of Tibet.[26] The same principles govern India's overall policy towards Sri Lanka.

Controversy over Repatriation

It has already been noted that the Government of Tamil Nadu began to pressurize the Government of India to repatriate the Sri Lankan Tamil refugees after the assassination of Rajiv Gandhi. The repatriation commenced in January 1992. Immediately, there was an outburst of criticism that India was 'pressurizing' the refugees to leave; that the repatriation was 'involuntary'; and that since peace had not returned to Sri Lanka, the repatriates would not be safe on the island. The

NGOs working among the refugees in India and human rights organizations like Asia Watch alleged that the hapless refugees were being 'forced' to leave and that their signatures had been obtained in option forms (unfortunately, the forms were printed in English), the contents of which they did not know.[27] According to Asia Watch, the repatriates faced 'direct and indirect coercion to return home, including arbitrary arrest, withdrawal of stipends and food rations.' Further, no international agency was permitted to visit the refugee camps to monitor whether the system was 'voluntary'. The refugees also had 'no reliable means' of ascertaining the actual conditions in their villages in Sri Lanka.[28] According to Asha Hans, 'The excellent Indian record of providing refuge to numerous neighbours has been blemished by the push factors used in repatriating the Sri Lankan refugees.'[29] By May 1992, 23,000 refugees returned to temporary transit camps in Sri Lanka.

Following international concern about the repatriation process and the continuing insecurity in Sri Lanka, the programme of repatriation was temporarily suspended. Negotiations soon started between New Delhi and the UNHCR, and in July 1992 an Agreement was reached which allowed the organization to establish a token presence in Chennai, with access to refugees at the point of departure, in the transit centres, but not in the camps themselves. The decision to permit the UNHCR to operate in Chennai and to monitor the repatriation facilities led to the safe return of the refugees to Sri Lanka.

The international context was also congenial. The end of the Cold War witnessed the return of 2.4 million refugees to their homelands. To quote the UNHCR Report:

> The ideal environment for the return of the refugees is one in which the causes of the flight have been definitely and permanently removed—for example, the end of the civil war or a change of government which brings an end to the violence and persecution. The ideal is rarely achieved. Instead, refugees return to places where political disputes will simmer and occasionally boil over, where fragile ceasefires break down, are repaired and then break down again, when agreements are broken and trust is removed. The great majority of returnees in the early 1990s have been going back to a situation of this kind—for example, in Angola, Mozambique, Cambodia, Sri Lanka and Afghanistan.[30]

The UNHCR officials, as stated earlier, are not permitted to visit refugee camps; however, any refugee can contact the UNHCR if he/she wants to do so. According to the UNHCR, they conducted interviews with 70 per cent of the refugees to verify the 'voluntary nature' of their return; they were convinced that the refugees had not been subjected to any 'covert coercion'. Only 19 families, comprising 68 persons, complained that they were repatriated 'under duress'. They were permitted to return to the refugee camps following the UNHCR initiative.[31]

The UNHCR presence in Tamil Nadu also facilitated better coordination between India and Sri Lanka. The UNHCR has been operating in Sri Lanka since 1987 and coordination between the two units, coupled with the cooperation of the bureaucracy on both sides, contributed to the overall success of the repatriation process. The UNHCR has been assisting refugees separated from their families by enabling reunions. As and when the UNHCR receives any complaint/ suggestion concerning the refugee camps, it immediately brings the matter to the notice of the Tamil Nadu Government and attempts to speed up the administrative machinery. According to UNHCR sources, their office in Chennai has received nearly 700 applications from the refugees for returning to Sri Lanka. Most of them relate to family reunion. With the conclusion of a ceasefire between the LTTE and the Sri Lankan Government and the prospects of negotiations becoming brighter, it is an opportune moment for the Government of India and the Government of Tamil Nadu to initiate the process of the voluntary repatriation of Sri Lankan Tamil refugees. According to media reports, the Department of Rehabilitation has asked Sri Lankan refugees staying in various camps in Tamil Nadu, who are desirous of returning to their country, to file their applications.[32]

The presence of the UNHCR in Chennai, though with a limited mandate, has enhanced the credibility of New Delhi in international forums. The Madras High Court in the case of *P. Nedumaran and Dr. S. Ramdoss* vs *The Union of India and The State of Tamil Nadu* stated: 'In so far as the consent of the refugees is concerned, when there is a world agency to ascertain whether the consent is voluntary or not, it is not for the court to consider whether the consent is voluntary or not. Nothing has been suggested against the competence or impartiality of the UNHCR in ascertaining the willingness of the refugees to go back.'[33]

The repatriates were understandably uncertain about their future in Sri Lanka. This was amply demonstrated when the first batch of refugees left by the *M.V. Akbar* from Chennai for Trincomalee on 20 January 1992. The LTTE condemned the repatriation as an 'inhuman act' and hours before the ship reached Trincomalee an LTTE ambush killed 20 Sri Lankan soldiers at Kuchchavali. The LTTE also blasted a part of the Sri Lankan Air Force base in China Bay in Trincomalee harbour, killing eight soldiers.[34] According to senior government officials who accompanied the repatriates, the panic-stricken Tamils immediately demanded that they should be taken back to Chennai. They refused to partake of food and declared that they would not disembark in Trincomalee. The officials did not want to abort the maiden voyage; they assured the repatriates that no one would be compelled to get down in Trincomalee; those who wanted to return to Chennai would be taken back. When the ship finally reached Trincomalee, the repatriates found friends and relatives waiting for them. All of them disembarked without any protest.

NEED FOR NATIONAL REFUGEE LAW

South Asian countries are signatories to major international humanitarian and human rights covenants. Three countries—India, Pakistan, and Bangladesh—are members of the governing body of the UNHCR. What is more interesting, important political leaders such as M.A. Jinnah, Liaqat Ali Khan, Zia ul Haq, Z.A. Bhutto, Pervez Musharraf, I.K. Gujral, and L.K. Advani were one-time refugees. Despite all these factors, none of the South Asian countries are signatories to the 1951 Convention on Refugees nor have they ratified the 1967 Protocol. South Asian countries have also not enacted any separate refugee legislation. As a result, the problems confronting the refugees are dealt with on an *ad hoc* basis.

There is one silver lining in the overall situation. The UNHCR in India has taken the initiative to sensitize the intelligentsia about the problems of refugees in South Asian countries. A number of seminars and workshops have been organized in collaboration with universities and organizations such as the SAARCLAW and the Indian Centre for Humanitarian Law and Research (ICHLR). Informal consultations have taken place and a Model Law on Refugees has been drafted by an Indian Group of Concerned Eminent Persons, under the Chairmanship of Justice P.N. Bhagwati, former Chief Justice of India. Justice Bhagwati has succinctly posed the problem as follows: 'Would the setting up of an appropriate legal structure or framework not help to provide a measure of certainty in the States dealing with the problem of refugees, and provide greater protection for the refugees?'[35] India and other South Asian countries must seriously ponder over this question.

Though South Asian countries are neither signatories to the 1951

Convention nor the 1967 Protocol, it must be pointed out that compared to many developed countries which are signatories, South Asian countries have been relatively generous towards asylum seekers. As Tapan K. Bose points out, South Asian states have given shelter and humanitarian relief to victims of forced migration, natural disaster, ethnic strife, and ecological disaster. To quote Bose, there are 'very few instances when asylum seekers have been blocked or refused entry into a South Asian State'.[36]

Why is India not a signatory to the 1951 Convention? An analysis of the Indian experience with refugees clearly shows that the policy of refugee determination cannot be done on an individual basis. The Indian experience is one of massive inflows of refugees, whether from Pakistan before and after Partition, Tibet after 1959, Bengalis from East Pakistan before the liberation of Bangladesh, or Sri Lankan Tamils after the communal holocaust in 1983. Other historical and political realities have also dissuaded India from signing the Convention. The 1951 Convention is Eurocentric and the refugee policies of the United States and the West European countries in the past were intertwined with Cold War politics. Equally relevant, as B.S. Chimni has forcefully argued, the Convention is 'being dismantled by the very states which framed the Convention'. Any talk of accession 'should be linked to the withdrawal of measures that constitute *non-entre* and temporary protection regimes'. Instead of 'burden sharing', the Western countries are resorting to 'burden shifting'.[37]

The question of signing the UN Convention has engaged the attention of the Government of India on several occasions: in 1967, in 1992-4, and just before India became a member of the Executive Committee of the UNHCR. The Ministry of External Affairs rightly considers the Convention and the Protocol as 'a partial regime for refugee protection drafted in a Euro-centric context'. As a backgrounder of the Ministry points out:

> They do not address adequately situations faced by developing countries, as it is designed primarily to deal with individual cases and not with situations of mass influx. They also do not deal adequately with situations of mixed flows, that is, they do not distinguish between political refugees and economic migrants . . . the Convention does not provide for a proper balance between the rights and obligations of receiving and source states. The concept of international burden sharing has not been developed adequately in the Convention. The idea of minimum responsibility for states not to create refugee outflows and

co-operating with other states in the resolution of the refugee problems should be developed. The credibility of the institution of asylum, which has been steadily whittled down by the developed countries, must be restored.[38]

Before the countries of South Asia arrive at a consensus on a regional convention on refugees, each state should enact its own national legislation on this subject. This legislation should not only spell out the rights of the refugees but it should also safeguard the territorial integrity and security of the state. Today the problems of the refugees are dealt with on an *ad hoc* basis. However, there are issues that cannot be addressed in this way. For example, do the refugees have the freedom to work? Do they have freedom of association? Refugee law, as Justice Bhagwati has pointed out, would 'help to provide a measure of certainty in the states dealing with the problem of the refugees. It would also provide greater protection to them.'[39] The legislation would enable all concerned to make a distinction between economic migrants and refugees. And, above all, it would incorporate the principle of *non-refoulement,* the basic tenet of international refugee law. Article 33 (D) of the UN Convention states: 'No contracting state shall return (*refouler*) a refugee in any manner whatsoever to the frontier of the territories, where his life or freedom would be threatened on account of his race, religion, nationality, membership of a particular social group or political opinion.'[40]

Since there is no refugee law in India, refugees are treated as aliens. They are covered by the Registration of Foreigners Act, 1939 (Central Act 16 of 1939) which is applicable to all foreigners. The Foreigners Act, 1946 (Central Act 31 of 1946) empowers the state to regulate the entry, presence, and departure of aliens in India. The Passport (Entry into India) Act, 1920 (Central Act 34 of 1920), the Passport Act, 1967 (Central Act 15 of 1967) govern the entry and departure of persons. Further, under the Constitution of India, certain fundamental rights – right to equality (Article 14); right to personal life and liberty (Article 21); and the freedom to practice and propagate one's own religion (Article 25) are guaranteed to citizens and non-citizens alike. These provisions, it must be pointed out, are in contrast to certain other rights such as the right to move freely throughout the country, the right to reside and settle in any part of India, the right to practice any profession in India, etc. (Article 19) which are available only to citizens. The judiciary has played a constructive role in protecting the interests of the refugees. In the famous case *NHRC* vs *State of Arunachal Pradesh*

(1996), the Supreme Court held that: 'The State is bound to protect the life and liberty of every human being, be he a citizen or otherwise.'[41] The NHRC also acts as a watchdog as far as refugee rights are concerned.

A study of the situation in Tamil Nadu with reference to the presence of a large number of Sri Lankan Tamil refugees is a clear illustration which drives home the point that India should not only take immediate steps to revamp the security machinery but that it should also enact a national refugee law. During recent years, there have been a number of serious lapses which have enabled the Tigers to become a law unto themselves. The assassination of Padmanabha and his EPRLF comrades in June 1990; the cold-blooded murder of Rajiv Gandhi in May 1991; the escape of Kiruban, a top LTTE leader, while being taken to Pudukkottai in April 1993; the escape of Charles Nawaz, a witness in the Rajiv Gandhi case in May 1993 from the Saidapet special camp; the daring escape of the LTTE cadres from the Tipu Mahal special camp in Vellore in August 1995—the list of failures is very long, and it brings no laurels either to New Delhi or to Chennai. If on that fateful night in Sriperumbudur, the female security personnel had physically frisked all the women who wanted to garland Rajiv Gandhi, perhaps we may not have lost a political leader of great promise in the prime of his life. Among the accused in the Rajiv Gandhi assassination case, half a dozen—Robert Payas, Jayakumar, Shanti (Jayakumar's wife), Vijayan, Selva Lakshmi (Vijayan's wife), and Bhaskaran (Vijayan's father-in-law)—were registered as refugees.

The absence of a well-defined national refugee law has created a number of anomalous situations. Three illustrations pertaining to Sri Lankan Tamils are given below. Among the 26 accused in the Rajiv Gandhi assassination case, six were registered as refugees. Judge Navaneetham awarded capital punishment to all the accused.[42] The Supreme Court confirmed the death sentence on four and awarded life imprisonment for three. The rest were convicted for lesser offences under the Arms Act, the Explosive Substance Act, the Foreigners Act, the Passport Act, etc. As they had already undergone imprisonment for these offences, the Supreme Court set them free.[43] While the acquitted Indian nationals were set free, the acquitted Sri Lankan Tamils are still placed in special camps. The Government of India can easily expel/deport them but what is evident is the lack of sufficient political will.

The second illustration refers to the *Ahat* case. The ship *Ahat* was registered in Singapore and flew a Honduras flag. It was allegedly carrying weapons and ammunition to the LTTE in Jaffna when the Indian Navy and the Coast Guard intercepted it. After an exchange of fire, the ship was set ablaze and some Sri Lankan Tamils, including the LTTE leader Kittu, committed suicide. Judge Lakshmana Reddy acquitted all the accused in the case and ordered the Commissioner of Police to hand them over to the State of Honduras.[44] The Special Investigation Team (SIT) and the Central Bureau of Investigation (CBI) went on appeal to the Supreme Court, which found the accused guilty of some charges and sentenced them to a total period of imprisonment of three years.[45] Here again, the accused had completed the term of imprisonment and, therefore, were set free. The State of Honduras did not want to take the Tamils; nor did the Tamils have Honduran passports. The Tamils also did not want to go back to Sri Lanka. One Tamil went to the Middle East. The rest are in 'safe custody' in Visakhapatnam.

The third case is a grim reminder of the ignorance of Tamil Nadu security officials about the international network which the Tigers have built up over the years. Bhaskaran, an LTTE guerrilla, was detained in the Saidapet special camp after Rajiv Gandhi's assassination. No charges were preferred against him, and Bhaskaran appealed to the authorities for permission to go abroad. The immigration authorities left Bhaskaran at the Meenambakkam airport. A few weeks later, Bhaskaran was found in Phnom Penh negotiating the purchase of surface-to-air missiles for the LTTE. What is more, he boasted to the journalists about how he had hoodwinked the authorities in Tamil Nadu.[46]

The examples given above should serve as a warning to New Delhi and Chennai. Even under the existing rules and regulations, aliens working against the national interests of India can be deported. There are judicial precedents too. In *Mohammad Sadiq* vs *The Government of India*, the court ordered the deportation of refugees under the Foreigners Act, 1946 since they had engaged in anti-national activities.[47] What is lacking is the political will to make difficult decisions. India, especially Tamil Nadu, cannot afford to be a 'soft state'. A national legislation on refugees combining the humanitarian needs of the refugees with the security interests of the state should be enacted. Let not history relive T.S. Eliot's message in the *Four Quartets*: 'We had the experience, but missed the meaning.'[48]

NOTES

1. Sadako Ogata, 'Foreword', *The State of the World's Refugees: Fifty Years of Humanitarian Action*, Geneva: Oxford University Press, 2000, p. xi.
2. U.S. Committee for Refugees, *Sri Lanka: Island of Refugees*, Washington, D.C.: U.S. Committee for Refugees, 1991.
3. Rohan Gunaratne, *International and Regional Implications of the Sri Lankan Tamil Insurgency*, Colombo: Alumni Association of the Bandaranaike Centre for International Studies, Colombo and International Foundation of the Sri Lankans, United Kingdom, 1997, pp.19-20.
4. 'Speech at Reddiar Sangham' (25 November 1927), *Collected Works of Mahatma Gandhi*, New Delhi: Publications Division, 1969, vol. 39, pp. 315-16.
5. R. Rangachari, *Periyapuranam – The Lives of the Sixty Three Saivite Saints*, Tiruvannamalai: Ramanna Asramam, 1997, p. 47.
6. *Ambrosia of Thirukkural*, New Delhi: Abhinav Publications, 1995, pp. 22-3.
7. *Shilappadikaram* (The Ankle Bracelet), tr. Alen Danielou, New Delhi: Penguin India Books, 1965, pp. 102-3.
8. Rohan Gunaratne, op. cit., pp. 19-20.
9. M.R. Narayan Swamy, *Tigers of Sri Lanka: From Boys to Guerrillas*, New Delhi: Konark Publishers, 1994, p. 175.
10. *Hindu*, 24 May 1991.
11. *Elephants and Others: Sri Lankan Refugees in Tamil Nadu and Sri Lanka* (Report of a Jesuit Research Service Visit to Tamil Nadu and Sri Lanka, 17 February-3 March 1994), May 1994, p. 4.
12. Sadako Ogata, 'Foreword', UNHCR, *The State of the World's Refugees: 1997-98: A Humanitarian Agenda*, New Delhi: Oxford, 1997, pp. x-xi.
13. R. Sampat Kumar, 'Returnees in Sri Lanka: Life Starts Again', *Refugees*, no. 63, April 1989, pp. 9-21.
14. Government of Tamil Nadu, Finance Department, *Policy Note, Demand No. 42, Miscellaneous 1996-97*, Madras: Government of Tamil Nadu, 1996.
15. Ibid.
16. For the UNHCR accounts of repatriation, see *Repatriation of Refugees from India to Sri Lanka, 13th August to 17th September 1993*, Colombo: UNHCR, n.d., and *Repatriation of Refugees from India to Sri Lanka, 28th January to 19th February 1994*, Colombo: UNHCR, n.d.
17. T.S. Subramaniam, 'Another Influx: Sri Lankan Tamils in Southern Tamil Nadu' and Amit Barua, 'Compulsions in Colombo', *Frontline*, 20 September 1996, pp. 49-50, 50-1.
18. Department of Rehabilitation, Government of Tamil Nadu.
19. T.S. Subramaniam, 'Another Influx: Sri Lankan Tamils in Southern Tamil Nadu', n.17.
20. *Hindu*, 21 February 1997.
21. Taraki, 'Refugees and Tragedy of Northern Seas', *Midweek Mirror*, 12 March 1997.
22. 'Caring for the Sri Lankan Refugees', *City Express*, 20 March 2002.
23. PUCL Report on the Conditions in the Special Camp for Refugees at Tipu Mahal, Vellore, Mimeograph, PUCL, Chennai, 1999.
24. Tamil Nadu Peoples Forum for Social Development, *Tamil Nadu Social Development Report, 2000*, Chennai: Tamil Nadu Peoples Forum for Social Development, 2000, pp. 23, 33, 42.

25. US Committee on Refugees, *1993 World Refugee Survey*, Washington, D.C.: US Committee on Refugees, 1993, p. 93.
26. N.L. Narasimha Rao, 'Indian Practice of International Refugee Law', unpublished M.Phil dissertation, School of International Studies, Jawaharlal Nehru University, New Delhi.
27. Asia Watch, 'Halt Repatriation of Sri Lankan Tamils', *Asia Watch*, vol. 5, no. 3, 11 August 1993, and T.S. Subramaniam, 'Homeward Bound', *Frontline*, 4 February 1992, pp.101-3.
28. Ibid.
29. Asha Hans, 'Repatriation of Sri Lankan Refugees from India', unpublished monograph.
30. UNHCR, *The State of the World's Refugees: The Challenge of Protection*, New York, 1993, pp. 103-4.
31. UNHCR, see n.16.
32. *New Indian Express*, 21 March 2002.
33. P.N. Bhagwati, 'Presidential Address', *Refugees in the SAARC Region: Building a Legal Framework*, New Delhi: UNHCR, 1997, pp. 19-23.
34. *Hindu*, 22 January 1992.
35. SAARCLAW and UNHCR, *Refugees in the SAARC Region: Building a Legal Framework* (Seminar Report), New Delhi: UNHCR, 1997, p. 23.
36. Tapan K. Bose, *Protection of Refugees in South Asia: Need for Legal Framework*, Kathmandu: South Asian Forum for Human Rights, 2000, p. 13.
37. B.S. Chimni, *The Law and Politics of Regional Solution of the Refugee Problem: The Case of South Asia* (RCSS Policy Studies 4), Colombo: Regional Centre for Strategic Studies, 1977, p. 7.
38. UN Division, Ministry of External Affairs, *Refugees* (No. UI/1515/8/99).
39. P.N. Bhagwati, see n. 33.
40. UNHCR, *Some Basic International Legal Documents on Human Rights and Refugees*, New Delhi: UNHCR, n.d.
41. 'National Human Rights Commission *v* State of Arunachal Pradesh and Others', *Bulletin of IHL and Refugee Law*, New Delhi, vol. 1, no. 1, pp. 147-59.
42. *Judgement in Rajiv Gandhi Case* (Designated Court No. I under the TADA Act of 1987).
43. *The Supreme Court Almanac*, New Delhi, vol. 3, nos. 3 and 4, 10-16 May 1999, pp. 241-516.
44. *Judgement by Judge B. Lakshmana Reddy* (Sessions Judge and Designated Judge under Tada), 29 June 1996.
45. *Hindu*, 24 August 1996.
46. Ibid., 21 September 1996.
47. Quoted in Bose, n. 36, p. 35.
48. T.S. Eliot, *Four Quartets*, New York: Faber and Faber, 1941, p. 39.

3. *Bhutan: Creating Statelessness— A Recipe for Regional Instability*

TAPAN KUMAR BOSE

The kingdom of Bhutan, or as the Bhutanese call it 'Druk-yul', which means the land of the thundering dragon, is situated in the eastern Himalayas. This mountain kingdom of 46,500 sq. km is completely landlocked. It shares its borders on the north with the Peoples Republic of China and on all other sides with India. Bhutan's early history is unclear. However, many archaeologists and historians believe that Bhutan was populated from a relatively early date—probably around 2000-1500 BC.[1] According to legends, till about the seventh century chiefs of Indian descent ruled different regions of Bhutan. It appears that most of these chiefs paid tribute to the king of Kamrup of the lower Bramhaputra valley in present-day Assam. After the death of King Bhaskaravarman of Kamrup, who was a contemporary of King Harshavardhana, the kingdom of Kamrup was weakened by internal feuds. As political confusion engulfed the region, various chieftains tried to free themselves from the control of Kamrup. Bhutan's reigning chiefs also became free at this time. The Tibetan invasion of Magadha also took place at this time. This brought most kingdoms of the region under the political control of Tibet. Within a century the people of Bhutan was converted to Buddhism. Since then Buddhism has played a central role in the history and culture of Bhutan.

Mediaeval Theocracy: The Rule of Monastic Principalities

According to most Bhutanese and western scholars, the real historical period of Bhutan begins with the introduction of Buddhism in Bhutan in the seventh and eighth century. Before the arrival of Buddhism, the Bhutanese practiced a form of animist religion known as 'Bon'. It is said that Mahayana Buddhism was firmly established in Bhutan during the eighth century when an Indian Buddhist monk Padmasambhava went to Bhutan. Padmasambhava later became known as Rimpoche.

He converted a reigning king of Bhumthang valley to Buddhism. Padmasambhava also incorporated several Bon deities into the Buddhist pantheon.[2] The growth of Buddhism in Bhutan was complemented by another factor. In the ninth century many Buddhist monks were forced to flee Tibet to escape the persecution of the anti-Buddhist king, Langdarma. While some of these monks took shelter in Kham in eastern Tibet several of them went over to Bhutan. After being compelled to run away from Tibet under the persecution of a non-religious king, the monks set up a system of mediaeval theocracy to make their position in Bhutan as secure as possible. As these monks set up several monasteries all over Bhutan they began to control the lives and property of the Bhutanese people. Every family was forced to send the brightest son to monk-hood. As the monasteries became firmly established and carved out their territorial areas of influence, many Buddhist schools of thought—the *Kadampa*, the *Kagyupda*, the *Sakyapa*, and the *Gelugpa*—emerged in Bhutan during this period.[3] For nearly seven hundred years, from the seventh to the seventeenth centuries, religious feuds between rival sects and monastic principalities continued to dominate Bhutanese social and political life. Religion continued to dominate all secular aspects of life. Even the wars were waged in the name of religion.

Establishment of Lamaist Theocracy

The unification of Bhutan took place in the seventeenth century when Ngawang Namgyal, a son of an abbot prince of a Drukpa monastery of Tibet, came to Bhutan and completely crushed all the rival sects and established his rule all over Bhutan.[4] He created a system of diarchy—the *Shabdung* or the *Dharma Raja* who was the head of *Chos* (religious) affairs and the *De-Srid*[5] or the *Dev Raja*—the head of temporal and secular affairs. He prescribed rules of conduct for all officers and laid down strict regulations for judicial and revenue administration. He was also responsible for dividing Bhutan into administrative regions, each under the rule of a local governor—*Penlops*—who owed their allegiance to the central authority established by him.[6] He created a Council of State (*Lhengya Tsok*) consisting of the Dev Raja, the Penlops, senior abbots of monasteries, and other ranked officials. The Shabdung was the real source of authority as he appointed the Dev Raja and the Penlops.

Ngawang Namgyal came to be known as Shabdung Rimpoche. It is said that he lived for about 150 years. However, most scholars agree that Ngawang Namgyal died at the age of 58 in AD 1651 but his closest associates kept the news of the event a secret. They announced that he had shut himself into meditation. This fiction was kept alive till about 1705. During this period of fifty years, his associates—the local governors, influential abbots, and monk warriors—ruled in his name. They were able to consolidate their position both politically and militarily. The borders of Bhutan were extended to its present limits. After the formal announcement of the death of Shabdung Rimpoche, his successive reincarnations continued to exercise supreme religious authority.

Till about 1907 Bhutan was ruled in the name of various Shabdungs who were incarnations of the first Shabdung Rimpoche—Ngawang Namgyal. However, none of his incarnations were strong or gifted in the art of statecraft. The process of identification of a child who is an incarnation of the departed monk-ruler became a contentious issue. The news of the deaths of the ruling Shabdungs was kept secret as parleys continued between the influential members of the state council. Feuding groups of abbots and governors tried to identify new re-incarnations and challenged each other's chosen candidates. On one occasion, two Shabdungs were installed at Punakha and Thimphu forts. The same feud continued over the appointment of *De-Srid* or the Dev Raja. After the formal 'death' of the first Shabdung in 1705 till 1917 only 6 incarnations were identified. During the same period, 55 Dev Rajas were appointed. Both the Shabdung and the Dev Raja had gradually become puppets in the hands of powerful ruling clans of east and west Bhutan.

The rivalry between the Penlops of Bhutan had weakened the central authority set up by the Shabdung Rimpoche. By the later part of nineteenth century trade with British India had become the most important source of revenue. The Penlops often fought over the share of the subsidy provided by the British. Towards the end of 1884, Ugyen Wangchuck, then Penlop of Tongsa declared war against the combined authority of the Shabdung and the Dev Raja. The Penlop of Paro supported him. The death of the chief of Punakha, the religious seat of Bhutan, and the defeat of the chief of Thimphu at the hands of Ugyen Wangchuck in the battle of Changlimithang, just below Thinphu in May 1895 made Ugyen Wangchuck the most powerful Penlop of Bhutan. With the support of his willing alley, the Penlop of Paro he become the de facto ruler of the whole of Bhutan. Though Ugyen

Wangchuck was friendly with the British, during the 1888-9 Anglo-Tibetan war, he chose to remain neutral, thus earning the gratitude of Emperor Kuang-hsu of China. The Emperor conferred the title of 'Chief of Bhutan' on him. Having secured the support of the Chinese, Ugyen Wangchuck turned his attention to the British. He knew that without the support of the British he could not establish his absolute control over Bhutan. In 1904, as a gesture of goodwill he accompanied Sir Francis Younghusband, leader of the British expedition team, to Lhasa. During the negotiations in Lhasa, he used his considerable influence on the high lamas and government functionaries of Tibet to sign the first Anglo-Tibet agreement in 1904. The grateful British in appreciation of his service conferred on him the title of 'Knight Commander of the British Empire in India' in 1905. In 1907, with the assistance of the British and the support of several powerful abbots, Penlop Ugyen Wangchuck became the first king of Bhutan. The Wangchuck dynasty has since ruled Bhutan. King Jigme Singye Wangchuck, the present ruler of Bhutan, is the fourth king of the Wangchuck dynasty.[7]

Transition to Modern Times

Mahayana[8] Buddhism continues to flourish vigorously in Bhutan today. In fact, after the takeover of Tibet by the Chinese in the 1950s, Bhutan became the only country in the world where Mahayana Buddhism is the state religion. Though Buddhism is the state religion of Sri Lanka and Thailand, the people in these countries follow the Hinayana[9] (Theravada) Buddhist path. The Chinese takeover of Tibet rekindled the West's interest in Buddhism during the Cold War. Centres of Buddhist Studies were set up in many Western universities during the 1960s and the 1970s. In the eyes of the West, Bhutan emerged as the last sanctuary of Mahayan Buddhism in this region as well as a bulwark against the spread of ungodly communism in this area.

Bhutan's ruling Wangchuck dynasty, which is successor to the seventeenth century Lamaist theocracy, is suspicious of the West and rejects the doctrine of individual freedom. It kept Bhutan isolated by restricting the entry of foreigners into Bhutan. Bhutanese citizens were not allowed to travel abroad without the permission of the government. Even today, the passport issued to Bhutanese citizens for travel abroad has to be returned to the authorities by its citizens on return to the country. Till about the 1960s, Bhutan government did not build roads. Modern communications and motorised transportation for the common people did not exist. Bhutan started building metalled roads around the sixties. In the last three decades Bhutan has built about 2,300 km of highway and arterial roads of which about 1700 km are black topped. Regular motorised transport for the common people and goods was introduced in Bhutan in 1962. Till then, the only source of transportation for the ordinary citizens were animal-drawn or man-pulled carts, mules, ponies, yak, and, of course, their own feet. Civil aviation arrived in Bhutan in 1983. Regular postal service was introduced in 1962. Telephone and telex services were also introduced at about the same time. Bhutan's mass media is still in an embryonic stage. A small radio station was set up in Thimphu with Indian assistance in 1991. The radio station broadcasts local news and educational programmes in Dzonghkha, English, and Nepali twice a week. Bhutan has only one newspaper *Kuensel* which is owned by the state. Prior to 1961 there were no modern educational facilities in Bhutan.[10]

Political Reforms

The 1950s were the most taxing times for South Asian regimes. The British who had ruled this region for two hundred years had departed only a few years earlier. The British Indian Empire had broken up into two nation states—India and Pakistan. Tibet, Nepal, Sikkim, and Bhutan, the Himalayan principalities over which the British exercised considerable influence through special treaties, were suddenly set free and left to fend for themselves. The success of the freedom movements in India, Pakistan, Burma, and Ceylon (Sri Lanka) was inspiring the peoples in all the countries of the region. In 1950, when India adopted its republican constitution, its echo was felt in Nepal. Within a year, the system of hereditary prime ministership by the Ranas was overthrown in Nepal. Under pressure of popular movements Nepal was moving towards a responsible and accountable government under a system of constitutional monarchy. By 1951 political parties were legalised in Nepal. China annexed Tibet in 1951. Though Bhutan felt protected by the 1949 Treaty of Friendship with India, it could not remain oblivious to the political changes taking place in neighbouring states.

The third king of the Wangchuck dynasty of Bhutan, Jigme Dorji Wangchuck, had just ascended the throne in Thimphu in 1952 when demand for political reforms began to surface. Bhutan at that time was an absolute monarchy. Jigme Dorji's father, the second Wangchuck king, had consolidated all political, economic, and judicial powers in the hands of the king. He had even abolished the office of the Penlops (regional governors) extending direct control of the king over the regions. In 1952 three Bhutanese citizens of Nepalese ethnicity, D.B. Gurung, D.B. Chetri, and G.P. Sharma established the Bhutan State Congress. The party was set up in Assam in India's northeast as political parties were banned in Bhutan. The main demand of this party was an end to the policy of discrimination against the Nepalese-Bhutanese vis-à-vis other ethnic groups in Bhutan.

The prevailing political situation in the region and the internal demand for political reforms forced King Jigme Dorji Wangchuck to introduce limited political reforms. In 1953 he created the *Thsogdu*, the National Assembly, with 130 members with the objective of involving different sections of Bhutanese people in the decision-making process. He also allowed the leaders of the Bhutan State Congress to return to Bhutan and some of them were nominated to the Thsogdu. A policy was also adopted to incorporate the Nepalese-Bhutanese into the political institutions, bureaucracy, and police.[11] As most of the economic demands of the Lhotsampa community were met, the political movement died down. Almost all the leaders of the Bhutan State Congress were allowed to return to Bhutan.

The present ruler of Bhutan, King Jigme Singye Wangchuck, ascended the throne of Bhutan in 1972, twenty years after the formation of the first Bhutanese political party in exile by the Nepalese-Bhutanese. During the first eight years of his rule, King Jigme Wangchuck continued the policy of associating the Nepalese-Bhutanese into the political system of Bhutan, which was started by his father, Jigme Dorji Wangchuck, in the 1950s. There is no doubt that the Nepalese-Bhutanese benefited from this policy and for a time they seemed to have abandoned their demand for political reforms.

The trouble started in the late 1980s when the present king initiated a policy of Bhutanisation. In June 1989 an extra-ordinary order was issued by the Bhutan Government under which all Nepalese-Bhutanese of southern Bhutan were required to wear the dress of the northern Bhutanese Ngalops—*Gbo* in case of men and *Kira* in case of women. Violation of this order was to be punished with fine and or imprisonment. Under this Royal decree called *Driglam Namza*, Bhutanese national language, Dzonhkha was made compulsory and the only medium of instruction in schools and offices. This was explained as necessary for preserving Bhutan's unique religious, political and cultural system from outside influence. The non-Buddhist Lhotsampas of south Bhutan revolted against this policy of promoting 'one nation, one people and one culture' by imposition of uniform dress code and one language. The resentment against this policy added fuel to the growing demand for political reforms in the southern and eastern parts of the country. Obviously, the exposure to the values of Western liberalism through the system of modern education that was introduced in the 1970s had motivated sections of the non-Buddhist Lhotsampas (Nepali-speaking Hindus) to ask for political reforms. They were no longer satisfied with the so-called economic benefits coming their way through the policy of association. The political movement of the Lhotsampas (Nepali-speaking Hindus) was most ruthlessly suppressed. About a third of Bhutan's population consisting of Nepali-speaking Hindus from south Bhutan were stripped of their citizenship. They were uprooted and expelled from the country. Their homes, lands, shops, and other properties were confiscated. These are the stateless people of Bhutan.

While the victims of Bhutan's ethnic cleansing are counting their days in the refugee camps in Nepal and in other shelters in Nepal and India and desperately clinging on to the hope that some day they would return to their homes, Bhutan and the international community seem to have forgotten them. It would seem that Bhutan instead of being punished for such an inhuman action has been rewarded. Bhutan's 'gross national happiness' programme and rudimentary political reforms are today praised by Western states and multilateral agencies such as the World Bank, the Asian Development Bank, and the UNDP. The World Wild Life Fund has acclaimed Bhutan's efforts in preserving nature and animal life. It has also helped covering up the suppression of a democratic movement and the systematic ethnic cleansing of Lhotsampas (Nepalese of south Bhutan) in the late 1980s and early 1990s.

Facts about Bhutan

Bhutan's exact population is anybody's guess. In 1985 Bhutan reported a figure of 1.3 million. Subsequently, in 1990, it was reduced to 0.6 million. King Jigme Singye Wangchuck told *Sunday* magazine that '. . . our official population figure is 1.3 million, but actually, it is closer to 600,000. People think that Bhutan deliberately gave wrong figure in the seventies, when we joined the United Nations. But in truth, someone had told my father that if he gave a figure less than one million, we would not be taken seriously by the UN.'[12] The United States State Department's website carries a profile on Bhutan. According to the State Department in 1999/2000, Bhutan's population was estimated to be 2.1 million. However, the Royal Government of Bhutan claims the total population of Bhutan in 2000 at 800,000. In 2001, Bhutan reported 5.07 per cent fertility rate and 0-percentage migration. In 2001, Bhutan's reported infant mortality was 109 per 1000 live births. Average life expectancy at birth was reported to be 45 years in 1991. However, in 1995 it was revised to 52.79 years. According to the 1991 *Asian Survey* (Berkeley), Bhutan's literacy rate was 25 per cent. In 1995, the Bhutan Government claimed that Bhutan's literacy rate had risen to 42.2 per cent.[13]

Bhutanese society is divided into three main ethnic groups: the Sarchops, the Ngalops also called the Drukpas, and the Nepalese. The Sarchops were the earliest inhabitants and they reside mainly in eastern Bhutan. Their origins can be traced to the tribes of north Burma and north-east India. The Ngalops who came after the Sarchops are of Tibetan origin. They brought Buddhism to Bhutan. The Sarchops and the Ngalops together constitute about 58 per cent of Bhutan's population. The third ethnic community are Nepalese Hindus who are called Lhotsampas. Before their large-scale eviction in 1992-9, the Lhotsampas constituted about 42 per cent of Bhutan's population. According to the Royal Government of Bhutan, the Lhotsampas or Nepalese now constitute about 27 per cent of Bhutan's population. Other minor communities and new migrants make up the balance of 15 per cent of Bhutan's present population. Of these, 75 per cent are Lamaistic Buddhist and 25 per cent are Hindus.

Economy

Bhutan is one of the poorest countries in the world. According to S.W.R. de A. Samarasinghe, Bhutan's decision to come out of its self-imposed isolation and to modernize was motivated to a large extent by the Chinese takeover of Tibet in 1951. He writes:

> Tibet (and to a lesser extent Nepal) is the only country with which Bhutan had had long standing ethnic, cultural, religious and trade links. Thus there arose a natural fear that cut off from the rest of the world with hardly any communications; Bhutan might lose its independence without the international community even being aware of it. Thus the move to modernisation was essentially a strategy to preserve its independence.[14]

It is interesting to note that prior to the 1950s, the money economy was virtually absent in Bhutan. The barter system was in wide practice. Powerful monasteries, landlords, and the royal family owned land. Basic socio-economic reforms such as the abolition of serfdom and land reforms were introduced in the 1950s. Prior to modernization, the Bhutanese economy was in low-level equilibrium. It was self-sufficient but trapped in a vicious cycle of a low-income, low-productivity, low-consumption, low-savings, and low-investment syndrome. In order to get out of this situation, the Bhutan government introduced economic planning for development. They adopted the Indian system of five-year plans. The First and the Second Five-Year Plans (1961-70) were implemented with 100 per cent financial aid from India. From the Third Five-Year Plan onwards the percentage of Indian aid began to decrease, although the actual amount increased. During the Sixth Plan (1988-92), India's contribution came down to 27.5 per cent, a figure which was at par with the amount of external aid received, mainly from the IMF, the World Bank, and the Asian Development Bank. Bhutan's own contribution to its five-year plans, which was zero per cent in 1961, increased to 45 per cent by 1992.[15]

The First Five-Year Plan (1961-5) aimed at developing the basic infrastructure like roads, power, communications, and transport. It also laid emphasis on agriculture and animal husbandry. The Second Five-Year Plan aimed at the further development of agriculture, infrastructure facilities, education, water supply, health services, transport, and such other nation-building activities. The Third and the Fourth Five-Year Plans laid emphasis on the productive sectors such as industry, hydro-power generation, and mining. During 1961-80, Bhutan also built a public sector which invested in industry, transport, trading of food grains, and communications. In 1981, Bhutan gained membership of the International Monetary Fund. The Fifth and the Sixth Five-Year Plans were designed according to the directives of the World Bank, the IMF, and the Asian Development Bank. Increased privatization of the economy and the promotion of export-oriented industrial projects became the main planks of these plans. As per the directive of the donors, Bhutan has now adopted a resource-based development strategy as a matter of necessity rather than choice.[16] The public sector which was considered the torchbearer of the Bhutanese development till the IMF and the World Bank dictated the Fifth Five-Year Plan has since been dismantled. Steps have been taken to transfer the government's commercial operations to the private sector. Bhutan's local transport system has been privatized. The Food Corporation of Bhutan, which was responsible for the local sale of food grains all over the country, has also been handed over to private hands. The government's holdings in industries and mines have also been diluted.

Bhutan's economy remains centred on agriculture, which employs an estimated 92 per cent of the total labour force and contributes about 38 per cent of the GDP. Agriculture consists largely of subsistence farming and animal husbandry. Rugged mountains dominate the terrain and make the building of roads and other infrastructure difficult and expensive. The industrial sector is technologically backward, with most production of the cottage industry type. Most development projects, such as road construction, rely on Indian migrant labour. Bhutan's hydropower potential and its attraction for tourists are essential resources. The Bhutanese Government has made some progress in expanding the nation's productive base and improving social welfare. Model education, social, and environment programmes in Bhutan are underway with support from multilateral development organizations. Each economic programme takes into account the government's desire to protect the country's cultural traditions and environment. Detailed controls and uncertain policies in areas like industrial licensing, trade, labour, and finance continue to hamper foreign investment. Major exports include cement, cardamom, fruit, vegetables, and timber products, most of which goes to India.

In 1999, Bhutan produced about 1.865 billion kWh of electricity from its hydroelectric plants using the existing abundant river system. It exported about 1.55 billion kWh of electricity to India. The sale of hydroelectric power is expected to cover the entire government budget within 10 to 15 years. The Government of India contributes nearly three-fifths of Bhutan's annual budget. Bhutan's per capita income in 2000 was estimated at US $1,100. In the same year, Bhutan reported a GDP growth rate of 7 per cent and an inflation rate (based on consumer prices) of 7 per cent (Please note that different agencies report varied figures about Bhutan's population and economy. As the Government of Bhutan does not publish regular reports and often relies on old estimates, it is difficult to arrive at the correct figures. The data published by the World Bank, the ADB, the UNDP, and other multilateral agencies also differ.)

Following the political reforms introduced in 1998, in 1999 the Government of Bhutan released its 2020 vision statement, which outlined Bhutan's significant development achievements since the 1960s when the average life expectancy of a Bhutanese citizen was 35 years.

Bhutan's vision statement is founded on the commitment to preserve its strong Buddhist ideals. This also includes maintenance of the 'monarchy' as the head of state and its 'independence'. With these objectives in mind, the Bhutanese ruling class devised a non-conventional measure of development—the 'Gross National Happiness' index. The Government of Bhutan argues that traditional measures of assessing progress and development such as GDP growth are inadequate in assessing the spiritual and emotional well-being of the people. Bhutan's governing elite claims that the political and economic reforms introduced under the 2020 vision statement are paying dividends. However, due to the non-availability of data about the rate of unemployment, differential consumption levels of the lowest and the highest income groups, the percentage of the population below the poverty line and the patterns of land holdings, it is difficult to make any proper judgement about the impact of the 2020 vision statement.

Political Situation

In 1865, Britain and Bhutan signed the Treaty of Sinchulu, under which Bhutan received an annual subsidy in exchange for ceding some borderland. As we have seen, under British influence a monarchy was set up in 1907. Three years later in 1910, a treaty was signed under which the British agreed not to interfere in the internal affairs of Bhutan but retained direct control over Bhutan's defence and foreign affairs. In 1924, the Secretary of State for India described Bhutan as an 'autonomous state under British suzerainty.'[17] In 1946, Bhutan presented a memorandum to the British Cabinet Mission seeking affirmation of its separate identity from other princely states in India. Immediately after the departure of the British, the Bhutanese grew suspicious of independent India's intentions towards their country. Briefly, the Bhutanese rulers had toyed with the idea of forging a federation of Sikkim and Bhutan in association with Tibet, the three Mahayana Buddhist countries, as a counter weight to India. However, the idea was soon abandoned and by 1948 Bhutan decided to directly negotiate with the new powers in New Delhi.[18]

India inherited parts of Bhutanese territory and control over her foreign policy from the British after her independence in 1947. However, on 8 August 1949 India accorded 'independence' to Bhutan through a new Indo-Bhutan Treaty of Friendship. Under the 1949 treaty, Bhutan is obliged to seek the advice of the Government of India concerning its foreign relations. India's advice is not binding, and Bhutan is free to decide whether to accept such advice. In addition, the

Government of India has undertaken not to interfere in the internal administration of Bhutan.

Bhutan is an absolute monarchy. It has neither a written constitution nor a bill of rights. The king is the head of government. A nine-member Royal Advisory Council assists him. The king appoints the members of the Royal Advisory Council. The cabinet system with a Council of Ministers was created in 1968 in response to the demand of a growing middle class which came into being as a result of modernization and economic development. The Council of Ministers is nominated by the king and its members are approved by the National Assembly. The Royal Advisory Council and the Council of Ministers are responsible to the National Assembly (Tshogdu), which consists of district representatives elected by direct popular consensus. At the village level, each family has one vote. The National Assembly meets at least once a year. The process of devolution of political power began at the district level during the 1980s. In an ostensible move towards democratization to allay international criticism, the King in June 1998 relinquished some of his executive powers to a cabinet of Ministers. The 1999 Royal Proclamation further empowered the National Assembly to remove the King by a two-thirds majority vote. The first High Court of Bhutan consisting of six judges was established in Thimphu in 1968. District courts were established in 1969. The High Court has both original and appellate jurisdiction. However, the King remains the ultimate court of appeal. The King appoints all judges of the High Courts and District Courts.

The King has remained active on security and foreign policy issues but has gradually extricated himself from the social policy issues that are handled by the Royal Council of Ministers. Since 1998, the Government has attempted to formalize these changes. Reforms to improve governance through greater transparency and accountability are ongoing. On 2 June 1999, on the occasion of King Jingme Singye Wangchuk's Silver Jubilee (25 years on the throne), the King lifted the ban on television and allowed access to the Internet. The King also plans to introduce a personal taxation system (at present the Bhutanese do not pay income tax) as part of his modernization push.

Restrictions on Foreigners

In July 1987, the National Assembly of Bhutan resolved that access to all monasteries; mountains and other holy places should be denied to tourists from 1988. It announced that from 1989, the number of foreign visitors should be strictly regulated and limited. Although there has in the past been a tourist quota (in 1996, for instance, there was a ceiling of 5,000 tourist visas issued), current practice is to let the comparatively high daily visa rate act as a self-regulating mechanism. The practice seems to be working: in 1997, only 5,365 tourist visas were issued, the highest number on record thus far. The standard visa rate is US$200 per day, which is inclusive of all accommodation, transport and meals. In addition, the services of a guide are usually included in the daily visa rate.

Refugees

The desire to protect Bhutan's unique identity and culture led to the forcible eviction of over 100,000 Lhotsampas, southern Bhutanese of Nepalese origin, between 1990 and 1992. Political analysts argue that the ethnic argument has been used to cover up the popular impulse towards democratic reform in Bhutan, which cuts across ethnic and religious divides. In this context, it should be noted that along with the ethnic Nepalese Hindu refugees, sections of the Sarchops of eastern Bhutan and a small number of Drukpa (ruling elite) student activists have also been pushed out of Bhutan. According to available information, from the late 1980s Bhutan saw a groundswell of democratic activism, especially by the educated ethnic Nepalese Bhutanese. A number of political parties such as the Bhutan People's Party and the Bhutan National Democratic Party and organizations such as The People's Forum for Human Rights, the United Liberation Front, and the Student's Union of Bhutan came into existence.

It is estimated that there are about 120,000 Lhotsampas, ethnic Nepalese refugees, in Nepal. Of these about 90,000 who are officially recognized as refugees, live in seven camps in eastern Nepal administered by the UNHCR. The World Food Programme is the main supplier of food grains to the refugees registered in these camps. Other supplies and services to the refugees are being provided by a host of international NGOs and foreign governments through bilateral aid to Nepal government. It is estimated that the Government of Nepal incurs an expenditure of about 100 million US dollars on the Bhutanese refugees living in the camps.

Bhutanese refugee organizations claim that there are about 20,000 unregistered Bhutanese (ethnic Nepalese Hindu) refugees living in some of the camps as well as outside in eastern Nepal. These are the relatives of the original refugees of 1990. Most of these persons claim that they had to leave Bhutan during 1993/4 because of systematic persecution by the Bhutanese authorities. In addition, there are about 35 Sarchops (ethnic Tibetan Buddhist) families living in Birtamod area of eastern Nepal since 1995/6. Most of these persons were associated with the democracy movement of the mid-nineties in eastern Bhutan under the leadership of Druk National Congress.

Bhutanese refugees had first taken shelter in India. Nepal and Bhutan do not share a common border. India was the 'first country of asylum'. Initially these refugees from Bhutan were housed in several relief camps set up by local people and the district administrations of Darjeeling and Siliguri. Within months, these camps were closed down and the hapless people were once again pushed out this time from India into eastern Nepal. Apparently, the decision to push the refugees into Nepal was taken by the Congress government in New Delhi at the behest of the Left Front government in Calcutta. India, which has a fairly good record of according refuge to persecuted people, was completely unsympathetic to the ethnic Nepalese refugees from Bhutan. Virtually, no efforts were made to determine their status or ascertain the cause of this massive influx. It seemed that India accepted Bhutan's explanation that these people were 'illegal immigrants' from Nepal and they deserved to be pushed back into Nepal. Having pushed these people into Nepal, New Delhi has conveniently been following a 'hands off policy' and suggesting to Nepal and Bhutan that the two countries should resolve this problem through bilateral efforts.

According to refugee sources, there are about 15,000 Bhutanese refugees in India. As India does not recognize these persons as refugees, they have had to find shelter among the local Nepalese-speaking community in north Bengal and Assam. According to unconfirmed reports, since the 1960s, about 7,000 refugees, belonging to the Sarchop community of eastern Bhutan, have been living in India's north-eastern state of Arunachal Pradesh. Apparently in the 1960s, the Sarchops were persecuted by the ruling Drukpa community as they followed the religious practices of the Gelugpa sect headed by the Dalai Lama. Their lands were confiscated for non-payment of revenue and the landless persons fled to neighbouring Arunachal Pardesh where they also received kinship support. (The South Asia Forum for Human Rights has undertaken a pilot survey of the non-camp and unregistered Bhutanese refugees in eastern Nepal, north Bengal, Assam, and Arunachal Pradesh. The survey is expected to be concluded by the end of 2002.)

ORIGINS OF THE CURRENT REFUGEE CRISIS

Drukpas and Lhotsampas have been living together peacefully for decades. A large number of Bhutanese citizens of Nepalese origin were in the government service holding important bureaucratic and diplomatic positions. They were employed as teachers in schools and technical institutions. Nepalese were nominated to the Royal Advisory Council. Nepali language was taught in the schools of southern Bhutan. Each year, the king celebrated 'Dashai', the Nepalese Hindu festival. The Nepalese from southern Bhutan were also elected to the National Assembly.

Some commentators and historians have talked about a latent animosity between the two communities. It has been indicated that the anti monarchy and pro democracy demonstrations in 1990 in southern Bhutan triggered the move to expel the bulk of the Nepalese population. However, looking at the level of preparedness of the government and the short period in which thousands of southern Bhutanese persons of Nepalese origin were made to sign the 'voluntary migration form' and sent out of the country after payments of paltry amounts of 'compensation', one wonders whether there was a plan for rearranging the population matrix of Bhutan.

The 1990 refugee crisis of Bhutan has its origins in King Jingme Singye Wangchuk's 1987 programme of national integration known as 'One Nation, One People'. In essence, the policy called for a revival of Drukpa Bhutanese identity and culture and the 'Bhutanization' of all ethnic groups in Bhutan. The programme sought to correct a perceived threat to Bhutan's cultural identity by counteracting foreign influences resulting from Bhutan's more open trading policy since the mid-1970s. The programme included such measures as enforcing the wearing of traditional garb in public by all Bhutanese, forcing them to cut their hair short in the Bhutanese style, forbidding the teaching of Nepalese in schools, limiting the number of foreign visitors, making certain holy places inaccessible to tourists, and discontinuing access to television broadcasts from India. Those who failed to comply were subject to a fine and imprisonment for a month.

This programme was strongly opposed by the Lhotsampas, the Nepalese-speaking Hindus who constitute up to 45 per cent of the total population of Bhutan. The ancestors of these people migrated from Nepal and the northern Indian provinces to Bhutan's fertile lowlands since the late 1800s. Immigration was prohibited in 1958, but Bhutanese authorities claimed that thousands of persons of Nepalese origin continued to cross the relatively porous border and settle down in southern Bhutan.

Bhutanese citizens of Nepalese ethnicity now living in the refugee camps in Nepal claim that the policy of ethnic cleansing was triggered by the realization that over 45 per cent of Bhutan's population belonged to the Nepalese community. They feel that the real objective of the 'Bhutanization' programme of 1988 was to evict hundreds of thousands of bona fide Bhutanese citizens of Nepalese ethnicity to eliminate any possible threat to the absolute monarchy.

In 1988, the King ordered a new census to register all citizens. He declared that all Lhotsampas must produce their land tax receipts from the year 1958. Those unable to produce these receipts were declared illegal aliens. This order effectively disenfranchised many Bhutanese of Nepalese origin. How fair was it to ask ordinary farmers and poor peasants to produce 30-year-old land tax receipts to prove their citizenship? This remains a moot question.

The 1988 census placed southern Bhutanese Lhotsampas into seven categories:

- Genuine Bhutanese citizen (able to produce land tax receipts dated prior to 1958);
- Returned migrants;
- People who were not present at the time of the census;
- A non-national woman married to a Bhutanese man;
- A non-national man married to a Bhutanese woman;
- Adoption cases (children who had been legally adopted), and
- Non-nationals (migrants and illegal settlers).

There were protests in southern Bhutan against this unfair census. In 1990, the unrest took on ethnic characteristics when a group of students of Nepalese ethnic origin founded the Bhutan People's Party (BPP). Though the party was banned, it evidently enjoyed broad support within the southern Bhutanese population who opposed the 'Bhutanization' policy. Apparently, some of the activists of BPP were encouraged by the successes of the pro-democracy movement in Nepal. In the face of official repression, the BPP reportedly became more militant and the demonstrations held in September 1990 turned violent.

The protests were suppressed by force. Hundreds of alleged anti-nationals were jailed. Their land and other immovable property were confiscated and in some cases, their homes were destroyed. A systematic reign of terror was let lose in southern Bhutan. Therefore, large numbers of southern Bhutanese began to flee. They crossed Bhutan's borders into India seeking refuge. India, technically the country of first asylum for the Lhotsampas, allegedly forced out of Bhutan, did not allow the Bhutanese refugees to stay in her territory. The Lhotsampas were chased out of Indian territory and forced to enter Nepal through its eastern border.

The inflow rates increased dramatically during 1992. Many refugees claimed that their citizenship had been revoked and they were forcibly evicted after being compelled to sign statements of voluntary departure. Others alleged that schools had been closed in southern Bhutan and houses destroyed. Many refugees claimed they suffered lengthy periods of detention without trial, rape, and torture before leaving Bhutan.

Currently, inflow rates to the camps are low, but the population of the camps in eastern Nepal is thought to be more than the official figure of 90,000. The Government of Nepal has no formal policy on refugees, but it has been tolerant of the inflow and has provided humanitarian asylum and land for the camps. As the Government of Nepal lacks the resources to provide additional support, the refugees are totally dependent on assistance from NGOs and other agencies assigned to the area by the United Nations High Commissioner for Refugees (UNHCR). Conditions in the camps have improved in comparison to the situation in late 1992, particularly in terms of sanitation, water supply, and preventive health measures. However, the presence of the camps has given rise to resentment from the surrounding Nepalese villagers whose residents resent what they perceive as the people in the camps enjoying better living conditions and services.

The Uncertain Future of the Refugees

The refugee issue seems unlikely to be resolved in the short to medium term despite the commencement of bilateral talks in 1993. Some of the recent steps taken by the King lend credence to the view that Bhutan is not interested in taking back the refugees.

Over the past five years, the government of Bhutan is implementing a programme of transfer of population—from northern Bhutan to south Bhutan. The land and the houses vacated by the Lhotsampas are being given away to the people from the hills from the central and eastern region. There is not a single Lhotsampa in the Royal Council. There is no representation of ethnic Nepalese in the council of ministers. Several members of the Council of Ministers of Bhutan have indicated that not a single refugee will be taken back whatever be the result of verification.

The Habitat International Coalition, an NGO based in The Hague, sent a fact-finding mission to South Bhutan between 23 September–1 October 2001. The team was to verify the claims of the Bhutanese refugees that their lands were given away to northern Bhutanese settlers under the Bhutanese government's resettlement programme. The team besides interviewing 25 refugee families from the camps in Nepal visited selected villages in Bhutan to verify the claims. In their preliminary findings, the team has indicated that they came across cases where the Royal Government of Bhutan has settled North Bhutanese on the lands of the South Bhutanese who were evicted after 1990. They have also said that not all the North Bhutanese settled in the Southern districts were landless persons as the government was claiming. Land was being given to army and police officers and/or their relatives especially land close to the road or the big houses. The team has said all the refugees interviewed by them in the camps in eastern Nepal wanted to go back to their lands from where they were thrown out. The refugees from Khudanabari camp (camp where verification has been completed) expressed their unhappiness with the verification process as it had ignored their land and housing property claims.

The refugees demanded that representatives of NGOs, the UNCHR and UNHCHR (office of the UN High Commissioner for Refugees and the office of UN High Commissioner for Human Rights respectively) be included as parties in all the talks and the joint verification process. The refugees also emphasized the urgent need for the Government of India to play an active role in resolving the Bhutanese refugee crisis.

The situation is further complicated by India's apparent apathy. Technically the country of first asylum for the people forced out of Bhutan, India has so far declined to mediate on the refugee issue. The Indian Government maintains that Bhutan and Nepal must solve this problem bilaterally, and has adopted a position of neutrality on the matter.

The Ongoing Verification of Bhutanese Refugees

Bhutan and Nepal have held several rounds of bilateral talks. Most of them have been unproductive. However, there were some encouraging signs after the visits by the High Commissioner for Refugees, Mrs Ogata and a European Parliamentary delegation to Nepal and Bhutan in early May 2000. During a visit to a refugee camp in eastern Bhutan Mrs Ogata had said that the much-awaited 'verification' of refugees by Bhutanese authorities was to begin soon and that the refugees would be able to go home. The beginning of the process of 'verification' of refugees by a joint team of Bhutanese and Nepalese officials in early 2001 kindled hope. The slow pace of the process, the inherent contradictions between 'verification' and 'harmonization' and the lack of response from the Bhutanese authorities have dealt a set back. The Joint Verification team has so far verified 862 houses from the Khudunabari camp consisting of 5,336 members. It took them 77 working days in the period between 26 March and 27 July 2001 (4 months). At this rate, it would take 6 years and 3 months to verify 100,000 members in all the camps.

After verification, the process of categorization will take place under four heads namely

1. Bhutanese forcibly evicted,
2. Bhutanese who 'voluntarily' migrated,
3. Non-Bhutanese, and
4. Bhutanese with criminal records.

The harmonization process will take place after the completion of categorization. It is not clear what the Bhutan government means by harmonization. If by this term is meant 'discussion' between the two governments in evaluating the verification data and placing them in slots it might take a few more years before the actual repatriation can begin.

Consequently, it would take more than ten years to complete the entire process of verification-categorisation and harmonization. It is not clear how long the Bhutan government would take to repatriate the 'verified' refugees. The refugees who have already waited for ten years will have to wait for a minimum of another ten years to go back. It appears that UNHCR had indicated its willingness to assist the joint Bhutanese-Nepalese verification process by providing logistical support and other arrangements for as many teams as may be required in the interest of expediting the process. But Nepal and Bhutan have not shown any interest in expanding the teams to expedite the process.

The Bilateral Process: Going Nowhere

While Nepal is unhappy with the current pace of verification, Bhutan does not seem to be unhappy. Some analysts believe that it suits Bhutan, as the very idea of verification was to postpone the repatriation itself. The Speaker of the National Assembly of Bhutan in a statement published in *Kuensel*, 14 July 2001, p. 6 said: 'that in the final analysis, it was the result of the process that counted most, not the pace of the process?' Worse still is the statement made by Deputy Minister of the National Environment Commission who alleged that the people in the camps were not refugees at all. He claimed that these people were lured by the prospect of making money as refugees. It is a strange statement coming from a minister of a government which is engaged in a verification process. It is difficult to believe that many of these refugees who possess proof of ownership of property worth hundreds of thousands of rupees have willingly gone into camps to get a daily dole of 400 grams of rice, 60 grams of pulses, and 25 grams of vegetable oil from the UNHCR.

Eight months have passed since the verification of the Kudenabari camp was completed. There is no indication when the verification process will be resumed again. From newspaper reports published in Kathmandu it seems that there were differences between the Bhutanese and the Nepalese teams on the process of categorization. It appears that the Nepalese team took the view that since an overwhelming majority of the refugees possessed documentary evidence of residence in Bhutan and had given affidavits of forcible expulsion from Bhutan, there could be no distinction between category 1 and 2, i.e. Bhutanese citizens unlawfully evicted and those who 'voluntarily' migrated. As for those involved in criminal activities in Bhutan, the Nepalese team reportedly held that it was for Bhutan to deal with those who had violated Bhutan's laws and Nepal was not involved.

It is possible that the verification process has stalled because of the difference of views on categorisation. Moreover, there is no move on the part of both Nepal and Bhutan to hold the next round of ministerial meeting. It seems Nepal has lost hope in the bilateral process. This was visible in the comment of the Finance Minister of Nepal Ram Sharan Mahat who represented Nepal in the eleventh round of bilateral talks. He was reported to have said that there was no point in meeting again to decide the dates of the next meeting, given what had happened in the previous rounds of bilateral meetings. A press report from

Kathmandu in January 2002 indicated that the Bhutanese leaders were not hopeful of any breakthrough in the forthcoming 12th ministerial-level meeting.

Need for a New Look: The Problem of Statelessness

It is time to take a new look at the Bhutanese refugee problem. By all accounts, it seems that the refugee creating country, Bhutan is not willing to take these persons back. Perhaps, the Bhutanese refugee problem needs to be understood more as a case of ethnic cleansing and creation of statelessness than as a refugee issue. There are nearly 140,000 (including the registered and unregistered refugees in Nepal and India) who have been made stateless. If Bhutan does not take these people back, and so far it has shown no willingness to do so, the question arises where should they go. Also should a state, which is part of the international community, be allowed to willfully make thousands of its own citizens stateless people? Nepal is one of the poorest countries of the world and cannot be expected to take on the burden of this additional population. This will be seen as an act of gross injustice to Nepalese people. India's apparent non-involvement is viewed by large sections of Nepalese as a pro-Bhutan position.

If Bhutan is able to get away with this immoral act of ethnic cleansing it will create a negative impact on this multi-ethnic region. It will further exacerbate the ethnic tension between Nepal's Hindi- and Maithili-speaking Madhesi population of the south and the Nepalese-speaking population of Nepal's north. Most hill people of Nepal see the Madhesis as pro-India. Nepal's Sadbhavana Party, which represents the Madhesis of Nepal's Terai, claims that about half a million Madhesis have been deprived of their citizenship by the government of Nepal. The hill people of Nepal often complain about illegal migration from northern Bihar, Uttar Pradesh, and Uttaranchal into the fertile plains of southern Nepal. What the Bhutanese have done to the Nepalese-speaking inhabitants of south Bhutan could also happen to the Hindi- and Maithili-speaking people of Nepal's Terai.

Apart from the moral and ethical arguments, there are security considerations for taking a fresh look at this crisis. Nepal, Bhutan, and north-east India are in the grip of armed insurgencies. The Indian army and other security forces have been engaged in counter-insurgency operations in the north-east for more than five decades. The military operations have not been very successful. Lately, the government of

India has been engaged in peace talks with some of the insurgent groups in the north-east. The government of Assam is also trying to engage the Bodo and ULFA insurgents into the political dialogues. If these peace initiatives are to be successful, the Bodo and ULFA militants who have been operating from inside Bhutan for several years have to be persuaded to declare a ceasefire and return to India. It has been reported in sections of the Indian press that in the early 1990s the Bhutan government had encouraged the Bodo and ULFA militants to operate from its territory as the Bodo and the ULFA were known to be anti-Nepalese. The Bodo insurgents have killed several Nepalese tea-garden workers.

Under pressure from the Government of India, Bhutan is now trying to get rid of the Bodo and ULFA insurgents from its territory. Despite the best efforts of the Government of Bhutan, it is clear that these militants are not going to leave Bhutan in the near future, at least not until the peace talks between them and the Indian authorities reach a substantial stage. As things stand today, a long drawn out conflict with the foreign militants within Bhutan appears inevitable. In 1997, Bhutanese forces brutally suppressed the democracy movement in eastern Bhutan. It has left the main inhabitants of eastern Bhutan, the Sarchops, unhappy and alienated from the monarchy. When the Bhutanese forces begin their operations against the foreign militants, the emergence of an anti-Bhutan alliance between sections of the foreign militants and disgruntled sections of the Sarchops cannot be totally ruled out. Under these circumstances, it is more important for Bhutan to win the confidence of its own dissatisfied people.

In Nepal, the Maoist insurgency has assumed serious proportions. Despite the declaration of a state of emergency and the induction of the Royal Nepal Army, so far the counter-insurgency operations have not been very successful. No senior leader of the Maoists has been captured and the insurgents are continuing to inflict heavy casualties on the police, the army, and other state functionaries in coordinated attacks in widely separated places. Nepalese and Indian media have carried several reports about Bhutanese refugee youth from the camps in eastern Nepal joining the Maoists. A study conducted by a researcher of the RCSS a few years ago reported that several youth from the refugee camps were reportedly trained by the ULFA. A recent CIA report on the region speculated about a growing link between the Nepalese Maoists, the refugee youth, and the ULFA.

No government can afford to ignore these security considerations.

Left to themselves, Bhutan and Nepal will not be able to solve the problem. Nepal has been asking for Indian intervention. It is obvious that India's so-called neutrality has been dictated by her perceived self-interest of controlling the growth of Nepali population in this region to avoid more Sikkim or Gorkhaland like situations. Bhutan is dependent on India. But India also depends on Bhutan for strategic reasons and the supply of large quantities of electricity. Bhutan also supports India in the international fora. However, the time has come for India to reassess its position on this issue in the light of the emerging security crisis. It is not too late for India to get involved in trying to resolve this problem in the best interest of all.

While the attempts to maintain the majority status of a particular community does not augur well for democracy, it is also important to address a numerically smaller community's fear of marginalization.

Moreover, it should be noted that most South Asia nation states are experiencing political turmoil as small minorities are trying to hold on to power in the name of representing the larger national interest.

Arguably, even Bhutan's fear of being overwhelmed by the Nepalese population can be allayed. It needs to be pointed out that in 1990 the Nepalese-speaking population of Bhutan was below 40 per cent. After the eviction, it has been reduced to 27 per cent. Bhutan should take back about 80,000 to 100,000 refugees belonging to category 1 and category 2. This is about 5 per cent of Bhutan's current population of 2.1 million. Consequently, there is no fear of the ethnic Nepalese population overwhelming the Drukpa majority. Moreover, a regulatory mechanism could be evolved for regulation and monitoring movement of populations in this area by India, Bhutan, and Nepal.

The regions of Nepal, Bhutan, and north-east India constitute a melting pot of ethnicity. The international borders in this region were drawn by an imperial power which had little regard for the ethnicity and the culture of the local population. People of Nepalese origin live all over this region, from the north-western corner of Nepal all the way to Mandalay province of Myanmar. The poor economy of this mountainous region has forced the Nepalese people to migrate in search of better economic opportunities. In the nineteenth century, they went to the malaria-infested regions of southern Bhutan to clear the forests and farm the cleared land. They also went to Assam and the Khasi and the Jayantia hills in Nagaland to work as labour in the tea gardens and in the agricultural farms. They went to India's north-east and to Myanmar (Burma) with their cattle as milkmen and settled down there.

Bhutan Fact Sheet

Area:	46,500 sq. km
Population:	2.1 million (1999)
Capital:	Thimphu (pronounced 'Tim-fu')
Type of government:	Absolute monarchy. No written constitution. No bill of rights. The king is advised by the nine-member Royal Advisory Council which together with the ministers also forms the Council of Ministers. The king nominates both the Royal Advisory Council and the Council of Ministers. Since 1999 they are responsible to the National Assembly (Tshogdu), which consists of district representatives elected by direct popular consensus (one family one vote). The National Assembly meets at least once a year. The king is also the final court of appeal. The king appoints the judges of the Supreme Court and high/appeal courts.
Opposition:	Political parties are outlawed in Bhutan. However, there are three active opposition groups composed of Nepalese-speaking Hindus, based in Kathmandu: Bhutan People's Party (BPP) formed in 1990. People's Forum for Human Rights formed in 1989. United Liberation People's Front formed in 1990. Druk National Congress (DNC) formed in 1995 in exile. United Front for Democracy (UFD) formed in exile in 1996/7
Languages:	Official language is Dzongkha, spoken mainly in western Bhutan. (Written Dzongkha is based on Tibetan script). Ethnic communities living in eastern Bhutan speak different Tibetan dialects. The Lhotsampas (southern Bhutanese of Nepalese origin) speak Nepalese. English is also spoken as its is taught in schools. English is also the language of instruction in all institutions of higher education.
Religions:	Mahayana Buddhism, mainly the Drukpa school of the Kagyuna sect, although Nepalese settlers practise Hinduism.
Currency unit:	Ngultrum (Nu)
Exchange rate:	US $1 - Nu 46.8 (2001) Nu is also linked to Indian Rupee and is traded at per
Real GDP growth:	6.9% (1999); 5.2% (2000)
Inflation:	7.6% (2001)

Source: Royal Government of Bhutan and State Department, Government of United States of America.

In recent times, the poor landless peasantry from northern Bihar has migrated into south Nepal. Skilled artisans from Bihar, Uttar Pradesh, and Uttaranchal have flooded the labour markets of Kathmandu and other towns of Nepal. This mobility of people and the cross-cutting ethnic links of the region needs to be taken into consideration while devising any solution to the problem posed by the forcible eviction of more than 100,000 persons of Nepalese origin from

Bhutan. Any attempt to dismiss this problem as a mere bilateral issue between Bhutan and Nepal or as an internal matter of a nation state will lead to a massive disaster engulfing the entire region. The search for a sustainable solution forces us to look beyond the traditional security considerations of the nation states. The mountainous terrain, the ethnic diversity of the region, and the histories of migration dictate that the nation states must rise above their narrow self-interests and devise a regional solution to this problem. This is also the chance for India to be the 'big brother' in a real sense.

Notes

1. See Dasho Rigzim Dorji, *A Brief Religious, Cultural and Secular History of Bhutan*, New York: The Asia Society Galleries, 1989, pp. 9-10. (Dasho is an honorific Bhutanese title for ranked officials.)
2. Ibid., p. 10.
3. Parmanand, *The Politics of Bhutan: Retrospect and Prospect*, New Delhi: Pragati Publications, 1992, pp. 10-11.
4. Dasho Rigzim Dorji, op. cit., p. 11.
5. The Bhutanese words *Chos* means religion and *Srid* means the world. In the traditional Tibetan government system after which the Bhutanese system was fashioned while *Chos-Srid* represented a diarchy in the organizational sense, in the ideological sense it represented a synthesis in the Mahayana school of thought, as *Chos* or *Dharma* was the main instrument for the release of the soul from the cycle of birth that tied humanity to *Samsara*. See A.C. Sinha, *Bhutan: Ethnic Identity and National Dilemma*, New Delhi: Reliance Publishing House, 2nd revised edition, 1998.
6. Nari Rustomji, *Bhutan: The Dragon Kingdom in Crisis*, New Delhi: Oxford University Press, 1978, pp. 5-6.
7. For a detailed discussion on the British frontier policy in the Himalayas in the nineteenth century, see Ram Rahul, *The Himalayas as a Frontier*, New Delhi: Vikas Publishing House, 1978 and Nagendra Singh, *Bhutan: A Kingdom in the Himalayas*, New Delhi: Thompson Press India Ltd., 1978.
8. The Mahayana school of Buddhism believes in the release of the entire humanity from the cycle of birth and rebirth through the path of *Dharma*.
9. The Hinayana school of Buddhism believes in self-*nirvana*, release from the cycle of birth and rebirth only for themselves, i.e. only for the followers of the school.
10. See the discussion on the political economy of Bhutan in Parmanand, op. cit., pp. 23-47. Also see B.S. Das, 'Economic Development and Social Changes in Bhutan', in Urmila Phadnis, S.D. Muni and Kalim Bahadur, eds., *Domestic Conflict in South Asia*, vol. 2, New Delhi: South Asian Publishers, 1986.
11. See Parmanand, op. cit., and Leo. E. Rose, *The Politics of Bhutan*, Ithaca, London: Cornell University Press, 1977.
12. Antara Dev Sen, 'The People Will Decide: Interview with King Jingme Singye Wangchuck', *Sunday* (Calcutta), 28 October 1990, p. 28.

13. Sukhdev Shah, 'Developing Bhutan's Economy: Limited Options, Sensible Choices', *Asian Survey* (Berkeley), vol. 18, no. 1, Spring 1991, p. 817. Also S.W.R. de A. Samarasinghe, 'Bhutan's Economy in Transition', *Asian Survey* (Berkeley), vol. 30, no. 6, June 1990, p. 561.
14. Ibid., p. 564.
15. Samarasinghe, op. cit., p. 572.
16. Shah, op. cit., p. 819.
17. Ram Rahul, op. cit., p. 90.
18. Ibid., p. 91.

4. *Still Waiting for a Better Morrow: A Decade of Burmese Refugees in Bangladesh*

C.R. ABRAR

The south-eastern tip of Bangladesh, the area between the districts of Teknaf and Cox's Bazaar, share a relatively short border (176 miles) with the Arakan state of Burma, a region predominantly inhabited by the Muslim Rohingyas. Since its inception, Bangladesh has experienced the influx of Burmese Rohingya refugees on two occasions, in 1978 and 1992. Each time, about a quarter of a million refugees crossed the border from the Muslim-dominated Arakan state of Burma.

In order to provide the readers with a comprehension of this complex problem, the first part of this paper deals with the background of the Rohingya problem. The second part discusses the responses of the Bangladesh government, the role of the UNHCR and the international Non-Governmental Organizations (NGOs) in the management of the refugee problem, traces the sources of tension between these agencies with regard to the protection and repatriation of the refugees, and the conditions of the vulnerable groups, particularly women and children. The third part deals with the impasse in the repatriation of the 21,000 refugees, the so-called residual caseload. The plight of the 'new arrivals' is also discussed. The conclusion highlights the problems caused by the absence of a national refugee law and calls for the·adoption of such legislation.

Background of the Rohingyas

The Rohingyas inhabit the northern part of Arakan state, currently known as Rakhine state. They constitute almost half the total 3 million population of the state, the other half are Buddhists. The Arakan Yoma mountain range separates the region from mainland Burma and has contributed to higher interaction between Arakan and the territory that constitutes Bangladesh today.

Over the last one thousand years the expanses of land that constitute Chittagong in Bangladesh and Arakan in Burma today, had changed hands a good number of times between the feuding warlords and kings of adjoining Bengal, Tripura and Arakan. It was the Arab merchants on their way to China who established first contacts with the Arakanese. Historian Mahbubul Alam points out that around AD 951 Chittagong was annexed by the Arakanese king and was named after him. Between the tenth and the sixteenth centuries the Chittagong, Sandwip and Ramu region was either under the control of the Muslim Sultans of Bengal or under the rule of the Arakanese kings. One may therefore argue that Bengal's relationship with the Arakan region can be traced to ancient times and there was constant fluctuation in that relationship. The Arakanese accepted Bengal's tutelage and paid taxes when Bengal was powerful and when the locus of power shifted to Arakan, eastern part of Bengal was made its vassal. All these led to increased interaction between the peoples of the region, including traders and religious preachers. There was influx of Muslims into Arakan from as far away as north India, Afghanistan, Persia, Turkey, and the Arabian peninsula. They merged into the existing Muslim society and gave rise to the growth of a group, the Rohingyas. A distinct dialect emerged as a result of the mixture of Persian, Urdu, Pushtu, Arakanese, and Bengali.

Two incidents involving two royal asylum seekers have significantly moulded the history of Arakan and its relations with Bengal. In 1404, the incident relating to the royal asylum seeker from Arakan, Narmikhelia, and his subsequent winning back of the throne and his conversion to Islam, significantly contributed to Muslim penetration and presence in Arakan. However, in the mid-seventeenth century the events surrounding the Mughal prince Shah Shuja, who sought asylum in Arakan, and later became involved in the court intrigues there, led to the erosion of the Muslim influence in Arakan.[1] In 1785 the Burmans overthrew the Arakan king and annexed it. The subsequent efforts of the Rangoon-based kings to consolidate their rule in Arakan met with resistance and brought about reprisals in 1791 and in 1796, tens of thousands were murdered and Bengal experienced a massive influx of Arkanese. It may be pertinent to state here that it was the refugees from Arakan who constituted the bulk of the original settlers between Teknaf and Cox's Bazaar. Hiram Cox, after whom Cox's Bazaar was named, was appointed by the East India Company as the superintendent for the rehabilitation of the refugees.

The First Anglo-Burmese War (1824) resulted in the British annexation of the Arakan and Tenessarim and the Second and the Third Anglo-Burmese Wars, annexation of the whole of Burma. The establishment of British rule in Burma created conditions for the return of the refugees. A large section of them returned. Nicolaus argues that together with the refugees, new settlers flowed into Burma. After its incorporation Burma was administered by the British as a province of India. The movement of people that took place between Bengal and Burma at the time was considered to be internal movement. The Burmese government views it as illegal migration and hence denies citizenship to the majority of the Arakanese Muslims. The historical reality is that Muslims had a significant presence in the Arakan region since the twelfth century.

The advance of the Japanese Army to the region during the Second World War led to the exodus of tens of thousands of Indians from Burma and of Muslims from Arakan. As communal riots flared up between the Buddhist and Muslim communities in Arakan, some 22,000 Rohingyas were forced to take refuge in the adjoining British Indian territories, i.e. Cox's Bazaar, Teknaf, Ukhia, and Ramu. The Muslim Arakanese were loyal to the British, rendering valuable service to the British war efforts, including reconnaissance and espionage, while their Buddhist counterparts took the side of the Japanese.

Following the end of the war, the failure of the British to deliver on a promise for a separate Muslim National Area— that would comprise Maungdaw, Buthedaung, and the part of Rathedaung bordering East Bengal—led to a major disappointment among the members of the Muslim community. As the Buddhist-dominated local administration began to wrest control over the region, alienation among the Muslims grew. A section of the Muslims formed the North Arakan Muslim League in Arakan and called for support on M.A. Jinnah, the architect of Pakistan. But this support was not forthcoming as Jinnah assured General Aung San that he was not keen on the idea. In 1948, an armed rebellion of the militant Muslims broke out that further eroded the relations of the Muslims with the Buddhist Rakhine and also their relations with the central government of Burma. The moderate Muslims stayed away from the rebellion. The Muslim militancy contributed to the formation of a belief that they were disloyal to the Burmese state. This resulted in the removal of the Muslims from various positions, such as the civil service, the police, and headmanship of village. Muslims were banned from military service, and not only did their educational and employment opportunities suffer but restrictions were also placed on their movement and their properties were confiscated.

1978 INFLUX

The 1978 influx was triggered by Operation Nagmin (Dragon King Offensive) of the Burmese military. The operation was ostensibly launched to identify citizens and 'foreigners' living in the country along the lines of the Burmese Emergency Immigration Act (1974). The Burmese authorities claimed that the Rohingyas 'absconded to Bangladesh in order to escape the Nagmin Project'. Following negotiations between the two governments, an agreement was reached on the repatriation of the refugees to Burma. The repatriation operation commenced on 1 August 1978 and ended on 29 December 1978. A total of 187,250 refugees were repatriated under the bilateral arrangement without the involvement of any third party, such as the UNHCR or any other international agency. It has been alleged that inadequate preparation and ill-planning of the repatriation process resulted in the death of 10,000 refugees.

1991 INFLUX

In 1991, Bangladesh experienced another influx of Rohingyas from Burma. The number of these people soon reached 250,000. The influx at this time was mainly because of the policies of denial of citizenship rights of the Rohingyas, the imposition of forced labour upon them by the Burmese state, arbitrary taxation and extortion by the Burmese army, forced relocation, development of 'model villages', and restrictions on the freedom of movement in Burma.

Refugee Management

Faced with this sudden influx the GoB took necessary steps to provide temporary shelter, food, medicare and health and sanitation services. A large number of officials were mobilized from different parts of the country to manage the refugees and shore up the relief activities. Temporary camps were set up and initiatives were taken to register incoming refugees. In September 1992, a census was conducted to ascertain the number of refugees. The census reported that 250,877 had crossed the border.

The overriding principle that guided the policy of the GoB towards the refugees was to seek their quick and safe return. The GoB sought international help for hosting the refugees. Initially, 20 camps were established. The UNHCR provided the refugees with food rations and non-food items. They were also provided with basic healthcare. The GoB, however, did not allow the refugees to pursue education since it perceived that this advantage or benefit may lead them to believe that they would stay in the country for a long period.

Through bilateral negotiations, the GoB signed a Joint Statement with the State Law and Order Restoration Council (SLORC) of Burma in April 1992. Burma agreed to the repatriation of those who could establish their *bona fide* residency prior to their departure for Bangladesh. The UNHCR and Burma also signed a Memorandum of Understanding (MoU) in November 1993, which stipulated the assurance of voluntary repatriation. So far some 238,000 refugees have been repatriated. But the government of Burma has been refusing to take back a major portion of the burden of more than 21,000 refugees, now residing in two camps in Cox's Bazaar. Despite its initial hospitality, the attitude of the GoB towards the refugees changed following the signing of the MoU with Burma.

In 1992 and 1993, concerns were expressed by the UNHCR and human rights groups over the coercion and forcible repatriation of the refugees. The relations between the UN agency and the GoB deteriorated sharply after the UNHCR withdrew from the repatriation process on 22 December 1992, following the refusal of the GoB to allow the UNHCR access to the camps. The UN agency accused the Bangladesh government of breaching the terms of the accord of October 1992. The GoB suspended forcible repatriation following a major international outcry. After prolonged negotiations it reached a MoU with the UNHCR that ensured 'free access to officials of the UNHCR to independent interview of refugees in transit camps . . . to determine the voluntary character of their decision to return' (1/a) and 'for conducting independent interviews with prospective returnees for certifying the voluntary nature of repatriation.' Under the MoU, the GoB undertook to commit that 'no refugees will be coerced into leaving against his/her will' (4/f) and that the UNHCR would have free access to and presence in all refugee camps at daytime.

The UNHCR signed a separate MoU with the Burmese government on 5 November 1993 under which the latter committed to cooperate to facilitate the voluntary return and to carry out the voluntary repatriation and integration of Burmese residents from the Arakan state. The repatriation process gradually gained momentum. This was also accompanied by a policy shift by the UNHCR, from providing information to promoting repatriation. Such a shift in policy invited criticism from the NGOs. A major factor contributing to this situation has been the lack of information about the situation prevailing in Burma, in general, and in Arakan, in particular. The reports of the UN Special Rapporteur for Burma and accounts of Amnesty International and Human Rights Watch Asia regarding human rights abuses in Burma—such as forced labour, forced relocation of villagers, and restrictions on the freedom of movement—have raised serious concerns about the safety of the returnees. UNHCR's policy of promoting repatriation was further criticized by the NGOs on the ground that the refugees were not fully informed of their choice. A survey[2] conducted by MSF found that 65 per cent of the refugees interviewed were still not aware of their right of refusing repatriation. The survey also claimed that 61 per cent of the refugees interviewed declared that they had concerns regarding the repatriation, of which 48 per cent stated that they could not express these concerns.

By December 1997, more than 200,000 refugees were repatriated to the Arakan, and the UNHCR reported that only 21,000 refugees were living in two camps, Nayapara and Kutupalong. It has been alleged that in the preceding months, that is, April, May, and July 1997 the Bangladesh authorities used force to intimidate the refugees to repatriate. The GoB has also put intense pressure on the UNHCR to hasten the repatriation process. Earlier, the Burmese authorities had informed Bangladesh and the UNHCR that it would not accept any more returnee refugees after 15 August 1997. The GoB's strong-arm tactics were intended to send back as many refugees as possible by that date. In addition, it might also have been meant to convey the message that it was willing to force the refugees back to Burma if the UNHCR could not arrange a 'voluntary' repatriation.

In 1997, the forcible repatriation of more than 300 refugees by the GoB across the Naf river triggered a violent reaction in the refugee camps. A section of the militant refugees took control of the two camps and restricted entry into them, allowing only a select group of UNHCR and NGO officials. They also forced some refugees to forego rations. It was only after more than a year, in 1998, that the authorities succeeded in restoring order. In the interim period all repatriation activities ceased.

On 15 November 1998, the Burmese government expressed its willingness to permit the repatriation of the Rohingya refugee families on certain conditions. These conditions included the demand that the families would be subjected to a re-verification of their residence in Arakan, that only fifty families would be allowed to repatriate per week, and that only complete families would be allowed to go back. Later, another condition was added: that the Burmese authorities should be allowed to confirm the willingness of each refugee to return.

In June 1999, faced with acute budgetary shortfalls the UNHCR informed the Government of Bangladesh that it would close its assistance programme by the year-end. However, because of ongoing protection concerns the agency still continues its operation, albeit with much reduced number of personnel.

The UNHCR acknowledges that it was sending people to a not very ideal condition and the situation was not very congenial in Burma. It, however, felt that refugees would be better placed there than languishing in camps, where they have limited opportunities in terms of developing themselves as full human being. The UNHCR would like the NGOs that were critical of the UNHCR's role to offer durable solutions to the problem rather than simply critiquing its position.

While protection remained a major issue of contention between the UN refugee agency and the NGOs, cordial relations existed between the parties in managing the assistance programme for the refugees. At the peak of the refugee situation a total of 32 NGOs were deployed to manage a vast array of assistance programmes: health, nutrition, nutrition of child and lactating mothers, sanitation, construction of shed, water testing, purification and supply, therapeutic and supplementary feeding, rice husk supply, religious education and repair of sheds. Both local and international and religious and secular NGOs were involved in the assistance programmes.

WOMEN REFUGEES

About 70 per cent of any refugee caseload is constituted by women and children. The Rohingya caseload is no exception. The Rohingya women have experienced abduction, physical torture, and rape at the hands of the Burmese military and also by the Rakhine Buddhists. A recently conducted study[3] suggests that abduction, forced labour, and the killing of the male heads of the household by the Burmese military have created immense psycho-social stress in these women. Many of these women have had to take responsibility for their families following the death or arrest of their husbands or after their husbands deserted or abandoned them. In many instances, these women themselves took the decision to cross the border. They came to Bangladesh by crossing the hilly border area on foot. Some of the women Rohingya refugees experienced sexual violence during the flight.

Camp life for the Rohingya refugee women is also fraught with problems. The practice of polygamy is widespread in the camps. A number of refugee women were abandoned by their husbands after their arrival in Bangladesh. Instances of rape and other kinds of exploitation of women by the male members of the camp refugee community were also reported. Although refugees should enjoy the highest protection facilities from the authority of the asylum country and all others concerned, analysts note that the 'Rohingya refugee women did not receive the level of protection that was due to them under the UNHCR's mandate. Violence committed against the Rohingya women also did not receive the kind of attention it deserved from the Government and the civil society of Bangladesh' (Khandekar and Haider, 1999: 58).[4]

Khandker and Haider (1999) further argue that women headed families with young and adolescent female members experienced the worst cases of persecution and physical torture from the Burmese security forces and even from members of their own community. They were completely unprotected during their movement through remote hilly areas. The women who did not get refugee status and settled in the camps were particularly vulnerable to abuse.

In the camps location of the toilet facilities, water sources and lighting condition have also became sources of insecurity for the Rohingya refugee women. There have been a number of instances when refugee women were attacked at night on their way to use such facilities. Often rape and physical abuse, committed by personnel of the law enforcing agencies and members of the refugee community, go unreported for fear of reprisal. The unregistered refugees, clandestinely living in camps, are often targeted. Insecurity of women is further increased by the way the programmes were designed. The system of distribution of ration through camp leaders, the *majhees*, had often led to forcing female heads of households to trade sexual favours to receive their rations. After complaints and campaigns by NGOs changes in the system were brought about and women were allowed to receive their own rations.

The insensitivity to the needs of women refugees is further reflected in the near-absence of female doctors in the camps. It has been reported that diseases like STDs went untreated for a long time due to the absence of female doctors. Likewise, the decision to provide women refugees sanitary napkins, taken in 1996, is yet to be implemented due to lack of funds.

The Residual Caseload

Over the last three years the repatriation process has virtually come to a standstill. Between January 1999 and December 2001, only 454 families comprising of 2,740 individuals were sent home. Two factors that contributed to this situation were: restrictive policies of the Burmese government with regard to entry of those willing to return and the unwillingness of a section of the refugees to return home due to lack of improvement in conditions at home.

The condition of the residual caseload of more than 21,000 refugees has become a major area of concern of several agencies. This section of the Rohingya refugees faces an uncertain future ten years after their arrival in the host country. A recent report of the MSF notes,

> Throughout their decade of exile, the Rohingya refugees have endured conditions that have fallen far short of the commitment guaranteed to them in the UN Refugee Convention of 1951. Today, the refugees still live in emergency-like conditions that are substandard and unhealthy. Not allowed to leave the camp freely, they have been confined to overcrowded, tight spaces, with insufficient water, inadequate shelter, and few educational opportunities.[5]

FOOD AND NUTRITION

Malnutrition has been identified as one of the prime concerns of relief agencies since 1992. The level of malnutrition has consistently been worse than for average Bangladeshis. A survey conducted in November 2001 reported that 58 per cent of the refugee children and 53 per cent of the adults are chronically malnourished.[6] In another informal survey in January 2002 the refugees identified food to as their number one concern.[7] Several factors may be assigned for food shortage. Refugees claim that they cannot access their full ration due to problems in the distribution system. In many instances the failure or the refusal of authorities to register the newly born has led to non-supply of food items to the additional member. Refugees are also denied food when their family books are confiscated and are essentially left to their own devices to secure food. They, along with the unregistered refugees, both living inside and outside camps, often depend on their families, relatives and friends who are registered in camps for their food supply. As food is the only source of income, refugees often sell or barter it for procuring other items such as vegetables, fish or other groceries and things that are not included in the ration list. Trading in food items also results in shortage.

HEALTH AND HEALTH CARE

The general condition of the refugee health has been viewed as stable. Overcrowding in the camps and lack of space has led to rise in respiratory tract infections and other communicable diseases such as diarrhoea, skin disease, common cold, and chicken pox. Although the mortality rates in the camps remain low, there has been a major increase in neo-natal deaths, a phenomenon that can be attributed to the malnourishment of the mother.

The high birth rate in the camps has been a major concern for the Bangladeshi authorities. In recent years the number of births have outnumbered the rates of death and repatriation combined. The Bangladeshi authorities called on NGOs working on health issues to institute family planning practices that are contrary to medical ethics.

HOUSING AND WATER

The 'temporary shelters' constructed hurriedly to accommodate refugees in 1991 still house the refugees. Although repairs are done every two to three years most of the shelters fail to withstand the monsoon rains. The authorities, with whom the responsibility for maintaining the shelter rests, have generally resisted improving the living conditions of the refugees on the grounds that such an effort would undermine their steps to repatriate them.

Water supply has always remained a major problem in Nayapara camp. It becomes more acute during the dry season. The vast majority of the refugees in Nayapara camp and a few in Kutupalong camp reported that in view of the short supply of water they could only meet their water needs from water sources located outside the camps and by digging wells inside the camps.

The 'New Arrivals'

The new arrivals constitute an important component in the highly complex Rohingya refugee operation. Field investigations reveal that tens of thousands of Rohingyas have crossed the border since the 'window' was closed in 1992. Many of these people are the 'reverse cases', or those who were repatriated earlier. Estimates of this category of undocumented Rohingyas range from 10,000 to 200,000.[8] All those who entered the country after May 1992 have been deemed by the Bangladesh government to be illegal migrants. An unofficial sample on survey of 350 household heads was conducted by the UNHCR. After cross checking 26 cases with the Burma office of the agency, it termed the group as economic migrants. Another 1998 survey by the UBINIG, a national policy research organization, claimed that 158 of its 200 respondent families reported 'army torture' to be the principal cause for their flight to Bangladesh.[9] The issue of 'newly arrived' persons from Burma has become a major challenge for those involved in the Rohingya refugee operation.

The refusal by the GoB to allow the newly arrived persons access to the status determination procedure has placed the lives of innumerable numbers of Rohingyas in great uncertainty. Not only do they fall victim to the arbitrary treatment of the law-enforcing agencies but they also fall prey to unscrupulous traders and traffickers in human beings. Without the care of any formal protection structure they lead their lives in great misery.

The case of the Rohingya refugees, particularly those of the newly arrived refugees, underscores the importance of the adoption of a national law for refugees. If such a law, with provisions for formal determination procedures, was put in place, then the newly arrived refugees could get an opportunity to present their cases before the concerned agencies. The enactment of such a law would also help the government to identify the genuine cases of those who fled persecution and those who came for economic or other reasons. It would also significantly reduce the suffering of one of the most marginalized communities in the region.

Conclusion

This paper provides a broad overview of the complexities of the decade-old Rohingya refugee operation. It presents the historical background of this Arakanese Muslim group whose members have been denied their citizenship in Burma and who have been periodically subjected to a whole range of discrimination. The paper also traces the history of the refugee flows from Arakan to the south-east tip of Bangladesh and the movements of people from the latter area to the former region. The paper then focuses on the responses of the Government of Bangladesh to the refugee flows in 1991 and its interaction with the UNHCR and with NGOs in managing the refugee problem. The paper also examined in detail the issue of the protection of the rights of the refugees, particularly in the context of sponsored repatriation. The paper briefly discusses the condition of the residual caseload and also of those asylum seekers who have not been given an opportunity to go through the status determination procedure. The paper argues for the adoption of a national law for refugees, a measure that to a great extent will equip the Bangladesh authorities to admit asylum seekers and treat refugees more efficiently and humanely and which will minimize the vulnerability of the genuine asylum seekers.

NOTES

1. For a brief account, see C.R. Abrar, 'Repatriation of Rohingya Refugees', in *Regional Consultation on Refugee and Migratory Movements*, Colombo, Sri Lanka: UNHCR, 1995.
2. For a detailed analysis of the issue, see 'Awareness Survey – Rohingya Refugee Camps – Bangladesh', 15 March 1995, Médecins Sans Frontières, Holland (unpublished).
3. S. Rozana Rashid, 'A Comparative Study of Vulnerability and Coping Mechanism of Rohingya Refugee Women and Chakma IDPs', mimeo, 2002.
4. Tushar Kana Khandker and Zulfiquar Ali Haider, 'Protection of Refugees: Case of Rohingya Women', in C.R. Abrar, ed., *On the Margin: Refugees, Migrants and the* Minorities, Dhaka: Refugee and Migratory Movement Research Unit, 1999.
5. Médecins Sans Frontières, Holland, '10 Years for the Rohingya Refugees in Bangladesh: Past, Present and Future' (unpublished paper), 2002.
6. 'Draft Nutritional Survey in Kutupalong and Nayapara Camps among the Rohingya Refugees', November 2001, p. 2 (publisher details not available).
7. Conducted by MSF, Holland.
8. MSF, 2002, op. cit., p. 24.
9. UBINIG, 'Vulnerability and Insecurity: Study on the Situation of Rohingya Women and Children in Cox's Bazaar and Teknaf' (publisher details not available).

5. *Towards a National Refugee Law for India*

T. ANANTHACHARI

Among the segments of our national life which require national level legislation, the 'refugees' issue deserves priority attention. The reasons for saying so are many. India is one of the few countries in the world which does not originate or generate refugees though it has, for the past few centuries, received refugees not only from its immediate neighbourhood but also from countries much farther away. It is also noteworthy that in the Indian subcontinent, India is surrounded by countries which are theocratic in their constitution and yet India has chosen to remain a secular country. This will always raise expectations from her in the matter of receiving and treating refugees on humane and humanitarian considerations rather than on mere legalistic and expediency basis.

India currently hosts well over 253,000 refugees comprising Tibetans, Sri Lankans, Bangladeshis (Chakmas), Afghans, Iraqis, Iranians, and a host of various other nationalities. It is extremely interesting that Iran and Iraq may be politically poles apart but India is the meeting ground for refugees from both these countries. It should also be pointed out that refugees who have come into India over the centuries belong to a variety of religions, some of them no doubt Hindus. The fact that India is a secular country and, equally importantly, that Indians are a tolerant people has been a major factor in infusing a sense of confidence in India's inherent values when people running away from fear due to persecution on a variety of grounds seek refuge in the country. It also strongly points to the inherent humaneness of the Indians, a quality without which it would be difficult to accommodate such a large number and variety of refugees in spite of our own economic concerns and numerous problems of governance which continue to surface due to, among other reasons, the enormous pressure of population in the country.

It is important to recognize that in spite of the fact that almost all the neighbouring countries in the Indian subcontinent have been the sources of large-scale flows of refugees from their territory, India has been an exception. This is all the more relevant because South Asia alone accounts for nearly 10 per cent of the total refugee problem all over the world. And, also because India shares borders with all its neighbours and the latter do not have common borders among themselves, India is the logical destination of refugees from our neighbours. Therefore, it is a dire practical necessity that India should have a regular legal framework to deal with refugees. At present, in the absence of a specific law to regulate and administer the problem of refugees in India, a lot of *ad hocism* has crept in which has not benefited the refugees; at the same time this does not offer any specific advantage to the country. Such an *ad hoc* approach does not permit of consistency and uniformity in dealing with individual refugees or groups of refugees. The absence of guidelines based on a firm policy often tempts individual refugees to approach the UNHCR for protection.

It is worthwhile to examine the manner in which 'refugees' have been handled so far in India, particularly at the time of their entry into the country.

When over 6.5 million people took refuge in the newly born state of India following the partition of the subcontinent in 1947, the Government of India took the necessary legislative and administrative measures by adopting The Rehabilitation Finance Administration Act, 1948 and the Displaced Persons (Claims) Act, 1950. It should be noted that those taking refuge in India after crossing the newly created India-Pakistan border were called 'displaced persons' and not 'refugees'. Under these two Acts, a 'displaced persons' meant 'a person who, being displaced from any area (now forming part of Pakistan) on account of civil disturbances or fear of such disturbances, has settled and is engaged or intends to engage in any business or industry in India.' Thus, these persons are not covered by international or regional conventions. The fact is that no procedure for the 'recognition' of these persons crossing the border was put in place nor was it insisted upon. In order to administer the above-mentioned Acts, a special ministry was created at the centre (with branches in all the states), whose primary concern at that time was to look after these 'displaced persons', including matters such as transport, communication, provision for earning a livelihood, if necessary by allotting agricultural land.

When the Dalai Lama and his followers (approximately 13,000 in number) crossed over to India in 1959, the spiritual and temporal leader of the Tibetans was given 'asylum' and his followers were registered as 'refugees' and were given registration certificates by merely following a preliminary screening procedure. In 1971, in the case of over 10 million people belonging to East Pakistan (later Bangladesh), who crossed over to Indian territory to escape the Pakistan Army, the Government of India established 'refugee camps' to accommodate them till their return to their homeland. After the birth of Bangladesh in December 1971, most of these refugees, in accordance with the prior understanding, went back to their now independent country, although some of the refugees became assimilated into the local population and managed to remain in India. The fact is that considering the particular situation then prevailing in East Pakistan, the Government of India acted in the best possible humanitarian manner and allowed the fleeing Pakistani nationals to take refuge in India. The Government of India undertook this mission notwithstanding the fact that there was no formal refugee regime in vogue in India at the time. However, it may be seen that the action taken by the Government of India fulfilled for all practical purposes the requirements of *non-refoulment*, a principle central to any law on refugees.

As a result of the prevailing situation and the war with Pakistan in 1971, about 44,000 refugees from the Sindh province of Pakistan were accommodated as refugees in India. The following year, in 1972, Ugandan citizens of Indian origin were given refugee status under the Foreigners from Uganda Order, 1972, which was specially promulgated to meet that situation. The same was the case with over 3,000 Burmese refugees who crossed over to India in 1988 when the Government of Myanmar (formerly Burma) suppressed the pro-democracy movement in that country. In accepting the Burmese as refugees, a spokesman of the Ministry of External Affairs, Government of India justified this action on the basis of 'well accepted international norms' defining refugee status and also in the light of the liberal attitude adopted by the Government of India in the past in interpreting these norms. The result was that no genuine refugee was turned back. Once again the cardinal principle of *non-refoulment* was obviously kept in mind.

In 1979, India handled the Chakma refugees, this time fleeing from the territory of Bangladesh to avoid persecution on grounds of race and religion, by setting up camps near the border and permitting their entry into India on the basis of local and preliminary screening. This procedure was followed in the absence of any specific legislation dealing with the determination of 'refugee status'. A similar policy was put into operation when, in July 1983, a mass exodus of Sri Lankan Tamils took place as the result of repressive military actions in Sri Lanka directed selectively against the Tamils there.

Besides these mass movements of people into Indian territory from across international borders, there have also been numerous instances of individuals or smaller groups of foreign nationals seeking refuge in India. Refugees from Iran, Iraq, Sudan, and some other African countries fall under this category. In all these cases, the Government of India has accepted the recognition of their refugee status by the UNHCR under the mandate of this international organization. Similar is the case of the more than 10,000 Afghan nationals who are living in and around Delhi after being accorded refugee status by the UNHCR, of course, with the approval of the Government of India.

These instances clearly show that the Government of India has deliberately been following a policy of exercising its prerogative on a case to case basis. While in the event of a large-scale exodus, as in the case of the Tibetans and others referred to above, the government seems to have followed the policy of recognition by specific order, while in the case of smaller groups and individuals the question of according refugee status seems to have been left in the hands of the UNHCR, although subject to the government's approval, if such refugees recognized by the UNHCR were to continue to stay in India as refugees. It is pertinent to point out at this juncture that the subject of the 'protection of refugees' is not adequately covered by any international legislation. The Convention Relating to the Status of Refugees, 1951 and its Protocol, 1967 are the appropriate instruments available at present. It should be noted that even though these are UN instruments, India, as well as all its South Asian neighbours, have not as yet signed and ratified these instruments.

In the absence of any specific legislation in India to cover 'refugees', the various provisions of a variety of acts and regulations have to be applied to refugees. The Foreigners Act, 1946 (which empowers the central government in respect of the entry of aliens into India, their presence, and their departure herefrom), the Registration of Foreigners Act, 1939 (which provides for the registration of foreigners entering, being present in, and departing from India), the Passport (Entry into India) Act, 1920 (which empowers the government to impose the condition of possession of a passport for entry into India), and the Passport Act, 1967 (which primarily deals with the issue of passports and travel documents to regulate the departure from India of citizens of India, and which applies in certain cases to others also) are brought into play to deal with refugees, who are in any case 'foreigners' and 'aliens'. Besides the above pieces of legislation, the Extradition Act, 1962, the Foreigners Order, 1948 (which deals with the power to grant or refuse permission to enter India or to depart from India), and the Citizenship Act, 1954 are relevant in the context of refugees. In addition to the above-mentioned legal instruments which are in respect of foreigners, refugees are also subject to the various provisions of criminal laws, *inter alia*, the Indian Penal Code, the Criminal Procedure Code, and the Indian Evidence Act.

Given the security situation prevailing in the country, particularly in the light of the role of some of India's neighbours in organizing violent and disruptive anti-India activities, including activities on Indian territory, the 'refugee problem' has sometimes come to be viewed in the light of national security considerations rather than in the light of its underlying humanitarian aspects. In this connection, the aspect of security needs to be duly addressed in any legislation that may be thought of to govern refugees in India. Studies conducted on the impact of refugees on the security/instability of host countries have highlighted the need to be vigilant against the adverse influences of refugees in matters relating to the security and stability of the host countries. Such instances have frequently occurred in India. Mahendra P. Lama in his paper 'Managing Refugees in South Asia' (Occasional Paper 4, Refugee and Migratory Movements Research Unit, University of Dhaka, Bangladesh, April 2000) argues that:

> national security is compromised when one or more of the three dimensions viz., the strategic dimension, regime dimension and structural dimension is threatened or eroded. The strategic security is threatened when refugees are armed and when government loses control of refugees; structural dimension is threatened by increasing demands on and the conflict over scarce resources and regime security threatened when refugees enter the domestic political process and create pressures on the government.

In the case of the refugees from Sri Lanka, the first two factors came into play when the Sri Lankan refugees were arming themselves freely on Indian territory and on many occasions sought to resolve the sectoral rivalries among themselves by resorting to violent and armed clashes. As already mentioned, such a development ultimately led to the assassination of Rajiv Gandhi in 1991 in the outskirts of Chennai.

There are other aspects too which make the law enforcement vis-à-vis refugees a complex and complicated matter. While law and order is a state subject under the Indian Constitution, international relations and international borders are under the exclusive purview of the Union government. This has resulted in a variety of agencies, both of the Central as well as the State governments, having to deal with refugee matters connected with law enforcement. Also, all policies governing the refugees are laid down by the Union government although the impact of the refugee problem as such has to be borne by the State administration to a greater degree, if not wholly.

A large number and variety of security agencies come into contact with refugees. Security personnel at the international borders, immigration personnel at the land check posts, international airports and seaports, besides a host of state police personnel, are all intimately connected with law enforcement affecting refugees one way or another. For all these security agencies, ensuring national as well as internal security is their first and foremost charge. They have to make sure that the laws of the land are enforced in regard to refugees without in any way ignoring or neutralizing security considerations. But, at the same time, it is also their responsibility that the humanitarian overtones so characteristically and inseparably associated with refugees in general, are not lost sight of. It is also well known that every single situation pertaining to 'refugees' is replete with human rights aspects as well. A proper understanding of the circumstances pertaining to specific refugee situations by the concerned law enforcement agency or even by an individual official would pave the way for taking care of both the security as well as the humane aspects—from both the humanitarian as well as the human rights angle. Viewed in this background, absence of a refugee-specific legislation is seen as a serious handicap. Since many refugees move from one place to another within the country (for example, Tibetan refugees in India), it has become a matter of practical importance that security and administrative personnel in the different states of the country are well versed with the various aspects of refugee matters, particularly the law enforcement aspect of the same. One single national legal instrument will facilitate such a requirement.

While all persons who are not Indian citizens are 'foreigners', including refugees, it is necessary to clearly distinguish refugees from other categories of 'foreigners'. Many Indians have considerable misgivings in this regard because of the failure to clearly understand the difference between 'refugees' and the various 'other categories of foreigners'. The consequence of this misunderstanding, particularly because of the large number of 'illegal immigrants' from Bangladesh who have spread into different parts of India, has tended to adversely influence the thinking of many Indians about the basic issues pertaining to 'refugees'. There are at least three well-defined groups of foreigners who are different from 'refugees'. These are: (i) temporary residents, tourists, and travellers; (ii) economic migrants; and (iii) criminals, spies, infiltrators, militants, etc. It is important that the distinction among these groups is clearly understood so that none of them is confused with or mistaken for a 'refugee'. Any law enacted to deal with refugees will naturally provide the required safeguards in this regard.

In the absence of a specific law to govern refugees, who have to be distinguished from other 'foreigners', there is considerable reluctance to treat refugees on a different footing as would be warranted by 'humanitarian' considerations. One of the aims of any national-level legislation would be to formally clarify this.

Recently, laws have been enacted to cater for the specific needs of children and unaccompanied minors. Juvenile homes have been given specific legal responsibility in this regard. Since it is common to encounter children and unaccompanied minors among refugees, it is necessary to make specific provisions in the legal statutes covering refugees to reflect the requirements of other national legislations in this regard.

Even though India is not a signatory to the 1951 UN Convention on Refugees and the 1967 Protocol, the country is a signatory to a number of United Nations and other international conventions on human rights. India's obligations in regard to refugees arises out of the latter conventions. India became a member of the Executive Committee of the High Commissioner's Programme (EXCOM) in 1955. The EXCOM is the UN organization which approves and supervises the material assistance programme of the UNHCR. Membership of the EXCOM indicates a country's particular interest in and greater commitment to refugee matters. India voted affirmatively to adopt the Universal Declaration of Human Rights which affirms rights for all persons, citizens and non-citizens alike. India voted affirmatively to adopt the UN Declaration of Territorial Asylum in 1967. India ratified the International Convention on Civil and Political Rights (ICCPR), as well as the International Convention on Economic, Social and Cultural Rights (ICESCR) in 1976. India ratified the UN Convention on the Rights of the Child in 1989. India ratified the Convention on the Elimination of All Forms of Discrimination Against Women

(CEDAW) in 1974. India accepted the principle of *non-refoulement* as envisaged in the Bangkok Principles, 1966, which were formulated for the guidance of member states in respect of matters concerning the status and treatment of refugees. These Principles also contain provisions relating to repatriation, right to compensation, the grant of asylum, and the minimum standard of treatment in the state of asylum.

As already emphasized, India does not have on its statute book a specific and separate law to govern refugees. It is desirable that the country should legislate a refugee-specific law incorporating the various aspects which have been highlighted in the foregoing paragraphs. In the absence of such a specific law, all existing Indian laws such as the Criminal Procedure Code, the Indian Penal Code, the Evidence Act, etc., apply to the refugees as well. At present, the relevant provisions applicable to a specific refugee case have to be culled out from among numerous laws. The fact that there is no single refugee-specific law in the country does not augur well for uniformly interpreting such laws whenever refugees are encountered in different part of India. At present, this aspect has been left to be resolved by judicial pronouncements in individual cases. All these instances strongly point to the desirability of adopting a refugee-specific legislation which can be uniformly and unambiguously enforced all over India.

It can be easily seen from the foregoing paragraphs that India, notwithstanding its own security concerns, particularly in the last two decades of the twentieth century, and despite increasing demographic pressure and attendant economic problems, continues to take a humanitarian view of the refugee problem. Even though India has not enacted a special law to govern 'refugees', this has not proved to be a serious handicap in coping satisfactorily with the enormous refugee problems besetting the country. By and large, India has honoured both the letter and the spirit of various UN and international conventions on the subject through executive as well as judicial intervention. As pointed out elsewhere in this paper, the spirit of *non-refoulment* is clearly evident behind many of the steps taken by the government. By these means, the country has evolved a practical balance between humane and humanitarian obligations, on the one hand, and security and national interests, on the other. It is in balancing these interests, which may sometimes appear to be competing against each other, that the security and law enforcement agencies face challenges on a day-to-day basis.

If and when a separate 'Refugee Law' for the country is enacted, it is important that this aspect be formally reflected in its provisions. The crucial thing is the need to provide adequate safeguards to enable the security agencies to verify the claims of an intending refugee before a decision is taken in his/her case without unduly and hastily denying the benefit of *non-refoulment* to the refugee(s). Such an inquiry is most likely to be a time- consuming exercise. Therefore, it is necessary that the proposed 'Refugee Law' should allow for a reasonable amount of time for the concerned court of law to carefully and meaningfully complete the inquiry into all cases, which should be decided on a case-by-case basis. Pending the completion of the inquiry, the refugee(s) may be detained in judicial custody. Another matter that deserves to be considered is whether in all those cases it is necessary to make public all these the details elicited during an inquiry, particularly if such a disclosure is likely to jeopardize the security of the nation or its relationship with a foreign country. Therefore, the need to make a 'secrecy' provision might also arise. Incidentally, in the USA, the statute relating to immigration and naturalization has a 'secrecy' provision.

Also, when an intending refugee is detained in accordance with the law, it is necessary to enable him/her to get appropriate legal advice. In this regard, the role of the legal aid cells at different levels, as also the role of the UNHCR, should be defined in the proposed legislative act itself. Since one of the aims of a national legislation would be to ensure uniformity of practice, and since refugees may be encountered in any part of India, it may be desirable to establish a 'nodal agency' for this purpose. This agency would ensure uniformity and may also help in establishing liaison relations between the security agency concerned, the refugee(s), and the legal aid mechanisms, including the UNHCR.

6. *Resolving the Refugee Problem: A Role for Human Rights Organizations*

D.R. KAARTHIKEYAN

Refugee movements are indicative of a world in turmoil, a world plagued by humanitarian crises. Refugees are persons who have been forced to flee their homelands because of the massive violation of their human rights, or those who have been forced to leave on account of man-made disasters (such as civil war, armed conflict, ethnic and racial strife, and political persecution) and natural or ecological disasters (including poverty). The existence of refugees is a matter of global concern and it is the responsibility of the entire international community to make sincere efforts to resolve their problems, both legally and politically.

In the aftermath of World War II, the United Nations was confronted with the tragic consequences of a devastating war which had uprooted and exiled millions across the world. This massive humanitarian crisis led to the creation of the office of the United Nations High Commission for Refugees (UNHCR) in 1950. Despite the creation of the UNHCR, the problem of refugees continued in the subsequent decades in Europe, Africa, and Asia. These crises resulted in millions of refugees stagnating for years in overcrowded camps in countries which lacked the capacity to absorb and rehabilitate these growing numbers of the homeless. As for the international community, with little hope of pursuing either the repatriation or the integration of refugees, the best that could be done in most cases was to provide humanitarian assistance to meet their most basic needs in the short term.

The partition of the Indian subcontinent in 1947 resulted in one of the greatest mass migrations of modern history. It is estimated that at least 15 million people migrated in both directions across the newly created international borders. The relocation of the population between the two countries of India and Pakistan following independence from colonial rule is symptomatic of the paradox in which they lived together in tolerance for several centuries. The refugees had to make enormous and frequently very difficult efforts to overcome the new situations which confronted them, were forced to negotiate their way in a new complex arena of social relations, and to undertake new initiatives to become self-reliant in their new surroundings. The creation, existence, and persistence of the refugee problem is the outcome of a complex interaction of colonial and national power in which millions of poor, ordinary, and powerless people become the inevitable victims of rapid change. The rehabilitation and assimilation of refugees in the national, political, social, economic, and cultural mainstream of the receiving country is one of the greatest success stories of modern India.

As civil conflict, political persecution, and natural disasters continue to plague many countries, millions of people are forced to live outside their countries of origin. Women and children make up the majority of the world's refugee population.

The challenge is not merely to manage the refugee movements so as to balance the rights of the refugees as well as the interests of the host state in a just and humane manner. This delicate balance can best be observed by eternal vigilance on the part of sensitive and dedicated human rights organizations.

International protection is guaranteed to refugees for humanitarian reasons. The basis of the principle of the protection of refugees is found in the statute of the office of the UNHCR and in the various refugee conventions.

The UNHCR was established by the General Assembly of the United Nations as a subsidiary organ under Article 22 of the United Nations Charter, and the body continues to play an active role in expanding the mandate of the office. The UNHCR does enjoy an international personality. As a subsidiary organ of the General Assembly, its 'personality' can be traced to the United Nations at large. Moreover, its statute shows that the office was entrusted by the General Assembly to act on the international plane.

The UNHCR's standing in regard to protection has been further reinforced by successive General Assembly resolutions urging all states to support the High Commissioner's activities. The UNHCR's statute mandates that it has to work with non-government agencies. It works with hundreds of NGOs throughout the world such as CARE and Save the Children.

Over the past four decades, the UNHCR's traditional role of providing protection has become much broader in scope and significantly more operational. At the same time, its focus of action is equally on the protection in the states of asylums of the refugees and their activities in the countries of origin.

Human instincts undoubtedly propel people to assist others in need since the dawn of civilization. Today the process of providing humanitarian assistance has became a highly organized enterprise involving law and regulations, defined roles and vested interests, major political implications, international organizations, and large sums of money.

Nevertheless, the efforts at providing refugee assistance remain heavily imbued with idealism and humanitarianism, a characteristic which is particularly noticeable in the case of private, religious, and charitable agencies. This idealistic and humanitarian motivation is largely based on the notion of rescuing the victims of persecution and violence.

The Magnitude of the Refugee Problem in South Asia

It is estimated that South Asia has over 1.3 million refugees.

AFGHANISTAN

At the end of 2000, over 3.6 million Afghans were living as refugees in countries other than their own. Of this figure, over 13,000 Afghan refugees were living in India.

At the end of 2000, Bangladesh hosted over 121,600 refugees.

An estimated 144,000 persons from Bhutan were living as refugees in neighbouring countries, including 129,000 in Nepal and more than 13,000 in India.

INDIA

India has offered safety and security to hundreds of thousands of victims of ethnic conflict in the last 55 years. At the end of 2000, more than 300,000 refugees were living in India. This included 110,000 from Tibet, 110,000 from Sri Lanka, 42,000 from Bhutan, 30,000 from Afghanistan, and more than 300 from other countries. Another 40,000 Afghans were living in India in refugee-like conditions.

Over 500,000 people were internally displaced in India as a result of political violence, including 350,000 Kashmiris and more than 157,000 others in north-east India. The 17-year-long conflict between the Sri Lanka Sinhalese, the Buddhist majority in the island, and the

Tamils, the Hindu minority, has resulted in more than 110,000 Sri Lankan Tamils fleeing to India. The number of Tibetan refugees in India keeps fluctuating as a result of deaths, births, and the arrival of an additional 2,000 to 3,000 refugees from Tibet each year. More than 40,000 ethnic Chin and 1,000 ethnic Naga refugees from Myanmar (Burma) were living in the north-eastern states of India.

Although South Asia has long had a hallowed tradition of generously receiving refugees and extending hospitality to them, none of the South Asian countries is a signatory to the 1951 Convention relating to the status of refugees or its 1967 Protocol. India was not a signatory to either the 1951 UN Convention or its 1965 Protocol, obviously because these conventions stressed the rights of refugees only, thus placing a disproportionate obligation on the refugee-receiving states. None of the South Asian countries has any national laws dealing specifically with refugees. The various governments of South Asia have dealt with refugee problems through bilateral negotiations. Refugees and asylum seekers in the region are treated like any other foreigners and are subject to the laws and regulations governing the entry, stay, and departure of foreigners. Obviously, the provisions of the Foreigners Act 1946 will not be adequate to meet the humanitarian and basic needs of refugees.

A seminar organized by SAARCLAW in collaboration with the UNHCR (New Delhi, 1997) examined the situation of refugees in the region. Most participants supported the need for the adoption of refugee laws. They also acknowledged the need for finding a humanitarian solution to this very serious problem. A common refugee legislation for the SAARC region would also need to be accompanied by clear citizenship laws for the region.

As observed by the Chief of Mission, during the seminar, UNHCR, New Delhi, the fundamental legal issues concerning the rights and obligations of both refugees and governments need to be addressed concurrently with the political aspects of a refugee problem. International refugee law was concerned both with protecting the rights of refugees as well as solving refugee problems.

While the country of asylum had the obligation to protect refugees, the country of origin had the obligation to create conditions so that refugees may return to their homes in safety.

The lack of a legal procedure to distinguish between illegal immigrants and refugees has resulted in increasing confusion regarding the two in the popular mind, thus straining the tradition of hospitality in the region.

There is a close relationship between the violation of human rights and the refugee situation. In addition to persons who fled their homes as the result of human rights violations, others who were forced to leave on account of man-made disasters, natural disasters, conflict situations, and poverty should also be classified as refugees.

Most of the causes behind the mass exodus of people around the world are due to human rights violations and such mass migration gave rise to human rights problems.

Hence, it should be borne in mind that refugee law is part of the much broader spectrum of international human rights law.

The codification, adoption, and implementation of refugee legislation is imperative to avoid *ad hoc* and delayed decisions. Such a legal framework must necessarily reconcile the conflicting interests of both the receiving country and the refugees. As Pandit Jawaharlal Nehru once said, 'The rule of law must strengthen the rule of life.'

While asylum may not be a final solution to the problems of refugees, it is an essential component of refugee protection.

One of the reasons why some Asian countries have chosen not to be signatories to the 1951 Convention or its 1961 Protocol is that these countries are not in a position to guarantee all the socio-economic rights of refugees as granted by these instruments.

However, India has always supported the basic principles for which the UNHCR stands. India's commitment may be seen in the way in which the country has treated the Tibetan, Sri Lankan, and Chakma refugees who have sought asylum within its borders. The Supreme Court of India has made a singular contribution in extending the rights of both citizens and aliens by imposing corresponding obligations on the state.

The problem of refugees, as stated by the eminent jurist Justice Shri P.N. Bhagwati, is a global one. It is the developing countries which continue to bear the major share of refugee inflows and are called upon to host large numbers of refugees and migrant populations. They find themselves overwhelmed by the burden imposed on them, given their scarce resources and energy diverted from their primary responsibilities of meeting the developmental needs of their own people. Their environment is devastated, resources are eroded, the economy is disrupted, law and order is threatened, and sometimes even the hospitality of the host country is abused.

Social, economic, and ethnic tensions exacerbated by the presence of refugees in areas where life is a perpetual struggle for existence for the locals themselves, result in widespread demands for the expulsion of refugees and sometimes even for entry across borders.

India must bear the expenses of feeding and housing Chakma refugees from Bangladesh, Tamil refugees from Sri Lanka, Arakanese refugees from Myanmar, and refugees from Tibet and Bhutan as well as refugees from other countries.

Virtually no country in South Asia has been free from the refugee problem.

When large numbers of people move across international borders, it is not usually possible to ascertain whether every person involved strictly meets the criteria of refugee status. Low-income countries simply do not have the logistical and administrative resources to undertake such demanding and complex tasks.

The country of asylum has an obligation to ensure that the refugees in its care are assured of the widest possible protection of all basic human rights as affirmed in the United Nations Charter, the Universal Declaration of Human Rights, and the 1951 Refugee Conventions. The refugees, in turn, are required to abide by the laws and regulations of the country which has granted them asylum and to conform to any measures taken by the authorities for the maintenance of law and public order.

The problem of forced displacement became considerably larger and more complex in the decade of the 1990s. But the number of refugees actually declined. The reduction in the number of refugees may be attributed to the success of large-scale repatriation movements which have taken place since the 1990s.

Article 1 of its statute provides that the UNHCR 'shall assume the function of providing international protection under the auspices of the United Nations to refugees who fall within the scope of the present statute'. Besides the Refugee Convention of 1951 and the additional Protocol of 1967, there are a number of regional conventions which further expand the definitions and rights of refugees to meet peculiar regional conditions.

The prevention of migration of refugees does not mean building barriers to stop the refugees from entering the intended country of asylum but it involves tackling the root causes which compel people to move in the first place. In seeking to prevent refugee movements, equal emphasis must also be placed on the economic and social conditions in which people live. Meeting the most important human needs on a priority basis, introducing employment criteria, adopting measures for poverty alleviation, education, and health can all help to reduce some of the pressures which lead to social unrest and upheaval which, in turn, may result in refugee flows.

Given the reality that most refugees both originate from and seek refugee status in some of the poorest parts of the world, neither the country of origin nor the country of asylum can be expected to discharge its respective responsibilities without the political and financial support of the international community.

In the final analysis, the existence of refugees is symptomatic of deeper social, economic, and political problems. The challenge is not how to keep people away but how to meet the needs of the victims and the communities which receive them, how to manage refugees in a way which satisfies their basic human rights while simultaneously addressing the concerns of the country of asylum. Solving the refugee problem involves a complex array of other problems: human rights, charity, immigration services, religious services, economic development, education, advocacy, and a host of support and other functions. Thus, the NGOs, including human rights organizations, play a crucial role in dealing with and solving the refugee problems at every stage.

No element has been more vital to the successful conduct of the programmes of the UNHCR in resolving the refugee problem than the close partnership between the UNHCR and the voluntary agencies. Such agencies act as the agents of private conscience and have become a permanent factor in refugee work in the last eight decades. The growing recognition of the role of NGOs and other human rights organizations in protecting and resolving the refugee problems requires their enhanced participation in dialogue with governments and national-level and state-level human rights commissions.

Internally Displaced Persons (IDPs)

According to a 2001 estimate, some 160,000 persons of various ethnicities were displaced in several parts of north-eastern India. This area of India, which is geographically and to some extent politically isolated from the rest of the country, is home to many tribal groups. The displaced populations in the north-east include an estimated 87,000 ethnic Santhals in Assam; 3,500 Bengalis also in Assam; 37,000 ethnics displaced from Mizoram into Tripura; 25,000 Bengalis in Tripura; and 3,000 ethnic Chakmas in Arunachal Pradesh.

Another important group of IDPs in India are the Kashmiris. As many as 350,000 Kashmiris, mostly Hindu Pandits, have been displaced since 1990 as a result of the long-standing conflict in Kashmir. Nearly 250,000 displaced Kashmiris are presently living near the city of Jammu, both in camps and in their homes. An estimated 100,000 Kashmiris are displaced elsewhere in India, primarily in the New Delhi area. Many displaced Pandits receive cash assistance and food aid from the Government of India. Former government workers continue to receive full salaries or retirement benefits. Nevertheless, some displaced Kashmiris complain that the government assistance is inadequate to meet their needs.

According to the UNHCR, more than 600,000 Sri Lankans were internally displaced. Another 110,000 Sri Lankans came to India as refugees. Most Sri Lankan refugees and displaced persons were Hindu Tamils, although Muslims and some Buddhist Sinhalese were also displaced. Sri Lanka hosted only 16 refugees, mostly Iraqis and Afghans. Sri Lankan refugees and displaced persons have been engaged in a bloody 17-year-long conflict that has claimed more than 62,000 lives. The conflict is between government forces that primarily represent Sri Lanka's Buddhists, the Sinhalese majority, and the LTTE, the Tamil minority.

An estimated 15,000 Lhotsampa ethnic Nepalese refugees from Bhutan are living in India. Most are located in the states of West Bengal and Assam. Under the terms of the Indo-Bhutan Friendship Treaty of 1950, India allows the Bhutanese to live and work freely in India. Therefore, the government does not acknowledge the Bhutanese as refugees, and nor does it assist them and nor does it require them to live in camps.

Nearly 14,000 UNHCR-recognized refugees live in urban sectors in India, mostly in New Delhi. At the end of 2000, a large majority (13,000) were from Afghanistan, while smaller numbers came from Myanmar, Iran, and Somalia. According to Indian refugee advocates, more than 40,000 other Afghans may be living in India in refugee-like circumstances.

In dealing with the refugee problem, the human rights organizations and human rights commissions have a vital role to play. They must be active in both spheres, that of preventing the exodus of the refugees from their home states in the first place and also, once the refugee problem has been created, they must be active in looking after the essential needs and welfare of the refugees in the asylum states.

According to the United Nations High Commissioner for Refugees:

Human Rights violations are a major factor in causing the flight of refugees as well as an obstacle to their safe and voluntary return home. Safeguarding Human Rights in [the] countries of origin is therefore critical both for the prevention and for the solution of refugee problems. Respect for Human Rights is also essential for the protection of refugees in [the] countries of asylum.

Even in the absence of specific legislation, refugees are entitled to enjoy human rights protection, a large number of which are enshrined in major international and regional human rights instruments and national constitutions. These include, for instance, the right of religious freedom, the freedom to hold and express opinions, and the freedom to organize and participate in public gatherings. Under international human rights law, all of these rights are guaranteed to both citizens and non-citizens. The Human Rights Committee explicitly states: 'Aliens have the right to freedom of thought, conscience and religion and the right to hold opinions and to express them. Aliens receive the benefit of the right of peaceful assembly and of freedom of association.' Of course, all these rights are subject to certain limitations.

Some of the international instruments constituting international human rights law are:

1. Universal Declaration of Human Rights.
2. International Convention on Civil and Political Rights.
3. Convention on the Rights of the Child.
4. European Convention on the Protection of Human Rights.
5. American Declaration of the Rights and the Duties of Man.
6. Declaration on the Elimination of All Forms of Intolerance and Discrimination Based on Religion and Belief.

India has been a receiving state for refugees over the centuries. Throughout its history India has welcomed all those who came as refugees and absorbed them as part of the people of India. They have intermingled, merged with, and become one with the common humanity of India. But this assimilation and amalgamation of different races and different ethnicities has been a historical development which has occurred naturally over the centuries without the benefit of any specific legislation mandated by the state. Even in the absence of legislation, India has always respected the principle of *non-refoulment*. It is only when the security of the state is threatened or when law and order is endangered that the state has been compelled to impose some restrictions on the movement of refugees or to curtail their rights.

However, *bona fide* asylum seekers have always been recognized and protected by the Indian government.

India has acceded to or signed most of the major international human rights instruments, many provisions of which are complementary to the principle of the protection of refugees. The Convention on the Elimination of all Forms of Racial Discrimination was ratified in 1969. In 1979, India acceded to the International Covenant on Civil and Political Rights and the International Covenant on Economic, Social and Cultural Rights (1986). In 1992, India acceded to the Convention on the Rights of the Child (1989). The Convention on the Elimination of all Forms of Discrimination against Women (1979) was ratified in 1993. In 1997, India signed the Convention against Torture.

However, there is no specific legislation dealing with the problems of refugees. These problems are dealt with by India and all other countries of South Asia on a purely *ad hoc* basis. This is purely due to a growing concern by the governments of the South Asian region that persons who may have committed crimes against humanity, war crimes, or other acts which are incompatible with the humanitarian nature of refugee status may enter the country and remain on Indian soil under the pretext of being refugees. It is necessary to emphasize that the absence of specific refugee laws and procedures may put the state at a disadvantage in reaching a proper decision regarding the determination of refugee status.

The Role of the Judiciary

Despite the absence of a formal legal instrument, the judiciary in India has played a major role in safeguarding the rights of refugees and asylum seekers. Indeed, some Indian judicial pronouncements have enshrined principles on the right to seek asylum, *non-refoulment*, and voluntary repatriation. The courts have arrived at their decisions without specifying or entering into a discussion on international refugee law. They have relied on applicable 'Rights Provisions' in the Indian Constitution, including Article 14 (Right to Equality) and Article 21 (Right to Life and Liberty), which have been determined to be applicable to refugees.

The decision of the apex court regarding the treatment of foreigners enunciated that foreigners are entitled to protection under Article 21. Where there was imminent danger to Chakma refugees, the state was directed to ensure that the rights and liberty of each and every one of them was protected (*NHRC* vs *State of Arunachal Pradesh*, 1996).

Article 51 in Part IV of the Constitution provides that the state is enjoined to foster respect for international law and treatment applications. The apex court does require the governments and courts to apply the principles of interpretation that further promote and do not hinder the aspirations of Part IV of the Constitution.

The courts in India have laid down guidelines in the area of refugee protection by reading Article 21 in its expansive significance in the light of the directive principles of state policy.

In the Vishakha Judgement of 1997, the Supreme Court held that any international convention not inconsistent with the fundamental rights and in harmony with the spirit of the Constitution must be read into the Constitution to enlarge the meaning and content thereof and to promote the objectives of constitutional guarantees. It was held in a series of outstanding pronouncements that the courts are under an obligation to give due regard to international conventions and norms in construing domestic law and particularly when there is no inconsistency between them, and there is a void in the domestic law.

Despite the absence of a legal framework, the Indian administrative and legal systems can be activated in favour of refugee protection by relying upon (i) the Indian humanitarian tradition; (ii) India's international legal obligations; (iii) the Constitution of India; and (iv) the humanist jurisprudence of the Constitution of India.

When Chakma refugees were being threatened with deportation, the National Human Rights Commission of India took the case to the Supreme Court. The NHRC also sent its team to examine the conditions in the refugee camps and thereafter it made appropriate recommendations to the concerned governments.

As the foundations of the refugee problem rested on human rights violations in the home country, appropriate measures are required to address these problems and to restore normalcy for ensuring effective repatriation. Minimum standards of treatment should be prescribed, a mechanism for redressal should be created.When these standards are not met, the country of origin should be held accountable for any refugee exodus.

There is a need to promote awareness of international refugee laws and standards. To ensure clarity, certainty, and uniformity in both substance and procedure, the several refugee-related ordinances which are issued from time to time should be codified, and the authorities and human rights organizations should comply with these regulations; it is also important to sensitize the public on various issues pertaining to the condition and status of refugees. Clear provisions dealing with the protection of refugee women and children as well as their safe and voluntary repatriation should be included.

The solution to a human problem must necessarily be based on humanism. Hence, the legal framework has to be based on human rights. In any civilized society, a human problem is a matter of common concern. Hence, the problem of refugees cannot be viewed in isolation. Therefore, the legal framework, which must necessarily be erected, should not only take care of and provide for the protection, welfare, rehabilitation, and repatriation of the refugees, but it should also reconcile the conflicting interests of the receiving country with the interests of refugee protection.

The basic cause for this problem is the abuse of human rights. Human rights are claims which every individual has or should have upon the society in which he or she lives. They are universal and are the due of every human being in every society. They do not differ with the country, culture, ideology, or with any political or economic system. They do not depend on gender, race, class, or status. They need not be earned or deserved. They are claims of rights, not merely appeals to grace or charity or brotherhood or love. They are claims of entitlement and the corresponding obligation rests with the political and administrative institutions.

Since human rights are basic, fundamental, and inherent, they need not specifically be conferred by any constitution or be legislated by an act. What the constitution or any specific law does is merely recognize the existence of human rights and provide the machinery for the protection of these rights and their enforcement and protection, whenever the need arises.

The 1951 Convention relating to the status of refugees and the 1961 Protocol have to be given legal sanction by enacting domestic laws which can be enforced in national courts.

The mere enactment of a law is not enough. The enactment of a law which is more readily acceptable is more effective. The existing position is that it is only to the extent that national courts can provide relief that it has been possible to do it.

So far the premise on which the judiciary has been acting to protect the interests of the refugees is that basic human rights are supposedly implied in every civilized system, and that unless there is an inconsistent provision in the domestic laws, basic human rights have been read into the provisions of the constitution and other enacted laws.

Therefore, it is as a result of judicial creativity that certain basic rights of the refugees have been taken care of through the medium of the courts. In India, the Supreme Court has held that certain basic rights such as the right to equality (Article 14), the right to life and liberty (Article 21), and the freedom to practice and propagate one's religion (Article 25) are available to non-citizen refugees as well. Due to this creative and humanistic interpretation of the law by the apex court, the rights of citizens as well as non-citizens have been expanded by the Indian courts.

The Role of the NHRC

When quit notices were issued to refugees in the north-eastern states of India by an activist students' organization, the Supreme Court granted relief when the NHRC approached the apex court for protection under Article 32 [1996].

The National Alliance of Peoples' Movement submitted a petition before the NHRC, seeking its intervention in the matter relating to the alleged human rights violations of the Bargi Dam Oustees in Madhya Pradesh. Later the NHRC sent a team to conduct an on-the-spot study. The NHRC also recommended to the Ministry of Rural Development, Government of India that at the policy level the central and state governments should re-examine and appropriately amend the relevant laws, regulations, and practices in order to ensure that when it comes to the acquisition of land for purposes related to national economic development, the provisions of the Constitution, and the pronouncements of the Supreme Court as contained in international instruments to which India is a party, should be fully respected. The Government of India had reported to the NHRC that a national policy on the resettlement and rehabilitation of displaced persons is under consideration at the highest official levels.

Human rights organizations brought to the notice of the NHRC that the Land Acquisition Act, 1984, which is still in force today, does not contain any provision for rehabilitation and, therefore, that this constitutes a grave violation of the human rights of the displaced persons who depend for their livelihood on the land and other resources. The NHRC considered the issue in depth and recommended that adequate provisions for the resettlement and rehabilitation of persons displaced in the process of land acquisition for various projects should be incorporated in the Land Acquisition Act itself. The Ministry of Rural

Development was advised to incorporate the rehabilitation and resettlement package in the Land Acquisition Act itself for the following reasons:

(1) The ILO Convention, to which India is a party, provides for the protection of the rights of indigenous and tribal peoples;
(2) The incorporation of the rehabilitation and resettlement (R&R) package in the law will ensure that the R&R of project-affected people is carried out in a systematic manner;
(3) The provisions of R&R in the law will avoid litigation, at times frivolous, in the matter, which would help in avoidance of delays and cost overruns of the projects;
(4) Once the R&R package is provided in the law, there will be uniformity in dealing with the cases by the court and this step would avoid undue interference by the courts;
(5) The R&R facilities should be provided in advance before the actual acquisition of land takes place;
(6) The NHRC noted that in a number of cases excess land is being acquired and that no consultation takes place with the people who are likely to be affected by the acquisition of land. A properly drawn up project document, containing estimates of the expenditure involved in R&R, would avoid the acquisition of excess land.
(7) For the purpose, of transparency and for the information of the people likely to be affected by the project, a committee consisting of representatives from the government, the industry/ agency for which the land is proposed to be acquired, and the project-affected people should hold detailed consultations before the acquisition of the land, as is the practice in the USA.

The NHRC has done valuable work in addressing the plight of refugees in specific instances, as in the case of the Chakmas and the Sri Lankan Tamils. Where necessary, the NHRC has taken individual issues concerning refugees to the Supreme Court, as was done in the case of *NHRC* vs *State of Arunachal Pradesh*, 1996. The NHRC has also made several recommendations to the central and state governments to relieve the distress and plight of IDPs such as the Kashmiri Pandits and also those who are displaced and dislocated by the construction of major irrigation projects.

I had conducted an investigation as Director General, NHRC into the enormous problems faced by thousands of persons who were dislocated and uprooted due to the construction of the huge naval project called Seabird on the Karwar coast of Karnataka. I reported several inadequacies in the rehabilitation arrangements. The NHRC directed the Government of India and the Karnataka Government to pay adequate compensation to every displaced person and also to adopt several other measures to improve the lives of the displaced persons and their families.

The important role which the human rights commissions and human rights organizations can play needs to be appreciated and encouraged. Of course, the role of institutions such as the human rights commissions and the judiciary is basically remedial. However, when the NHRC and the State Human Rights Commissions lay down guidelines, the authorities are meant to ensure the strict observance and implementation of these rules to prevent the suffering caused to such displaced persons in future.

7. *Bangladeshi Migrants in India: Towards a Practical Solution– A View from the North-Eastern Frontier*

WASBIR HUSSAIN

The turbulent north-east may be India's backwaters, but this area of 255,000 sq. km[1] shares a highly porous and sensitive frontier with unpredictable China, blow-hot-blow-cold Myanmar, semi-friendly Bangladesh, and traditional ally Bhutan. If the region is best known to the outside world for its separatist insurrections and ethnic strife, it is also known as a place which hordes of migrants from across the borders, primarily from Bangladesh, have made their destination over the years, and eventually their home. Inhabited by 39.02 million people,[2] north-eastern India has a 4,500 km-long international border, but is connected to the Indian mainland by a tenuous 22 km-long land corridor passing through Siliguri in the state of West Bengal in eastern India—a link also called the 'Chicken's Neck'. Four of the north-eastern Indian states together share a 1,879 km-long border with Bangladesh: Tripura 856 km, Meghalaya 443 km, Mizoram 318 km, and Assam 262 km. West Bengal, of course, has a 2,216 km-long border with Bangladesh. The seven states of the region came to be bracketed as the 'north-east' after India gained independence in 1947.

The unabated trans-border migration has altered, or is threatening to alter, the demographic complexion of some of these states, particularly Assam and Tripura. This has been the cause of much of the turmoil in the region, with the indigenous people facing the prospect of being reduced to a minority in their own homeland. The influx of Bengalis from the plains of the erstwhile East Pakistan, now Bangladesh, has reduced Tripura's tribal population to a minority. According to the 1991 Census, the indigenous tribal people of Tripura constituted only 28 per cent of the state's population of 2.76 million. Three decades earlier, the tribals comprised two-thirds of Tripura's population.[3]

The illegal Bangladeshi influx into Tripura and Assam may not surprise everyone considering the fact that the two states share several hundred kilometres of a porous border with that country. Besides, the illegal migrants get much-needed breathing space by staying put in the border areas on the Indian side which are inhabited by people of the same stock who speak the same language, thus making detection by the authorities difficult. But what is significant is the massive population explosion in Nagaland, a hill state with a 99 per cent tribal population which has no direct border with Bangladesh, but which is said to be facing the major brunt of the illegal Bangladeshi influx. The provisional figures released by the Census Commissioner of India in early 2001 revealed that Nagaland recorded a 64.41 per cent growth in population between 1991 and 2001, much above the national average of 21.34 per cent.[4] Up from the growth of 56.08 per cent in the years 1981 to 1991, Nagaland once again recorded the highest population growth in the country. A media report said that the figures supported the fear expressed by the Nagaland Chief Minister S.C. Jamir in 2000 that Nagaland, after Assam, would be the next state to be hit by large-scale illegal migration by Bangladeshis. The report quoted Jamir as saying at a meeting of the chief ministers of the north-eastern region with Prime Minister Atal Behari Vajpayee in Shillong in January 2000, 'Unless steps are taken to prevent the entry of people of dubious nationality into our state, Nagaland may face the same problem as that of Assam.'

The movements of people from East Bengal, later East Pakistan and now Bangladesh, into Assam and Tripura, and onwards to other states in the region, have transformed vast tracts of territory from land-abundant areas to land-scarce areas. In a region known for its lack of industrial activity, the large-scale influx of people from across the porous international borders has led to a conflict between the migrants and the indigenous people over the sharing of natural resources, as well as employment, both in the government and in the private sectors. Such clashes of interest have directly led to the growth of violent tribal insurgencies, as in Tripura, with guerrilla groups targeting the migrant settlers from the plains, who are seen as land grabbers. The anger of these insurgent groups is also directed against the Indian state, which these outfits accuse of being an 'exploiter', working against tribal interests.

Similarly, in Assam the issue of migration has led to the growth of Assamese sub-nationalism, at times bordering on xenophobia, mainly because of the fear among the indigenous communities of being overwhelmed by migrants from Bangladesh. The anti-foreigner (read anti-illegal migrant or anti-Bangladeshi) uprising in Assam, from 1979 to 1985, led by the All Assam Students' Union (AASU)—by far the most influential organization representing the Assamese people—was perhaps among the largest mass uprisings in independent India. According to a conservative estimate, the number of people killed during the agitation stood at more than 7,000, with another two million losing their homes.[5] The issue is as alive today as it was in 1985, when the agitation formally ended with the signing of an agreement on 15 August 1985, in New Delhi, between the AASU and the central government, then led by Prime Minister Rajiv Gandhi. The issue of migration and citizenship has, in fact, become the pivot around which the entire politics of Assam has come to revolve—an issue on which elections to the State Legislative Assembly can be won or lost.

The Crown, Tea, and Migration

In 1826, Assam came under British rule with the signing of the Treaty of Yandaboo that ended the Anglo-Burmese War. For 600 years, from AD 1228 to the signing of the Yandaboo Treaty, Assam was ruled by the mighty Ahom kings. To British officials such as Major John Butler of the 55th Regiment, Bengal Native Infantry, who had travelled widely in Assam between 1837 and 1851,[6] from the middle of the nineteenth century, the state presented itself as a region 'with vast expanses of uninhabited land'. In fact, the reality of the depopulated condition of Assamese society is reflected in the arguments of Ananda Ram Dhekial Phukan, one of the first well-known modern Assamese personalities. Phukan pleaded in the early 1850s that in order to improve the precarious condition of agriculture in Assam, European technology and implements should be introduced, and that the government should also import a sufficient number of men from Europe and Upper India into Assam.[7]

It was again in the middle of the nineteenth century that the possibility of large-scale production of tea in Assam on a commercial basis was confirmed. This 'discovery' led to unimaginable excitement in the London Stock Exchange: 'a madness comparable in intensity with that of the South Sea Bubble seized men's minds, and normally level-headed financiers and speculators began to scramble wildly for tea shares and tea lands in Assam'.[8] Traces of oil, too, were then discovered. This economic transformation was enough reason for the British colonialists to encourage migration into Assam, a trend that continued through much of the twentieth century.

Two distinct categories of migrants came in large numbers—workers for Assam's tea plantations, who came from present-day Bihar and Orissa, and oppressed peasants from East Bengal. The massive migration of tribals from the Jharkhand region (in Bihar and Orissa) significantly transformed the demographic composition in Assam. Such massive migration made the state, in demographic terms, the fastest-growing province in colonial India.[9] The population of the tea-garden employees in 1921 was 1.3 million or one-sixth of Assam's total population at the time.[10]

The British, to fill the coffers of the Crown, imposed heavy taxes on the peasantry, leading to peasant revolts in Assam in 1861 and 1891. Unable to enhance the rate of taxation any further, the colonialists tried to bring in larger tracts of land under agriculture to boost revenue generation. This amounted to encouraging the migration of peasants to Assam's wetlands from the thickly populated parts of East Bengal, mainly from the districts of Mymensingh, Rongpur, and Pabna (in present-day Bangladesh).[11] At that time, of course, this was an internal migration of a deprived community in search of greener pastures.

Nevertheless, fears about the adverse impact of migration were already being expressed. In 1920, the British tried to impose certain restrictions on migration and introduced what was called the Line System. This regulation prevented migrant peasants from purchasing land within specified areas and forced a large number of them to the riverine areas (*chars* in the local language), thus segregating them from the indigenous people. Being a loose regulation, the Line System failed to stop or check the influx of migrants into Assam. In fact, two Assamese and a Bodo tribal member from among the nine-member Line System Committee informed the British authorities that 'they did not anticipate that the new rulers (the British) would invite foreigners to come in such large numbers so as to swamp the indigenous population'. The note that these three members wrote said that it was the government's 'sacred duty' to protect the Assamese from this wave of East Bengali migration.[12]

Minorities in their own Homeland: The Major Fear of Assam

The rate of population growth in Assam during 1901-51 was the second highest (137.80 per cent) in the world, exceeded only by Brazil (204 per cent).[13] This trend of a high rate of population growth continued in Assam in the years that followed India's independence. Sociologist Monirul Hussain observes:

> It is a historical fact that the rate of growth of population in Assam has been much higher than that of India's average since the colonial period. Significantly in 1921, when the population growth rate was negative for India, Assam had shown a tremendously higher growth rate that is 20.47 per cent. And the gap of growth between India and Assam was as high as 20.77 per cent. In 1901, Assam's population constituted only 1.38 per cent of India's total population. However, by 1971, Assam's share nearly doubled at 2.67 per cent.[14]

Population watchers in Assam were beginning to get restive. Slogans such as 'Our land, their living space' were spreading quickly among the indigenous Assamese, making them uneasy.[15] The gravity of the situation was brought home by none other than the then Election Commissioner, S.L. Shakdher. At a conference of the Chief Electoral Officers of States, in 1978, he declared that reports from the north-east regarding foreigners being included in the voters' list were, indeed, alarming. Shakdher went on to add:

> In one case [Assam], the population in [the] 1971 census recorded an increase as high as 34.98 per cent over [the] 1961 census figures and this figure was attributed to the influx of [a] very large number of persons from foreign countries. The influx has become a regular feature. I think it may not be a wrong assessment to make that on the basis of [the] increase of 34.98 per cent between the two census, the increase would likely to be recorded [*sic*] in the 1991 census would be more than 100 per cent over the 1961 census. In other words, a stage would be reached when that State may have to reckon with the foreign nationals who may in all probability constitute a sizeable percentage if not the majority of population in the State.[16]

A by-election called for in 1979 following the death of a Member of Parliament (MP) was to trigger the first organized anti-foreigner movement in Assam, and this, in fact, went on to become the immense mass uprising known as the Assam Agitation. The circumstances of the by-election provide interesting insights. The deceased MP was Hiralal Patowari, representing the Mongoldoi parliamentary constituency in northern Assam. The Election Commission, therefore, ordered a fresh poll to fill the vacancy. Soon, officials started the exercise of revising the voters' rolls for the Mongoldoi constituency.

The exercise was reaching an end when the local electoral officer started receiving complaints that the names of many Bangladeshis had been included in the voters' list. Within several weeks, as many as

70,000 complaints were registered against illegal immigrants. A tribunal was set up by the state government to investigate the complaints. It upheld 45,000 complaints or 64 per cent of the cases out of a total electorate of 600,000.[17]

There were other voices also raised in protest, although there has been no group or organization in Assam openly backing illegal migration from Bangladesh. Religious and linguistic minority[18] leaders and organizations began to accuse the authorities of deleting the names of *bona fide* Indian minorities from the voters' lists on the grounds that they were Bangladeshis.

This was the beginning of a whole new 'politics of citizenship' in Assam, and this issue continues to dominate the state's murky politics even today. 'The organizations behind the Assam movement estimated the number of "foreigners" in Assam to be as high as 4.5 to 5 million, or 31 to 34 per cent of the total population of the state in 1971.'[19] The AASU galvanized the masses in Assam, successfully mobilizing them to come out onto the streets, and enforced general strikes and a boycott of elections. No correct voters' list (free from the names of illegal aliens), no elections—this was the slogan the AASU had put forward. The AASU-led anti-foreigner movement in Assam sought to halt the illegal influx of foreign nationals from Bangladesh as well as from Nepal, preventing these categories of people from taking part in the electoral process, and eventually detecting and deporting them. This was intended to protect the state, its people, and its culture against what it called the 'silent invasion from Bangladesh'.

After protracted negotiations, the Assam movement formally ended on 15 August 1985. The AASU and the Union government signed what came to be called the Assam Accord. This Accord fixed a cut-off date to determine who the illegal migrants in Assam were. This date was 25 March 1971, the day that Bangladesh was born. The Assam Accord states that all those migrants who have come and settled in the state on or before this date shall be regarded as citizens. And those illegal migrants who are found to have arrived in the state after this date are to be detected and expelled in accordance with the law.[20]

The government announced fresh elections in Assam for December 1985. The student leaders who were at the forefront of the anti-foreigner stir transformed themselves into political leaders by creating a new political party called the Asom Gana Parishad (AGP) or the Assam People's Party. The results of the polls that followed were on expected lines; the AGP rode to power with an absolute majority on the euphoria generated by the Assam Accord and on just one plank: ridding Assam of 'illegal aliens'.

The December 1985 elections also saw the emergence of the United Minorities Front (UMF), another product of the Assam Accord and the anti-foreigner agitation. The UMF bagged 17 of the state's 126 Legislative Assembly seats and projected itself as a party dedicated to fight attempts by the 'chauvinistic Assamese' to harass *bona fide* citizens belonging to the religious and linguistic minority groups by branding them 'Bangladeshis'. The UMF won these 17 seats mainly with the support of the minorities and the settlers who were gripped by the fear of being subjected to possible harassment once the AASU leaders-turned-politicians came to rule Assam.

The Assam Accord may have formally ended the anti-foreigner movement but politics in the state since then has revolved around the same highly emotive issues. It has created a divide between the communities and has also led to a mistrust among the people. A superficial view would suggest that Muslims in Assam are encouraging Muslim migrants from Bangladesh to come and settle in the state, thus increasing the population of this religious group. This is far from the truth.

Dhaka, though, is often accused of pursuing a hidden agenda—of Islamist expansionism—in engineering a migration of its people into Assam. Bangladesh's 'hidden agenda' theory is frequently supported by the reiteration of the recorded statements by some prominent Pakistani politicians in the past. Former Pakistan Premier Zulfikar Ali Bhutto's book, *Myth of Independence*, is often cited by commentators in Assam to highlight the fact that Pakistan was keen on including Assam in East Pakistan (now Bangladesh) during the partition of the subcontinent. Bhutto wrote:

> It would be wrong to think that Kashmir is the only dispute that divides India and Pakistan, though undoubtedly it is the most significant. One at least is nearly as important as the Kashmir dispute, that of Assam and some districts of India adjacent to East Pakistan. To these, Pakistan has very good claims. . . .[21]

Similarly, Sheikh Mujibur Rahman, the founding father of Bangladesh, wrote:

> Because Eastern Pakistan must have sufficient land for its expansion and because Assam has abundant forests and mineral resources, coal, petroleum, etc., Eastern Pakistan must include Assam to be financially and economically strong.[22]

A look at such passages reinforces the fear among the indigenous people in Assam, and keeps the issue alive. In November 1998, the Governor of Assam, Lt. Gen. (retd.) S.K. Sinha, presented a 42-page official report to the President of India on 'Illegal Migration into Assam'. Governor Sinha wrote:

> As a result of population movement from Bangladesh, the spectre looms large of the indigenous people of Assam being reduced to a minority in their home state. Their cultural survival will be in jeopardy, their political control will be weakened and their employment opportunities will be undermined. This silent and invidious demographic invasion of Assam may result in the loss of the geo-strategically vital districts of Lower Assam [on the border with Bangladesh]. The influx of these illegal migrants is turning these districts into a Muslim majority region. It will then only be a matter of time when a demand for their merger with Bangladesh may be made. The rapid growth of international Islamic fundamentalism may provide the driving force for this demand. . . Loss of Lower Assam [the area close to the Bangladesh border] will sever the entire land mass of the North East from the rest of India and the rich natural resources of that region will be lost to the Nation.[23]

Sinha's sweeping observations greatly angered the Muslim politicians belonging to different political parties, who called him a Hindu chauvinist. These leaders castigated Sinha for virtually doubting the patriotism of the indigenous Muslims by suggesting that a day might come when the districts bordering Bangladesh might witness the demand for a merger with the neighbouring nation. That is another story, but the fact that a top government functionary has decided to officially place on record the possible consequences of cross-border human traffic into Assam underlines the fact that the issue is, indeed, of paramount importance.

Government agencies in Assam, such as the tribunals functioning in accordance with the Illegal Migrants Determination Tribunals Act, 1983 (the IMDT Act), have been going ahead with their job of disposing off cases concerning illegal migrants. Assam is the only Indian state where the IMDT Act is in force to deal with foreigners. Elsewhere, the Foreigners Act, 1946, is applicable. Under the IMDT Act, the onus of proving one's citizenship lies with the accused, whereas under the Foreigners Act, the onus lies with the police and other government agencies. However, progress has been extremely slow and the number of cases disposed off, and the number of people declared as illegal migrants, has been negligible considering the figure of aliens living in the state as estimated by the leadership of the anti-foreigner movement.

The Ministry of Home Affairs in New Delhi has itself admitted that the functioning of the IMDT Act has been 'unsatisfactory'. The Ministry has cited the following statistics, during a presentation in mid-1999 in connection with a court case, to prove its assessment:

- Total enquiries (of suspected illegal migrants) initiated: 302,554;
- Enquiries referred to the Screening Committee: 296,564;
- Enquiry reports referred to the IMDT Tribunals: 31,264;
- Persons declared as illegal migrants by the IMDT Tribunals: 9,625;
- Number of illegal migrants expelled: 1,461.[24]

It may be noted that the *Demographic Yearbook* published by the Registrar-General's Office, which supervises the census operations in India, said in its 1981 Report that as many as four million persons, residents in India that year, had reported their birthplace as Bangladesh. This excluded figures for Assam where the census was not held in 1981 because of the anti-foreign nationals agitation.[25] Compared to such a large figure, the number of suspected illegal aliens formally declared as foreigners by the IMDT Tribunals and later expelled is indeed insignificant.

Students under the banner of the AASU, in their continuing effort to get the Assam Accord implemented in both letter and spirit, succeeded in persuading the Government of India to come up with a definition of the 'indigenous people' of Assam. A definition was arrived at during a meeting in April 2000 between the leaders of the AASU and senior officials of the Indian Home Ministry. 'Indigenous people' were defined as 'those whose names figure in the 1951 National Register of Citizens[26] and their descendants'. For the seven districts in Assam where the NRC of 1951 is not available, the electoral rolls of 1952 were to be taken as the basic document. In the case of these seven districts, those people who had their names enrolled in the 1952 voters' list and their descendants will fall under the category of 'indigenous' or 'Assamese' people.[27]

This official definition triggered a fresh round of controversy in Assam. Several individuals and groups in the state are unhappy with this development,[28] and argue that the AASU is not the sole representative of the people of Assam. They insist that it was unfair, to say the least, on the Union government's part to have worked on the exercise of evolving a definition of the 'indigenous people' of Assam by sitting with 'a few student leaders'.[29] The stage is now set for a major confrontation and, possibly, a legal battle as well.

The search for a definition was necessitated by the demand of the AASU for 100 per cent reservation in the State Assembly and the state's seats in the Lok Sabha[30] for the 'indigenous people of Assam'. This demand again had its genesis in the anti-foreigner uprising (1979-85) and was sparked off by the fear that the continued flow of illegal migrants could soon overwhelm the indigenous Assamese, with the migrants coming to dominate the state's politics. This fear found an echo in the Assam Accord, in which Clause VI states:

> Constitutional, legislative and administrative safeguards, as may be appropriate, shall be provided to protect, preserve and promote the cultural, social and linguistic identity and heritage of the Assamese people.[31]

Any move to protect or preserve the identity and heritage of the 'Assamese people' is welcome and there can be no two opinions about it. The dispute, however, is over the new cut-off date of 1951 (NRC) and 1952 (voters' list) chosen to determine who would be regarded as the 'indigenous people' of Assam. Already, the Assam Accord provides for 25 March 1971 as the cut-off date for the detection and expulsion of illegal foreign migrants. This means that people already residing in the state on or before this date are to be regarded as citizens of India residing in Assam. Now, it seems that the government has agreed to push back the cut-off date by another 20 years. These attempts at redefinition have, moreover, created resentment among a large number of ethnic and other minority groups in the state. Leaders of ethnic groups such as the Bodos and the Karbis feel that a cut-off date cannot be used to decide who is a native (indigenous) and who is not.[32] Minority organizations like the UMF say that it would go totally against the interest of the post-Partition migrants and the riot-affected people from parts of Assam who had fled to East Pakistan only to return later.[33] An estimated 300,000 Muslims from western Assam fled to East Pakistan in 1950, in the wake of communal riots. Following the Nehru-Liaquat Pact later in 1950, these people returned to Assam in batches, till about 1952. By this time the exercise of preparing the NRC of 1951 as well as the voters' list of 1952 was already over. The names of this category of people, the absentee Muslims, therefore, did not figure in these two documents.

There is another category of people whose names apparently do not figure in the NRC of 1951. They are the Bengali Hindu refugees from

East Pakistan. A large-scale influx of this group into Assam began only in 1950, and continued thereafter. These are the 'displaced persons', and the Assam Act XVI of 1951 made elaborate provisions for granting rehabilitation loans to them, thereby formally welcoming them into the state.

Nevertheless, infiltration has always been a problem in Assam. As early as 27 June 1962, the Prime Minister Jawaharlal Nehru speaking to the Assam State Committee of the Congress party in Parliament, said:

> You refer to Pakistani infiltration. This is perfectly true. But you will appreciate that this infiltration from Bengal to Assam has been taking place for a very long time past . . . this infiltration should be stopped and effectively dealt with . . . Probably it will be difficult now to deal with illegal immigrants who came before 1952. We might, therefore, fix 1952 as the date of our enquiry.[34]

The AASU or even the Union government may now find Nehru's 1952 cut-off date proposal handy. But the document that is proposed to be taken as a reference point to determine who is a native of Assam is the NRC of 1951, whose legitimacy in a court of law may be disputable. Legal opinions vary on whether the NRC can at all be accepted by a court as evidence under the Indian Evidence Act in support of a person's claim to Indian citizenship.

For readers outside Assam or to an international audience, these events or developments in a remote part of India may appear to be too local or even too intricate. But they demonstrate just how an issue like cross-border migration has come to dominate almost the entire politics of a strategically located state of over 26 million people.

Tripura: Tribal Resurgence

In May 2000, the north-eastern Indian state of Tripura, that juts into Bangladesh from Assam's south-east, witnessed political developments that can have a far-reaching impact on the state's already tense natives-versus-aliens conflict. A ragtag political party of tribals called the Indigenous People's Front of Tripura (IPFT) won the little-noticed elections to the 28-member Tripura Tribal Areas Autonomous District Council (TTAADC), an administrative structure established in 1982 to cater to the interests of the state's dwindling tribal population. The element of news here is that the IPFT, according to media and police reports, is backed by the outlawed National Liberation Front of Tripura

(NLFT),[35] a dreaded tribal separatist guerrilla group, that is fighting for an independent tribal homeland outside India. The main grouse of the indigenous tribals and militant groups such as the NLFT is over the increasing pressure on tribal lands and culture as a result of the ever-growing population of Bengali migrants from the plains. The tribals' anxiety in Tripura is the same as that of the natives of Assam: the invasion by 'outsiders', and is, in a sense, far more acute since the indigenous groups have already been reduced to a minority. The rise to power of a rebel-supported political party like the IPFT for the first time since the formation of the Tribal Council is a definite sign of tribal resurgence in the state. Tripura could well be among the few places in South Asia where the natives have been reduced to a minority by hordes of migrants in a span of under 50 years. B.G. Verghese observes:

> Tripura is the Northeast's nightmare being a state whose demographic transformation has rendered its original inhabitants a minority in what was once a proud tribal kingdom ruled by a succession of 183 Tripuri princes who held sway over a land that finds mention in the *Mahabharata* and [the] *Ain-i-Akbari* and whose history is recorded over the centuries in the Rajamala, the state chronicle.[36]

The Maharaja or the king of Tripura enacted legislation in 1917 and 1925 to acquire lands for tea cultivation. This encouraged migration. Moreover, the Tripura rulers had adopted Bengali for running their administration. This attracted Bengalis from East Bengal to the area. Artisans followed. Poverty, famine, landlessness, and the exploitation of *zamindars* (landlords) drove Bengali peasants and others in distress to Tripura. By 1931, the number of migrants from various other regions had risen to 114,383, the vast majority from Bengal or Assam.[37]

Even at that time, the rulers of the day had anticipated trouble for the state's tribes people. The Maharaja in 1931 and again in 1943 reserved land for use in agriculture by five tribal groups in the state: the Tripuris, the Reangs, the Jamatias, the Noatias, and the Halams.

The tribals in princely Tripura, where the 'Excluded Areas' and the 'Inner Line' provisions were introduced 'only in the 1940s through the creation of a tribal reserve, were the most apprehensive about a possible large-scale influx of Bengalis'.[38] Their fears came true with the partition of India and Pakistan, which brought about a dramatic transformation in Tripura's demographic profile. Tripura acceded to India on 13 August

1947 and a complete merger with India took place on 15 October 1949. Waves of migration from what became East Pakistan started into Tripura on a day-to-day basis. 'Attacks on Hindus in East Pakistan in the 1960s led to many refugees settling in Tripura. One estimate says that 600 persons fled to Tripura every day after the assaults.'[39] This in-migration forced the state government to seek the de-notification of the lands reserved earlier for the tribals. The systematic process of land alienation had begun, and with it the bloody conflict between the natives and the aliens or settlers.

By the mid-1960s, the tribals in the state were getting more and more restive. A tribal political party, the Tripura Upajati Juba Samity (TUJS), was formed in 1967. In the neighbouring province of Mizoram, the tribal chieftain Laldenga had formed a separatist guerrilla group called the Mizo National Front (MNF). The formation of the MNF stirred the imagination of the Tripura tribals, and men like Bijoy Kumar Hrangkhawl established the Tripura National Volunteers (TNV) in 1978. The activities of the TUJS were, thus, both political and militaristic. In the words of an analyst:

> On the one hand [it carried out] mass action through rallies and meetings and on the other [made] a concerted effort to build up a large body of volunteers trained in guerrilla warfare. Hrangkhawl was the crucial link in the delicate chain, the bridge between the party's legitimate and underground activities.[40]

By mid-1979, the TNV had carried out a series of attacks on the settlers as well as what they considered the symbols of governmental authority, such as the security forces. The declared aim of these activities was to protect the distinct identity of the tribals from the 'invaders from outside'

Tripura has also witnessed a sizeable infiltration of Buddhist Chakma refugees from the Chittagong Hill Tracts of Bangladesh. As Verghese notes:

> One of the components of the Bangladeshi influx is the Chakma refugees originally numbering around 70,000. These Buddhist tribals fled the Chittagong Hill Tracts in the 1980s after the Bangladeshi government settled thousands of plains Muslims in this relatively sparsely populated hill region.[41]

For the state of Tripura, the influx of the Chakmas created a dual set of problems. In the words of Partha S. Ghosh, the noted social scientist:

On the one hand it [had] to live with the problem of the intermittent flux of refugees. . . . On the other, the disturbed atmosphere on the border has encouraged its own extremist elements, particularly the TNV, to carry on their activities with impunity from their hideouts across the border.[42]

A look at the official census figures tells Tripura's story. During the first census of independent Tripura (1876-7), the tribal population stood at 67,906 as against the province's total population of 91,759. In 1901, the total population of Tripura was 173,325 and 92,477 were tribals. A look at Tripura's census figures from 1951 to 1991 clearly shows how the migrants have outnumbered the indigenous tribals.

Year	Population		Growth Rate	
	Total	Tribal	Total	Tribal
1951	639,929	237,953	24.6	36.8
1961	1,142;005	360,070	78.7	31.5
1971	1,556,342	450,544	36.3	25.0
1981	2,053,058	583,920	32.0	30.0
1991	2,757,205	853,345	34.0	46.0

Source: Annexure I of the Memorandum Submitted by the Tripura Upajati Juba Samity (TUJS) to Union Home Minister L.K. Advani, Agartala, 27 March 2000.

Today, violence is the order of the day in Tripura. From 10 April 1993 to 31 December 1999, a total of 1,018 persons (656 non-tribals and 362 tribals) were killed and 2,001 (1,663 non-tribals and 338 tribals) were kidnapped in the state.[43] In the following years of 2000 and 2001, as many as 692 civilians, 47 security force personnel, and 87 militants were killed.[44]

The situation is one of a bitter ethnic feud between the tribals and the settlers from the plains. The tribals are clearly in a fight-back mode, both politically and through an unlawful armed struggle. Union Minister for Home Affairs Lal Krishna Advani visited Tripura over 27-28 March 2000 to make an on-the-spot assessment of the situation. Tribal leaders representing the TUJS presented a memorandum to the Ministry of Home Affairs (MHA), the burden of which was the demand for the protection of tribals' rights. The TUJS articulated the following major demands:

- More power to the TTAADC.
- Barbed-wire fence along the state's 856 km-long border with Bangladesh to check the influx of aliens.

- Implementation of the Indira-Mujib Pact (the agreement between Indian Prime Minister Indira Gandhi and Bangladesh's main architect Sheikh Mujibur Rahman), under whose terms the post-1971 migrants from Bangladesh are to be pushed back.
- Introduction of an Inner-Line Permit system to check the entry of plainsmen to the Tribal Council area.[45]

Simply put, the tribals in Tripura today are bent on ensuring that their population in the Tribal Council area does not fall below the existing 70 per cent (as already mentioned, the overall tribal population in the state is as low as 28 per cent).

The Viewpoint from Dhaka

To put it simply, both the government and a majority of intellectuals and think tanks in Bangladesh deny that there has been any illegal influx of their people into Assam or any other part of India. They claim that the economy of the Indian states bordering Bangladesh is not sound and, therefore, does not have anything to attract their people to cross over. Dr. S.A. Malek, political adviser to former Prime Minister Sheikh Hasina asserted: 'Why should our people migrate to Assam or anywhere else in India? The living standards in Bangladesh today is [*sic*] quite satisfactory.'[46] Dhaka's non-government Track II policy influencers are, however, simultaneously making out a case for more *lebensraum* or living space for their country and people. Today, analysts and academicians such as former Foreign Secretary and former High Commissioner to India, Farooq Sobhan, and Chairman of the Grameen Bank in Bangladesh, Muhammad Yunus, talk about visa-less travel, border-less trade, and other policies that would remove restrictions on the movement of their population across the international border.

The idea of *lebensraum* has been variously articulated in Bangladesh for a long time, though the use of the expression itself is relatively recent. In the early 1990s, Sadeq Khan, a former diplomat, stated:

> All projections, however, clearly indicate that by the next decade, that is to say by the first decade of the 21st century, Bangladesh will face a serious crisis of lebensraum . . . if consumer benefit is considered to be better served by borderless competitive trade of labour, there is no reason why regional and international co-operation could not be worked out to plan and execute population movements and settlements to avoid critical demographic pressure in pockets of high concentration. . . . A natural overflow of population pressure is very

much on the cards and will not be restrainable by barbed wire or border patrol measures. The natural trend of population overflow from Bangladesh is towards the sparsely populated lands in the South East, in the Arakan side and of the North East in the Seven Sisters side of the Indian sub-continent.[47]

Of late, this idea of a free movement of people seems to have enough buyers within Bangladesh, and has been strongly articulated by several leading thinkers, economists, and former diplomats there.[48] There was strong support for a regime of 'hassle-free' cross-border migration of people. S.A. Malek, despite his denials of cross-border migratory pressures within his country, readily agreed with the view that an effective sub-regional cooperation between eastern India, Bangladesh, Bhutan, and Nepal under the aegis of SAARC (South Asian Association for Regional Cooperation), but distinct from it, would be beneficial for the people of this sub-region insofar as matters of trade and travel are concerned.[49]

Similarly, opinions were expressed by Muhammad Yunus[50] in favour of sub-regional linkages between eastern India, Bangladesh, Bhutan, and Nepal. He goes on to talk of a possible European Union-type of structure. Nevertheless, even as he speaks of borderless trade and visa-less travel in the sub-region, Yunus does not think that there is any economic incentive for Bangladeshis to migrate to Assam or any other north-eastern Indian state. Yunus asserts instead that 'Bangladeshis would rather like to migrate to such Indian cities as Chennai, Delhi or Hyderabad where the economies are looking up.'[51]

Farooq Sobhan suggests that a document like an identity card should suffice for people to travel between the two nations. He also favours a 'work permit' mechanism for workers to stay and work in both countries. Sobhan, however, concedes that there was 'some' Bangladeshi migration into India's north-east: 'I see no reason why we should not acknowledge that there has been some migration to Assam.'[52]

The refrain among a section of Bangladesh's elite seems to be the same. Professor Amena Mohsin,[53] for instance, asserts: 'Migration is a normal and natural phenomenon and cannot be stopped. The need today is to evolve ways to legalize it.' Erecting a barbed-wire fence along the Indo-Bangladesh border to check migration of people cannot serve anybody's purpose, she observes.[54]

The Bangladeshi assertion, however, that the state of the country's economy is not so bad as to encourage large-scale migration is untenable. According to the Centre for Policy Dialogue, a Dhaka-based think tank:

The state of the economy in the financial year (FY) 1999, representing the period from July 1, 1998 to June 30, 1999, presents a mixed record depending on the time perspective within which it is viewed. If we look at the events specific to FY 99, the economy performed better than might have been expected. If, however, we take the long view then a variety of governance problems appear to have aggravated Bangladesh's development crisis, which poses serious hazards for the country in the days ahead.[55]

Bangladesh was hit by devastating floods in the first half of 1999, the worst such disaster in contemporary memory. Yet, its economy revived quite well, mainly due to the impressive recovery in crop production (GDP growth in 1999 was estimated at 5.2 per cent according to the CPD study). But the CPD study also notes:

. . . without prejudice to the impact of the floods, the inability to enhance the revenue effort by the Government of Bangladesh remains a longer term problem. A revenue-GDP (Gross Domestic Product) ratio of below 12 per cent puts Bangladesh in the class of Sub-Saharan Africa.[56]

On the subject of poverty alleviation, the CPD study notes:

The agenda for poverty alleviation remains at best on the rhetorical agenda of this government [the government of the day] as it has been on the agenda of its predecessors . . . The inherited approach to poverty alleviation, based on a plethora of donor funded projects under implementation by a variety of ministries as well as the entire NGO community, remains the order of the day with successive governments. . . .

But the study admits that this is not working: '. . . poverty levels remain stabilised at around 50 per cent. . . .[57] The poverty agenda lacks any overreaching goal based on a vision defined in categorical targets backed by specific programmes with identified budget allocations to realise these targets.'[58] Clearly, all is not well for the poorest of the poor in Bangladesh and this, perhaps, explains the desire in Bangladesh for a serious initiative to achieve sub-regional economic cooperation and population movements that can transcend national boundaries.

Three Rivers and a New Sub-regional Grouping

The Indian Chamber of Commerce (ICC), the largest trade and commerce body in eastern India with its headquarters in Kolkata, has already launched a definite initiative for sub-regional cooperation. It has roped in industry leaders, economists, bankers, and foreign policy think tanks from eastern India, Bangladesh, Nepal, and Bhutan and has launched what has been called the Greater Ganga-Brahmaputra-Meghna Initiative (GGBMI) for an Eastern South Asian sub-regional economic cooperation.[59] The initiative, however, is yet to take a definite shape.

The Manila-based Asian Development Bank (ADB) is supporting this initiative and has already appointed a staff consultant to prepare a preliminary study of the benefits of sub-regional cooperation and the agenda ahead. The World Bank has also agreed[60] to support the project by sharing its research on transportation logistics for the sub-region. USAID would make available the work done on energy resource sharing in the sub-region.[61]

The transnational initiative of the ICC on the 'emerging East' began in 1997 and is now gathering momentum with several countries showing interest in the idea. Canada has also expressed its interest in sharing their experiences of regional economic cooperation. The steering committee of the GGBMI met in Kathmandu in November 1998 and in New Delhi in 2000 to give shape to the project and push ahead with the idea. Convinced that sub-regional cooperation with SAARC and SAFTA (South Asian Free Trade Area) would lead to a win-win situation for all the member countries involved, the Delhi meeting zeroed in on the following benefits of such an initiative:

- Increase in market size and scale of economies;
- Reduction of non-tariff barriers;
- Improvement of physical and institutional linkages; and
- Improvement of access to raw materials and natural resources.[62]

All the 18 key people who attended the Delhi meeting (steering committee members and special invitees like representatives from the ADB) were convinced that the initiative would succeed only if the 'political mindset' in each country could be influenced to appreciate the benefits of such sub-regional cooperation. The conveners of the member countries in India, Bangladesh, Bhutan, and Nepal are to meet the political leadership in their respective countries on the issue.

The ICC is the coordinating body for the GGBMI and the nodal body for India. In Bangladesh, it is the Federation of Bangladesh Chambers of Commerce and Industry. In Nepal, the nodal body is the Federation of Nepalese Chambers of Commerce and Industry. The Bhutan Chamber of Commerce and Industry will coordinate the initiative in Bhutan.

The ADB has described its own role in the initiative as that of an 'honest broker'. It would carry out the master plan and the feasibility studies, finance the projects, and mobilize co-finance and investments once the project is put in place. During a recent presentation on the GGBMI, ADB officials cited some examples of existing 'growth triangles', including the Greater Mekong sub-region; Indonesia-Malaysia-Singapore; Indonesia-Malaysia-Thailand; Southern China-Hong Kong-Taiwan, and the Central Asian republics.[63]

Another development which still has to cross many a hurdle before being converted into a policy decision is the possibility of opening a corridor between Bangladesh and India. Indications to this effect were provided by the Commerce Minister of Bangladesh Amir Khasru Mahmud Chowdhury. While speaking to the press, on 23 December 2001, Chowdhury indicated that Dhaka would allow Indian manufacturers to sell their products in the north-eastern states using Bangladesh territory. 'It is neither transit nor transshipment. It is as simple as re-export through back-to-back Letters of Credit (LoC).'[64] The minister felt that the arrangement would provide Bangladesh a chance to introduce its merchandises to the north-eastern states of India. Similar re-export arrangements exist in the garment trade sector in Bangladesh, and Singapore and Hong Kong have long been benefiting from such business arrangements. There is no reason why, with adequate political will from both the sides, India and Bangladesh cannot work out many such arrangements.[65]

Stopping the Flow: A Challenging Task

One thing is by now quite clear—the migration of people from across the border can only be contained and not stopped by erecting barbed-wire fences, although New Delhi has set in motion the task of fencing a 3,200 km-long stretch of the Indo-Bangladesh border with 2007 being set as the target year of completion. In a written reply in the Lok Sabha, the External Affairs Minister Jaswant Singh, on 18 December 2001, disclosed that out of the total length of the land border, 854 km along the Indo-Bangla border have been fenced, while the balance 2,432.8 km is scheduled to be fenced by 2006-7.[66] A set of imaginative economic and administrative measures backed by strong political will alone can deal with or probably end the problem of illegal Bangladeshi migration to India.

A school of thought has been advocating for quite sometime now that work permits be given to illegal Bangladeshi migrants. Journalist and author Sanjoy Hazarika is among those who have been persistently arguing in favour of giving work permits or job cards to Bangladeshis. Hazarika recommends[67] that all Indians resident in the north-east must first be provided with multi-purpose identity cards. Once these identity cards are given to Indian nationals, Hazarika says, Bangladeshis wishing to work in the region or elsewhere in India can be issued work permits.

Even Prime Minister Atal Behari Vajpayee created quite a flutter in Assam in May 2001[68] when, addressing an election rally in the southern town of Silchar, he said that his government was considering the option of issuing work permits to illegal Bangladeshi migrants living in the country. The ruling Congress party in Assam led by Chief Minister Tarun Gogoi was quick to oppose the move as also the AASU, by far the most vocal of the anti-Bangladeshi pressure groups in the North-east, or for that matter in the country as a whole.

The work permit idea, to my mind, will not work and could, on the contrary, open the floodgates for a wave of new migration from Bangladesh into India. I say this because those illegal Bangladeshi migrants who have already settled in Assam or elsewhere and who have over the years managed to obtain one or more crucial documents such as ration cards, and perhaps enrolled themselves in the voters' list, would certainly not come forward to declare their Bangladeshi nationality should the work permit system come to be introduced. After all, a huge unspecified chunk of these illegal settlers is believed to have already managed to dodge election authorities scanning the voters' list in Assam for the names of foreign nationals year after year since 1979. Now, it will be too much to expect this group of settlers to stick their necks out by coming forward to avail of work permits if and when such a document is issued.

But illegal Bangladeshis who may have already entered India in recent months or those looking for an opportunity to cross the border would certainly be tempted to avail of the work permits. This section of people, after all, will have nothing to lose since they would still not have settled down and established roots in India. If erecting a border fence will not work and issuing work permits to Bangladeshis will not work, then one can talk of the same old story: improved policing of the border. That is easier said than done in view of the terrain of the Indo-Bangladesh border. Charges of corruption among the people manning the border is another story. What then could be a workable solution?

Now, a question can be raised that if deportation is impossible, much less detection, can the 'Assamese Muslims of East Bengal origin', as the old settlers from East Bengal and East Pakistan are referred to, be accepted as a part of the greater Assamese society. This category of people is still regarded as aliens, but there appears to be a case for accepting them as an integral part of the greater Assamese society. At least there seems to be a rethinking in this direction on the part of those who uphold the vision of a pan-Assamese social milieu.

By far the strongest indication of this shift in attitude was seen at the special annual session, in February 2002, of the Asom Sahitya Sabha (ASS), the apex socio-literary body in Assam, held for the first time in a migrant-dominated area in the state. Delivering his presidential address at the session held in the town of Kalgachia, in the western district of Barpeta, Sabha President Homen Borgohain, one of Assam's front-ranking literateurs, declared that the 'Assamese Muslims of East Bengal origin' are an integral part of the greater Assamese society and urged upon his organization (the Asom Sahitya Sabha) as well as the people in general to initiate steps for the development of this section of the society.

Borgohain said: 'Had they [Assamese Muslims of East Bengal origin] tried to keep their Bengali origin intact, then the indigenous Assamese people would have become a minority in their own homeland.'[69] Borgohain added that despite the fact that the Assamese Muslims of East Bengal origin comprised more than one-fourth of the state's population,[70] not a single session of the Asom Sahitya Sabha was held prior to this time at any place dominated by this section of people. He also appreciated the attitude of these people who have willingly given up their original mother tongue and have come to accept Assamese as their only language of communication.

If the settlers from East Bengal and East Pakistan can be accepted as part of the 'greater Assamese society', there is no reason why settlers from Bangladesh who had entered Assam on or before 25 March 1971 (the cut-off date for the detection and expulsion of illegal migrants that figures in the Assam Accord) cannot be regarded as such. Perhaps the Asom Sahitya Sabha itself or Borgohain on his own was actually hinting at this when he talked of bracketing that particular group of migrants with the 'greater Assamese society'. This approach, to my mind, has the potential to present a workable solution to the problem of infiltration from across the border. A political arrangement giving amnesty and recognition to the settlers that also provides for a mechanism to stop the further influx of illegal migrants must be brought about sooner than later. With the expansion of opportunities within the limited space available already triggering off a war for survival among the migrants themselves, this section of people—the old settlers—could well be used as a buffer to stop the influx of new entrants.

I almost wholly agree with the views of a senior Assam police officer that we must not brand the riverine areas (*chars*) along the Brahmaputra or other rivers in Assam as the land of the Bangladeshis. Doing so would amount to pushing them into the hands of anti-national elements who would love to nurture them and political parties which would love to cultivate them as block vote banks. If an assimilationist approach is not adopted, the police officer says, the situation could well prepare the ground for a possible civil war, as those immigrants would rather rush to the fold of Islamic fundamentalism, which has been slowly gaining ground in Assam, rather than face ethnic cleansing or be subjected to mass deportation.

While arguing for the adoption of the assimilationist approach, I would like to place on record my belief that such a move has to be conditional. Accepting or formally recognizing the settlers as part of the 'greater Assamese society' and immediately granting all rights to them[71] would be disastrous. My recommendation is that at least for a specific time period, the settlers should be barred from participating in elections, both in exercising their franchise or contesting for political office. Besides, demands by organizations such as the AASU for 100 per cent reservations for the 'indigenous people' of Assam in the State Assembly, in Parliament, and in local bodies can be considered. After all, the constitutional safeguards for the majoritarian groups is a must in Assam today, if anything, to allay their fears and apprehensions of being overwhelmed by the migrants. The delicate issue here is to arrive at an acceptable definition of the term 'indigenous people'. If the assimilationist approach comes to be backed by at least the big players—the AASU, the Asom Sahitya Sabha, and the government—the old settlers from erstwhile East Bengal or East Pakistan must be regarded as people 'indigenous' to Assam.

The migration of people from one place to another may be a natural phenomenon and a common human experience. As an instance, one may point to the 'browning of America', where between 1846 and 1930 an estimated 50 million people from Europe emigrated and settled. In South Asia, an estimated 25 million people are believed to have been involved in the processes of mass population movements during the last 50 years. But when a sizeable group of people migrate in waves to a particular area, the host region gets affected, both politically and economically. India's north-east is a victim of this cross-border human traffic. This has led the indigenous people to take up arms and secede from India, as we see in Tripura. In Assam, xenophobia has gripped the people, with some sections casting doubts on the nationality of even *bona fide* citizens belonging to the religious and linguistic minority communities.

Clearly, the issue of migration (popularly referred to in the region as the issue of infiltration from Bangladesh) has become a major political and economic problem, not only in the north-east of India but in the country as a whole. For instance, Bangladeshi migrants living in New Delhi clashed with the police in June 2000 over the arrest of a man belonging to the community. This was enough to force the issue of the Bangladeshi influx into India into the national limelight, propelled by enormous media coverage. The issue has not only come to dominate local politics in the region but it has also drawn the attention of the central government. For instance, a report of the Ministry of Home Affairs, Government of India, while noting the change in the demographic composition of the areas bordering Bangladesh, made the following observation: 'The large-scale influx of illegal Bangladesh[i] immigrants has led to large tracts of sensitive international borders being occupied by foreigners. This has serious implications for internal security.'[72] The seriousness with which the Government of India views the problem of infiltration is indicated by its decision to fence the entire 4,096 km-long stretch of the Indo-Bangladesh border spread over five states at a cost of Rs. 1,334 crore.[73]

The issue of migration into north-east India cannot be brushed aside as an uncalled-for fear on the part of the indigenous people of the region. There is a combination of factors on both sides which is responsible for the continuing influx of illegal migrants; one such 'push' factor is the steep and continuous increase in the population of Bangladesh and a sharp deterioration in the country's land-man ratio. The 'pull' factors on the Indian side include ethnic proximity and kinship which provides easy shelter for the migrants; a porous border with Bangladesh; better economic opportunities (Dhaka's denials notwithstanding); and interested religious and political elements which encourage migration.

Of late, it is being increasingly felt that market linkages and hassle-free trade and business activity in the sub-region of eastern India, Bangladesh, Bhutan, and Nepal could greatly boost the economy of the area. If this happens, it is felt that the migration of people for economic reasons would come to a halt or would be reduced considerably. But for any such sub-regional initiative to reach its logical end, the mindset of the political leadership in the countries in the area will have to change.

Notes

1. Located at: Longitude 89.46 degree E to 97.30 degree E and Latitude 21.57 degree N to 29.30 degree N.
2. *Census of India*, 2001.
3. See Annexure I in 'Memorandum Submitted by the Tripura Upajati Juba Samity (TUJS) to Union Home Minister L.K. Advani', 27 March 2000. The Memorandum was signed by Shyama Charan Tripura, Chairman, Advisory Committee of the TUJS.
4. *Times of India*, 15 August 2001 and www.rediff.com/news/2001/mar/27assam.htm
5. Monirul Hussain, *The Assam Movement: Class, Ideology and Identity*, New Delhi: Manak Publications, 1993, p. 10.
6. Sanjib Baruah, *India Against Itself: Assam and the Politics of Nationality*, New Delhi: Oxford University Press, 1999, p. 44.
7. Hussain, *The Assam Movement*, p. 41.
8. Percival Griffiths, *The History of the Indian Tea Industry*, London: Weidenfeld & Nicolson, 1967, p. 96.
9. Kinsley Davis, *The Population of India and Pakistan*, cited in Hussain, *The Assam Movement*, p. 43.
10. Edward Gait, *A History of Assam* (1905), Calcutta: Thacker, Spinck & Co., 1933, p. 414.
11. Hussain, *The Assam Movement*, pp. 41-2.
12. Baruah, *India Against Itself*, p. 67.
13. Susanta K. Das, *Spotlight on Assam*, cited in Baruah, *India Against Itself*, p. 50.
14. Hussain, *The Assam Movement*, p. 60.
15. Wasbir Hussain, 'Cross-Border Human Traffic in South Asia: Demographic Invasion. Anxiety & Anger in India's Northeast', *Faultlines: Writings on Conflict & Resolution*, Bulwark Books & The Institute for Conflict Management, New Delhi, vol. 7, p. 111.
16. The Conference of the Chief Electoral Officers of States was held on 24 September 1978, in Ootacamund, Tamil Nadu.
17. Sanjoy Hazarika, *Strangers in the Mist*, New Delhi: Viking Penguin, 1994, p. 138.
18. Muslims are a religious minority in Assam and constitute nearly a third of the state's population of 26 million, while Bengalis are regarded as the chief linguistic minority.
19. Baruah, *India Against Itself*, p. 118.
20. For the full text of the Assam Accord see: www.satp.org/India/Documents/Assam_Accord%201985.htm# Assam_Accord
21. See Governor of Assam, 'Report on Illegal Migration Into Assam', submitted to the President of India by the Governor, Lt. Gen. (retd.) S.K. Sinha, November 1998, p. 6. The Report can also be accessed at http://www.satp.org/India/Documents/Assam_Illegal%20Migration%20into%20Assam.htm

22. Sheikh Mujibur Rahman, 'Eastern Pakistan: Its Population and Economics', cited in 'Report on Illegal Migration into Assam', p. 6.
23. 'Report on Illegal Migration into Assam', pp. 17-18.
24. Ministry of Home Affairs, North-East Division, 'Supplementary Status Report on Illegal Immigration of Bangladeshi Nationals', New Delhi: Government of India, n.d.
25. Hazarika, *Strangers in the Mist*, p. 32.
26. The National Register of Citizens is a contemporaneous register prepared by the officers appointed under the provisions of the Census Act in the course of census operations.
27. *Northeast Daily* (Guwahati), 12 April 2000.
28. The groups and/or individuals who have expressed their disagreements include the United Minorities Front, the All Bodo Students' Union, the Autonomous State Demand Committee, and Member of Parliament (Lok Sabha) representing Kokrajhar, S.K. Biswmuthiary.
29. *Northeast Daily*, 17 April 2000.
30. The Lower House of the Indian Parliament.
31. See the text of the Assam Accord: www.satp.org/ India/Documents/ Assam_Accord%201985.htm#Assam_Accord
32. Bodo leader U.G. Brahma and Karbi leader Holiram Terang, quoted in *Northeast Daily*, 17 April 2000.
33. UMF leader Hafiz Rashid Choudhury, quoted in *Northeast Daily*, 17 April 2000.
34. See M.V. Kamath, 'Neglected Assam', *Illustrated Weekly of India*, Bombay, 20-26 January 1980.
35. *Northeast Daily*, 10 May and 25 May 2000.
36. B.G. Verghese, *India's Northeast Resurgent*, New Delhi: Konark, 1997, p. 166.
37. S.R. Bhattacharjea, 'Tribal Insurgency in Tripura', cited in Verghese, *India's Northeast Resurgent*, p. 167.
38. Subir Bhaumik, *Insurgent Crossfire: North-East India*, New Delhi: Lancer Publishers, 1996, p. 67.
39. Hazarika, *Strangers in the Mist*, p. 123.
40. Bhaumik, *Insurgent Crossfire: North-East India*, p. 197.
41. Verghese, *India's Northeast Resurgent*, p. 179.
42. Partha S. Ghosh, *Cooperation and Conflict in South Asia*, New Delhi: Manohar, 1995, p. 78.
43. Reply by Tripura's Home Minister in the State Assembly to a question by an opposition leader on 14 February 2000.
44. South Asia Terrorism Portal, http://www.satp.org/satporgtp/countries/india/states/tripura/data_sheets/index.html
45. See 'Memorandum Submitted by the Tripura Upajati Juba Samity'.
46. Interview with the author, Dhaka, June 2000. Also see *Northeast Daily*, 16 June 2000.
47. *Holiday*, Dhaka, 18 October 1991.
48. The author gathered these impressions during his visit to Dhaka in June 2000.
49. Interview with the author, Dhaka, June 2000. Also see *Northeast Daily*, 16 June 2000.
50. Muhammad Yunus is well known for having revolutionized the banking system in Bangladesh, a country of 130 million people, by advancing micro-credit to poor

villagers without any collateral. His Grameen Bank model has come to be used in countries as diverse as China, the United States, Kenya, Malaysia, the Philippines, Togo, Tanzania, and South Africa among others.

51. Interview with the author at Dhaka, June 2000. Also see *Northeast Daily*, 16 June 2000.
52. Interview with the author at Dhaka, June 2000. Also see *Northeast Daily*, 16 June 2000.
53. Professor Amena Mohsin teaches international relations at Dhaka University.
54. Interview with the author at Dhaka, June 2000. Also see *Northeast Daily*, 16 June 2000.
55. See the chapter 'State of the Bangladesh Economy, 1999: An overview', in *A Review of Bangladesh's Development 1998-99*, Dhaka: University Press, 2000, p. 1. The Centre for Policy Dialogue is a non-government initiative to promote an ongoing process of dialogue between the principal partners in the decision-making and implementing processes.
56. Ibid., p. 4.
57. Ibid., pp. 8-9. The population of the country is around 130 million.
58. Ibid.
59. The Ganga, the Brahmaputra, and the Meghna are among the major rivers of the subcontinent. These rivers can be linked as a super waterway. The new sub-regional initiative began in October 1997 and took shape a year later, in November 1998. Document supplied by the Indian Chamber of Commerce.
60. Ibid.
61. Ibid.
62. Presentation by the Asian Development Bank at the meeting.
63. *Northeast Daily*, 28 June 2000.
64. Dhaka will be the open corridor for Indian goods to the north-east, *Hindustan Times* (North East Special), 23 December 2001.
65. However, the trade talks scheduled to be held on 26 December 2001 between Bangladesh and India were postponed after both sides developed differences on the agenda of the talks. 'Indo-Bangla trade talks postponed', *Assam Tribune*, 26 December 2001.
66. 'Indo-Bangla border: Fencing to be complete by 2007: Jaswant', *Assam Tribune*, 20 December 2001.
67. Sanjoy Hazarika, *Rites of Passage, Border Crossings, Imagined Homelands, India's East and Bangladesh*; Penguin Books, 2000, pp. 261-2.
68. *Assam Tribune* (Guwahati), 3 June 2001.
69. *Sentinel* (Guwahati), 13 February 2002.
70. The 2001 Census put the population of Assam at 26 million.
71. A large chunk of the settlers have already come to enjoy the basic rights through different means.
72. Disclosed to the author by official sources.
73. *Northeast Daily*, 24 May 2000.

8. *Refugees in South Asia: Security Threat or a Security Tool?*

SUBA CHANDRAN

The meaning of the term 'security' has undergone a significant transformation in recent years, especially since the end of the Cold War. This is because the end of the Cold War has resulted in a complete shift in threat perceptions at the international, regional, and national levels.[1] During the Cold War era, the traditional realist view of security focused mainly on the state, power, and military security, and hence importance was given to the maintenance of the military status quo, the sustenance of the regional and international hierarchies, the protection of boundaries, and the prevention of war.

The end of the Cold War made security concerns based on these considerations less significant.[2] Military preparedness in terms of maintaining troops and absorbing new military technology has high social, economic, and environmental costs today.[3] The increasing threats arising out of the domestic sources of instability in terms of economic, ethnic, and environmental tensions have shifted the focus of security from the military to the non-military sphere.

National security is considered as

> an integral concept: its internal and external dimensions are closely linked. They influence and impinge in many diverse ways. Incitement of disaffection and exploitation of the resultant discontent among ethnic and religious minorities by outside forces breed violence, militancy, insurgency and terrorism within the country. For this purpose, national loyalties are subverted, and conditions of instability and insecurity created through indoctrination and smuggling of arms, money, narcotics etc.[4]

I

Refugees: Threat Perceptions

With the expansion of the concept of security, refugees today are regarded as a source of non-military threat to national security. While scholars and policy makers have devoted time and resources to the study of refugees per se, not much work has been done on the implications of the presence of refugees on the security of the state that hosts them, nor has much attention been paid to the effects on the security of the state from where the refugees originally came. Attempts to fill this void in the scholarly literature only began in the second half of the 1990s.[5]

It has been argued that the presence of refugees poses threats to the social, economic, and political institutions in the host state. Refugees are considered as security threats for the following reasons:[6]

- The inherent tensions among the various refugee groups—each with its own clan, regional, religious, and ethnic loyalties—have security implications for the host country.
- Refugees are involved in petty crimes and become a part of the local underworld, thus increasing the law and order problems in the host country.
- The struggle for scarce economic resources results in competition between the local population and the refugees.
- The presence of refugees exerts its own influence over local politics.
- Refugees pursue their armed struggle against their home state, thus affecting the relations between the host country and the originating country.

These issues need to be probed in more detail. At the outset, when discussing the security threats posed by the refugees, a distinction needs to be made among them. In almost all the cases in South Asia, the movements of refugee populations have been based on an ongoing violent armed conflict in the country of origin. Second, as discussed earlier, in most of the cases, whether in Afghanistan, Sri Lanka, or Myanmar, a number of groups were/are involved in the conflict against the state, on the one hand, and against themselves, on the other hand. To sustain their armed conflict, these groups at times take refuge as refugees with or without the knowledge of the host country. This group comprises the militant refugees, which must be clearly differentiated from the civilian refugees, who form another group.

For example, among the Sri Lankan refugees in India, most of the refugees who fled to India in the first phase, which began with the 1983 riots, were civilian refugees, whereas a significant number of militant refugees (mainly belonging to the militant organizations fighting the LTTE) came to India during the second phase that began in 1990.[7] Even the LTTE had its presence and sympathizers all over Tamil Nadu, which was vital not only for its own survival but also important for the successful waging of its war against the Sri Lankan Army. Many of the LTTE cadres hid and operated in many parts of Tamil Nadu as refugees. Thus, a clear distinction must be made between the civilian refugees and the militant refugees. The state and the central governments, for various reasons, did not have complete control over these civilian refugees and militant groups.

A second distinction also needs to be made among the refugees themselves, between those who stay at specific refugee camps and those who succeed in finding their own resources for survival. Not all these refugees stay in the camps. At the beginning of 2002, there were around 63,000 Sri Lankan refugees living in 111 camps all over Tamil Nadu and there were around 20,000 non-camp refugees. In Pakistan, at the beginning of 2001, there were around 1.2 million registered refugees, besides an unknown number of unregistered refugees living all over the country.

In addition, there are a number of militants living in special camps either as refugees or otherwise in select camps. In Tamil Nadu, there are around 1,600 Sri Lankan militants living in five special camps located at Vellore, Pudukkottai, Salem, Chinglepet, and Chennai. It should also be noted that there are a number of other militants and foreign nationals who live in the host country unnoticed by the official authorities. For example, an unknown number of militants belonging to the various *mujahideen* groups and the Taliban live in Pakistan.

These divisions need to be kept in mind when examining the threats posed by the refugees to the security of the host nation.

II

Refugees and Social Security

Threats to social security from refugees, according to the experts, assume the following forms: drug addiction and drug trafficking, increasing law and order problems, trafficking in arms and women, etc.[8] These assertions need to be further investigated.

First, let us examine the problem of drug addiction and drug trafficking by the refugees. The most quoted figures regarding the connection between refugees and drug addiction comes from Pakistan. In 1979, there were no heroin addicts in Pakistan, but the number jumped to four million in just two decades.[9] The rise in heroin addiction in Pakistan is directly linked to the presence of Afghan refugees in Pakistan.[10] Al Asif, a major Afghan refugee area near Karachi, was considered to be a 'den of vice' where it was claimed 'arms and drugs were freely available and the area was frequented by a majority of the criminal elements'.[11]

Second, the refugees are also accused of gun running and arms smuggling. In the case of the Sri Lankan Tamil refugees, they possessed weapons without any valid licenses and took 'the law into their own hands, in view of [the] lack of direct control over their activities by the state authorities.'[12] Some of these camps have an independent existence, despite being settled by the government. For example, all the Sri Lankan groups 'had their own camps, which were virtually prohibited zones for outsiders: One could do anything in these secluded fortresses, no question asked. Even when some one was tortured to death, the screams would reach nowhere.'[13] The jobless youth in the coastal areas of Tamil Nadu found smuggling an attractive alternative and, even worse, the local population was often unwilling to share information regarding these illegal activities with the authorities.[14] The Afghan refugees living around Karachi are well known for their 'guns-for-hire service', whereby they rent weapons on a daily or an hourly basis.[15]

Third, there are inherent conflicts among the refugees themselves based on their different and competitive religious, ideological, and group loyalties. These loyalties result in open fighting among the various groups living in the host state. For example, the Sri Lankan refugees in Tamil Nadu were openly involved in armed fights.[16] In June 1990, the LTTE carried out an attack in Madras, killing 13 members of the Eelam People's Revolutionary Front (EPRLF), including its leader K. Padmanabha.[17]

Finally, the refugees are also involved in criminal acts, ranging from major robberies to murder, which adds to the law and order problem of the host state. Ms Jayalalithaa, the Chief Minister of Tamil Nadu, blamed the Sri Lankan refugees for armed robberies and the rising crime rate in Tamil Nadu.[18] They are involved in petty crimes and thus '. . . become a part of the local underworld and criminal groups in the host country. Trafficking in drugs, arms and women has been found to be a common feature of the poorer section of South Asian refugees . . . (for example) the Southern Bhutanese refugees in India.'[19]

The above-mentioned threats posed to the social security of the host nation need to be examined against the background of the distinction made, first, between civilian refugees and militant refugees, and, second, between camp refugees and non-camp refugees.

First, an in-depth analysis of the problem of drug trafficking and drug addiction in South Asia reveals that the role of refugees is only marginal. South Asia is situated between two major opium-producing regions: the Golden Triangle comprising Myanmar, Thailand, and Laos and the Golden Crescent comprising Pakistan, Afghanistan, and Iran. The opium produced in these two regions has been traditionally trafficked through South Asia to Europe and America. Much before the Soviet troops invaded Afghanistan, the Khomeini-led revolution in Iran had resulted in the disruption of the traditional western route for the drugs, as a consequence of which the drugs were trafficked through Pakistan, mainly its Makran coast. In addition, the illegal cultivation and trafficking of opium inside Pakistan has a long tradition and history. For example, in the North Western Frontier Province of Pakistan, opium has always been illegally cultivated in the approximately 4,000 acres of the Dir, Buner, and Swabi districts and in the Khyber, Bajaur, Mohmand, and Draksai agencies.[20] In the NWFP, drug trafficking is pursued by clans such as the Jaduns, the Yusufzais, the Khattaks, and the Afridis, who continue to be involved in the drug trade even today irrespective of what is happening in Afghanistan and regardless of the presence of Afghan refugees in Pakistan.[21] These tribal groups have powerful connections with the Pakistani political elite and even with the Pakistani Army.[22]

Putting the entire blame on the refugees for the problems of drug trafficking and drug abuse inside Pakistan is not justified. It should also be noted that there is no drug abuse and illegal drug trafficking at any significant level in Tamil Nadu, where the Sri Lankan refugees were/are present. On the other hand, there is a significant drug abuse problem in some of the states in the north-east of India, where there are no refugees. According to a UN Drug Control Programme (UNDCP) estimate, there are about 50,000 drug abusers in Manipur, 24,700 in Nagaland, and 13,800 in Mizoram.[23]

The second major charge leveled against refugees is that they are involved in gun running, resulting in the proliferation of small arms in the local society. This charge also needs to be probed further. The proliferation of small arms and light weapons in Indian and Pakistani society is the result of a number of factors, and blaming the entire problem on the refugees is an over-simplification of a complex situation. First, in the case of India and Pakistan, it was the deliberate policy of both governments to arm certain groups to achieve their political objectives in Sri Lanka and Afghanistan respectively. Second, an independent arms mafia has always existed in South Asia, possessing a well-connected network, which enables the smuggling of small arms throughout the region. Third, there was an increasing demand for small arms in both Indian and Pakistani society, fueled by terrorist and sectarian organizations which have been fighting with their respective governments for the last few decades.

The Research and Analysis Wing (RAW) of India has been accused of training the various Sri Lankan Tamil militant groups in Dehra Dun since September 1983.[24] Of the various militant groups trained by the RAW, the TELO was able to impart training to the maximum number of people and it also succeeded in obtaining more weapons than the other groups.[25] In an interview, Anton Balasingam, chief ideologue and spokesman of the LTTE, claimed that, 'TELO got more weapons than all of us—they had closer contacts with RAW. We were becoming the pre-eminent group in Jaffna, and India was trying to balance us with the others.'[26]

From September 1983 to July 1987, India is said to have trained 'an estimated 1,200 Tamils in the use of automatic and semi-automatic weapons, self loading rifles, 84 mm rocket launchers, heavy weapons, and in laying mines, map reading, guerrilla warfare, mountaineering, demolitions and anti-tank warfare. . . . Select members of EROS, LTTE, EPRLF and ENDLF were also given special training in diving and under-sea sabotage.'[27] The militant groups also set up camps in the districts of Madras, Madurai, Tiruchi, Pudukkottai, South Arcot, Salem, Coimbatore, Thanjavur, and Ramanathapuram.[28]

In Pakistan, the proliferation of small arms is a result of many factors,[29] and is not merely due to the presence of Afghan refugees in the country. The main factor was the *jihad* against the Soviet-backed government in Kabul by the *mujahideen* who were provided with all types of weapons, ranging from machine guns to Stinger missiles. Between two to three billion US dollars were spent on arming the *mujahideen*, a task undertaken by the CIA and the ISI. These weapons did fall into other hands, which was the main reason for the easy availability of the number of small arms that one now witnesses in Pakistan. Second, guns have always played a major role in the daily affairs of most of the tribal groups in the NWFP. The famous Darra market[30] catered to the needs of the local tribes, and it later expanded to cater to the demands that came from both inside and outside Pakistan.

III

REFUGEES AND ECONOMIC SECURITY

The belief that refugees constitute an economic threat is directly linked to two factors. The first factor is the numerical size of the refugee population, and the second factor is the ability of the host state, especially in economic terms, to provide the refugees with the basic living conditions.

All the countries in South Asia are in various stages of economic development; none of them has the ability to provide adequate infrastructure to its own citizens.

SOUTH ASIA IN THE GLOBAL FRAMEWORK

	Population (millions)		Real GDP (PPP dollars millions)		Absolute Poverty (millions)		Illiterate Adults (millions)	
	1960	1993	1960	1993	1960	1993	1960	1993
World	2,996	5,508	5,303	30,542	n/a	1,314	735	853
South Asia	564	1,191	365	1,632	n/a	527	234	396
Share of South Asia in the world (%)	19	22	6.9	5.3	n/a	40	32	46

Source: Mahbub ul Haq, *Human Development in South Asia, 1997*, New Delhi: Oxford University Press, 1997, p. 8.

Here are some relevant facts pertaining to South Asia. It is the most populous region in the world. Its share in the absolute poverty at the global level is 40 per cent, whereas its share in the global income is a mere 5.3 per cent.[31] In terms of per capita income South Asia, at $ 309, is the poorest region in the world.

PER CAPITA INCOME OF VARIOUS REGIONS
GNP per capita (US $)

Region	Per capita
South Asia	309
Sub Saharan Africa	555
East Asia (including China)	825
All developing countries	970
Arab States	1,725
Latin America and the Caribbean	2,966

Source: Mahbub ul Haq, *Human Development in South Asia, 1997*, New Delhi: Oxford University Press, 1997, p. 11.

Given these human development indicators in South Asia, refugees are sure to pose an economic burden on the host society. Despite various economic limitations, South Asian countries do accommodate refugees on their soil and feed them even at a very high cost, and this achievement deserves to be commended. Before and during the Indo-Pak war of 1971, India did support the refugees from East Pakistan at a fairly high cost. According to *Time* magazine:

> The cost of feeding and attempting to house the refugees is currently $1,330,000 a day—an expense that Mrs. Gandhi's government can ill afford if it is going to fulfill the campaign promise of *garibi hatao* (eradicate poverty). The food required by the refugees is rapidly depleting existing food stockpiles and threatens to create a famine for the Indians themselves. The refugees are also taking work away from the Indians; in West Bengal, the refugee peasants are hiring out as agricultural labourers for a quarter of the wages [that the] local labourer is paid.[32]

During the 1980s, Pakistan spent more than a million dollars a day to house and feed refugees. There were around 2.4 million registered refugees whose maintenance cost around a million dollars, and when the unregistered refugees are included, the number would be more than the estimated figures.[33]

A major reason for Pakistan, and especially for some of its provinces, to refuse to build any extra camps for the Afghan refugees[34] was mainly based on economic considerations. In an interview, Lt. Gen. (retd.) Iftikhar Hussain Shah, governor of the NWFP, claiming that the large number of Afghan refugees had devastated the provincial economy, said, 'We have made it clear to the UNHCR and also conveyed to the federal government that no more land would be provided for new refugee camps. . . . It is a matter of our economy.'[35] The economic factor has been the main reason for Pakistan to continually reject the UNHCR demands to have more camps for Afghan refugees.[36] According to Pakistani authorities, around 280 camps have been set up in various parts of the country since 1979. It costs 30 million rupees to set up a new camp, and an additional 5 million rupees is needed every month to feed the refugees in a camp.[37] According to Pakistani officials, 'The UNHCR is just interested in registering them, who would take care of their logistics and food afterwards is not the UNHCR's concern.'[38] This is why the visit of Ruud Lubbers, UN High Commissioner of Refugees, in May 2001 to Pakistan failed to reach any agreement regarding the registration of the thousands of refugees living in the makeshift camp in Jalozai.[39] Pakistan prefers that the UNHCR set up camps to rehabilitate the displaced Afghans inside Afghanistan, which the UNHCR dismisses as a 'silly idea' and 'not the solution'.[40]

A second factor which also contributed to Pakistan's changed policy towards the Afghan refugees in the period before 11 September 2001 was that the international community was unwilling[41] to contribute to the maintenance of these refugees.[42] After the 11 September terrorist attacks in the United States, the international community started pouring huge amounts of aid to solve the problems of the Afghan refugees.[43]

While talking about the economic burden that the refugee population poses to the host state, it is also essential to focus on the economic benefits that these outsiders bring. One should recognize that the economic benefits may be insignificant when compared to the costs involved, but nonetheless there are certain benefits from the presence of refugees in the host nation. It is said that:

> On the benefit side, the aid community has brought millions of dollars into the region, hiring local citizens and buying locally produced supplies and materials. Inexpensive Afghan labour has held down prices of agricultural and manufactured goods, thus benefiting local consumers.[44]

However, these economic benefits may be far from adequate to mollify the local population. As the local people and the refugees compete for the limited resources available, the locals may not recognize or may refuse to acknowledge the fringe benefits brought about by the presence of aliens living in their country.

The readiness of the refugees to work for minimum wage reduces the labour wages in the area, thus affecting the livelihood of the local population. Second, in certain instances, as in the case of the Sri Lankan refugees, they received not only cash doles but also other essential items at subsidized rates, whereas the local population received nothing.[45] Besides, the refugees have monopolized certain market areas. For example, the Afghan refugees have succeeded in monopolizing the transportation sector in Peshawar and, to a certain extent, in Karachi.[46] In Karachi alone, there are around one million Afghans, comprising Pushtoons, Tajiks, Uzbeks, and Hazaras, who are engaged in the transport sector, daily labour, and hawking.[47] Any accidents involving Afghan drivers or buses owned by Afghans result in increasing the tensions between the local population and the Afghans. Besides, the Afghans are involved in land grabbing, encroachment, etc. and the local population is finding it difficult to evict them, so that their lands could be sold.[48] The Afghans have illegally settled in approximately 7,500 acres of land around Karachi which is worth around Rs. 37.5 billion, and this land is now unavailable for sale.[49] Half of the 300,000 population of Chaman, a small town near the Pakistan-Afghanistan border, consists of Afghan refugees.[50]

IV

Refugees and Political Security

The contention that refugees constitute a threat to the political security of the host state is a significant factor that needs to be further examined. Does the mere presence of refugees in a state result in the creation of political instability and insecurity? To what extent did the Afghan refugees in Pakistan and the Sri Lankan refugees in Tamil Nadu contribute to the political instability in these two countries?

Refugees are considered as a threat in three levels: strategic, regime, and structural.[51] When the refugees are armed and when the state loses control over the refugees, it affects the strategic security of the state; when there is a conflict over scarce resources, it affects the structural security of the state; and when the refugees get involved in domestic politics, it affects the regime security of the state.[52] It is even considered that in South Asia 'there are "dramatic examples" not of the familiar story of wars producing refugees, but rather of refugees producing wars'.[53] These are serious contentions which need to be probed further. Once again, these assertions need to be investigated keeping in mind the differences between the militant refugees and the civilian refugees.

Why do the refugees take to arms? Where do they find such sophisticated arms? Where do they get military training? Is the host state not aware of these issues? What is the role of the host state in providing arms, military training, and safe havens? In other words, what are the various reasons and compulsions which lead the host state to decide to arm a section of the refugee population?

The two most frequently quoted instances of refugees being a security threat to the state are the Afghan refugees in Pakistan and the assassination of Rajiv Gandhi by Sri Lankan Tamils.

The security threat posed by the Afghan refugees to the polity of Pakistan is explained as follows:

> The presence of [a] large number of Afghan refugees caused many political problems in Pakistan. These included the growth of terrorism, and [a] sharp

cleavage among the political parties regarding the Afghan refugees and their eventual return. Until the advent of the eighties, organized terrorism was virtually absent in Pakistan. . . . The NWFP has been particularly at the receiving end of terrorism. The Kabul regime had managed to penetrate into the great reservoirs of resistance; namely the refugee groups.[54]

The perception of a threat emanating from the refugees to the political security of the host state is based on the following three assumptions: first, the growth of organized terrorism in the host country; second, the impact of refugees on domestic politics; and third, the transformation of the local population into a minority in their own land. These three dimensions of the security threat supposedly posed by refugees to the political security of the host country need to be probed further. We will examine the role of refugees in the growth of organized terrorism with respect to three specific issues: terrorism in Pakistan, the assassination of Rajiv Gandhi, and ethnic conflict in the north-east of India.

There is no denying the fact that Pakistani society is facing a serious threat from what they call 'organized terrorism'. To what extent are these terrorist activities the result of the presence of refugees in Pakistan? In other words, is the present level of violence related to Pakistan's direct involvement in the Afghan *jihad*?[55] Pakistan had actively supported the various *mujahideen* groups in the 1980s by providing them with weapons and training, and in the 1990s, Pakistan contributed to the extension of this *jihad* by creating, supporting, and sustaining the Taliban.[56] Or is the present level of violence in Pakistan related only to the presence of Afghan refugees in the country? Second, how far is the sectarian violence, which is considered to be the main threat to Pakistan's stability, the outcome of the presence of Afghan refugees in Pakistan? Third, to what extent have the Afghan refugees contributed to the ethnic and tribal violence that Pakistan is facing in Sind and the NWFP? Fourth, to what extent have the Afghan refugees contributed to Pakistan's Kashmir policy which has resulted in the institutionalization of *jihadi* groups in Pakistan? Fifth, why is it that Afghan refugees in Pakistan are seen as a major threat, as the root cause of all the ills that Pakistan is facing, whereas the same number of Afghan refugees present in Iran are not considered to constitute a similar grave threat to national security?

It is also interesting to note that, besides the differences among the refugees and the host country[57] there were also differences in the refugee assistance programmes in Iran and Pakistan.[58]

AFGHAN REFUGEE POPULATION IN PAKISTAN AND IRAN DURING 1979-99
(as on 31 December of each given year)

Year	Pakistan	Iran
1979	402,000	100,000
1980	1,428,000	300,000
1981	2,375,000	1,500,000
1982	2,877,000	1,500,000
1983	2,873,000	1,700,000
1984	2,500,000	1,800,000
1985	2,730,000	1,880,000
1986	3,156,000	2,350,000
1987	3,156,000	2,350,000
1988	3,255,000	2,350,000
1989	3,272,000	2,350,000
1990	3,253,000	3,061,000
1991	3,098,000	3,187,000
1992	1,627,000	2,901,000
1993	1,477,000	1,850,000
1994	1,053,000	1,623,000
1995	1,200,000	1,429,000
1996	1,200,000	1,415,000
1997	1,200,000	1,412,000
1998	1,200,000	1,401,000
1999	1,200,000	1,325,000

Source: *UNHCR The State of the World's Refugees, 2000*, New Delhi, Oxford University Press, 2000.

An examination of the evidence relating to the questions posed above will make one realize that the Afghan refugees play only a minor role in the creation of the ills which plague Pakistani society.

Long before the terrorist attacks of 11 September 2001 occurred, there was a realization in Pakistan and elsewhere that Pakistan was becoming a major hub for the activities of the Islamic extremist groups involved in terrorist activities both inside and outside the country.[59] These extremist groups comprised mainly the former *mujahideen* who had fought against the Soviet Union and most were Pakistanis and not Afghan refugees. These groups along with the Taliban had close links with the ISI, which had been using the former to achieve its security objectives.[60] Besides these extremist organizations, there was also the Pakistani underworld, with its headquarters in Karachi, which was engaged in trafficking in drugs, arms, and women.[61] The Karachi underworld is even suspected of having links with the 11 September terrorist attacks.[62]

Besides the *jihadi* factor, the second factor that has contributed to the present state of chaos in Pakistan is sectarian violence. The Sipah-i-Sahaba Pakistan (SSP)[63] and the Tehrik-i-Jafria Pakistan (TJP)[64] along with other sectarian groups are engaged in fomenting major sectarian conflicts that have destroyed social harmony and wrecked peace in the country.[65]

Another instance which highlights the role of refugees in disrupting national security was the assassination of Rajiv Gandhi in 1991, a crime for which the Sri Lankan refugees were blamed to a great extent. However, an in-depth analysis of the events leading to Rajiv Gandhi's assassination will prove that the Sri Lankan refugees were only one part of the conspiracy. Many groups were involved in carrying out the assassination and the subsequent provision of shelter for those who carried out the assassination. Broadly speaking, the people behind the assassination of the Indian prime minister may be classified into three groups. The first was the core group, comprising the LTTE leadership and selected cadres.[66] Sivarasan, Dhanu the human bomb, Subha, Murugan, and others entered India illegally. The second group, comprising LTTE cadres such as Vijayan, Selvalaxmi, and Baskaran, entered India long before the arrival of the assassination team and registered themselves as refugees in Rameswaram.[67] The objective of this group was to provide the necessary logistical support to the assassination team. For various reasons, the LTTE did not want to use or involve its then existing political support groups. The third group consisted of some Sri Lankan refugees and Indian citizens who were sympathetic to the LTTE cause. Except for a few people in this third group, the others were unaware of the conspiracy, but they did help the conspirators after the assassination took place.

Another security threat posed by refugees in the arena of domestic politics is seen in the case of Afghan refugees in Pakistan, whose presence has been used by the local political parties in the country to further their own political purposes and to serve their political objectives, and in the process becoming their vote banks.[68]

Another contention is that the presence of refugees may numerically reduce the local population to a minority in their own land. This threat may assume serious dimensions if the host population and the refugee population do not belong to the same ethnic community.

The Afghan refugees in Pakistan were settled mainly in the NWFP and Baluchistan. The continuous inflow of the Afghan refugees increased the fears among the Baluch leaders that the Afghan refugee population belonging mainly to the Pashtun community would upset the balance between the Pashtuns and the Baluchis in Baluchistan. It was feared that the Baluchis would become a minority in Baluchistan.[69]

The same fear was reflected in a report submitted by Lt. Gen. (retd.) S.K. Sinha, Governor of Assam, to the President of India in 1998. The report warned that the:

> silent and invidious demographic invasion of Assam may result in the loss of geo-strategically vital districts of Lower Assam . . . The influx of these illegal migrants is turning these districts into [a] Muslim majority region. It will then only be a matter of time when a demand for their merger with Bangladesh may be made. The rapid growth of international Islamic fundamentalism may provide the driving force for this demand. The loss of Lower Assam will sever the entire land mass of [the] North East from the rest of India and [the] rich natural resources of the region will be lost to the nation.[70]

The local population in India's north-east felt 'threatened by an increasing sense of being marginalised in their home land by a culturally and ethnically different group'.[71] In Arunachal Pradesh, the presence of Chakma refugees led the Arunachal Pradesh Students Union (APSU) to demand the removal of the Chakmas from the country. This development has two further implications. First, state politics are exploited in terms of the issue of 'sons of the soil versus aliens'. The other political parties in the state, whether willingly or unwillingly, have also had to focus on this issue for their own political survival. Second, the assertion of such demands by the local population in the host state upsets the refugees, and the fear of being expelled leads the refugees, in turn, to assert themselves against their hosts. In Arunachal Pradesh, for example, 'in a bid to protect themselves from being ousted, the Chakmas have built links . . . with militant organisations causing the balance of forces to change and posing problems for internal security'.[72]

V

Conclusion

The perception that refugees constitute a threat to the host state is based on three considerations: social security, economic security, and political security.

As discussed above, the assertion that refugees are a social threat—because of their involvement in drug addiction and drug trafficking, proliferation of small arms, smuggling, and their involvement in the underworld—is clearly being over emphasized. While it is true that in certain cases refugees are indeed involved in the above-mentioned activities, it is totally unjustified to lay the entire blame for the social problems of the host country at the door of the refugee population. Trafficking in drugs and small arms, which result in drug addiction, narco-terrorism, and the proliferation of small arms in the local society is an independent development, and would continue to exist irrespective of the presence of refugees in a particular region.

Second, the assertion that refugees constitute an economic threat or burden cannot be disputed. The fact that refugees are an economic threat is directly linked to three factors: the size of the refugee population; the ability of the host state to provide food and shelter to the outsiders; and the level of international economic aid.

REFUGEE POPULATION BY ORIGIN AND COUNTRY OF ASYLUM
(as on 31 December 1999)

Country of Origin	Country of Asylum	Number
Afghanistan		
	Iran	1,325,000
	Pakistan	1,200,000
	Netherlands	20,300
	Germany	16,600
	India	14,500
	UK	3,500
	Denmark	2,300
	Kazakhastan	2,300
	Other	11,700
Bhutan		
	Nepal	107,600
Myanmar		
	Thailand	99,700
	Bangladesh	22,100
	Malaysia	5,100
	Other	900
Sri Lanka		
	India	66,400
	France	15,900
	Canada	9,700
	Germany	9,200
	UK	8,300
	Switzerland	4,300
	Other	2,500

Source: The State of the World's Refugees, 2000, Annex 6, pp. 316-18.

Third, the perception that refugees constitute a political threat rests on three factors: the level of involvement of the host state in the conflict; the integration of the refugees in the local population; and the politicization of the refugee population by the local political parties and other interest groups.

The threats posed by the refugees to the security of the host state are directly linked with the involvement of the host state in the affairs of the state from where the refugee population originates. The following tables provide data on refugee populations and the countries of their asylum. It is no coincidence that the host states that face security threats from refugees are the same states that are actively involved in the conflicts in the refugee-producing country.

The de-politicization of the refugee issue in local politics by political parties and interest groups along with the non-use of the refugee card in the diplomatic arena of bilateral relations would greatly reduce the intensity of threats posed to the political security of the host nation.

Notes

1. In recent years many works examining the changing dimensions of security have appeared. See M. Klare and D. Thomas, eds., *World Security: Trends and Challenges at Century's End*, New York: St. Martin's Press, 1991.
2. For perspectives on security in the post-Cold War period, see Edward E. Azar and Chung Moon, eds., *National Security in the Third World: The Management of Internal and External Threats*, Hants: Edward Elgar Publishing Limited, 1988; George A. Cooray, ed., *New Dimensions of Security after the Cold War*, Colombo: Institute for International Studies, 1997.
3. Ann J. Tickner, 'Revisioning Security', in Ken Booth and Steve Smith, eds., *International Relations Theory Today*, University Park, Pennsylvania: Pennsylvania University Press, 1995.
4. K.S. Dhillon, 'India 1947-1997 Internal Security: A Status Report', in P.R. Chari, ed., *India Towards Millennium*, New Delhi: Manohar, 1998, p. 89.
5. For the implications of the presence of refugees on security, see Warren Zimmermann, 'Migrants and Refugees: A Threat to. Security?', in Michael S. Teitlebaum and Myron Weiner, eds., *Threatened Peoples, Threatened Borders*, New Delhi: Universal Book Traders, 1997; Myron Weiner, 'Security, Stability and International Migration', *International Security*, vol. 17, no. 3, Winter 1992-3, pp. 92-126. For excellent analyses of the impact of refugees on security in South Asia, see Lokraj Baral, *Regional Migrations, Ethnicity, and Security: The South Asian Case*, New Delhi: Sterling Publishers, 1990 and Lokraj Baral and S.D. Muni, 'Refugees, South Asia and Security', in Lokraj Baral and S.D. Muni, eds., *Refugees and Regional Security in South Asia,* New Delhi: Konark Publishers, 1996, pp. 24-33.
6. Lokraj Baral and S.D. Muni, 'Refugees, South Asia and Security', in Baral and Muni, eds., *Refugees and Regional Security in South Asia*, p. 25.

7. By 1990, following the departure of the Indian Peace Keeping Force (IPKF) from the country, these non-LTTE militant and political organizations which had been fighting in Sri Lanka realized that they faced a serious threat from the LTTE. Hence, these groups decided to leave the island and take refuge in Tamil Nadu.
8. See Mahendra P. Lama, *Managing Refugees in South Asia: Protection, Aid, State Behaviour and Regional Approach*, Occasional Paper 4, RMMRU Unit, Dhaka, 2000, pp. 19-27; Lokraj Baral and S.D. Muni, 'Refugees, South Asia and Security', in Baral and Muni, eds., *Refugees and Regional Security in South Asia*, pp. 24-33.
9. See D. Suba Chandran, 'Drug Trafficking and the Security of the State: A Case Study of Pakistan', *Strategic Analysis*, vol. 22, no. 6, September 1998, pp. 903-22.
10. See Mahendra P. Lama, *Managing Refugees in South Asia: Protection, Aid, State Behaviour and Regional Approach*, pp. 22-3; Pervaiz Iqbal Cheema, 'The Afghan Refugees and Pakistan's Security Problems', in Baral and Muni, eds., *Refugees and Regional Security in South Asia*, pp. 178-93.
11. Syed Shoib Hasan, 'Under the Spotlight', *Herald*, October 2001, p. 32b.
12. K. Mohandass, *MGR: The Man and the Myth*, Bangalore: Panther Publishers, 1992.
13. M.R. Narayan Swamy, *Tigers of Lanka: From Boys to Guerillas*, New Delhi: Konark Publishers, 1995, p. 175.
14. Manoj Joshi, 'The ignored signals', *Frontline*, 17-30 July 1990, p. 18.
15. Syed Shoib Hasan, 'Under the Spotlight', *Herald*, October 2001, p. 32b.
16. This aspect of the internal divisions among the Sri Lankan refugees and the militant population and their open fights in Madras and elsewhere in Tamil Nadu is examined in K. Mohandass, *MGR: The Man and the Myth*, Bangalore: Panther Publishers, 1992, pp. 140-9.
17. See R. Parthasarathy, 'A massacre in Madras', *Frontline*, 17-30 July 1990, pp. 13-14.
18. Bertram Bastiampillai, 'Sri Lankan Tamil Refugees in Tamil Nadu: Trouble to the host', in Baral and Muni, eds., *Refugees and Regional Security in South Asia*, p. 207.
19. Baral and Muni, 'Refugees, South Asia and Security', in Baral and Muni, eds., *Refugees and Regional Security in South Asia*, p. 26.
20. See D. Suba Chandran, 'Drug Trafficking and the Security of the State: A Case Study of Pakistan', *Strategic Analysis*, vol. 22, no. 6, September 1998, pp. 903-22.
21. Among the various tribal groups that are involved in illegal drug cultivation and trafficking, the Afridis are considered professionals as they are involved in the process right from the beginning, from cultivating to processing and then transporting the drugs to the international markets. See D. Suba Chandran, 'Drug Trafficking and the Security of the State: A Case Study of Pakistan', *Strategic Analysis*, vol. 22, no. 6, September 1998, pp. 903-22.
22. For the nexus between the political elite, the Pakistan Army, and the drug traffickers, see Zahid Hussain, 'Narco Power: Pakistan's Parallel Government', *Newsline*, December 1989; Aabha Dixit, 'Narco Power: Threatening the Very Roots of Pakistan', *Strategic Analysis*, May 1991, vol. 13, no. 15; D. Suba Chandran, 'Drug Trafficking and the Security of the State: A Case Study of Pakistan', *Strategic Analysis*, September 1998, pp. 903-22; 'Heroin in Pakistan: Sowing the Wind', C.I.A Report published in the *Frontier Post*, 31 August 1993.
23. http://www.undcp.org/india/country_profile.html

24. M.R. Narayan Swamy, *Tigers of Lanka*, p. 107.
25. Thomas Abraham, 'The Emergence of the LTTE and the Indo-Sri Lanka Agreement of 1987', in Kumar Rupesinghe, ed., *Negotiating Peace in Sri Lanka: Efforts, Failures and Lessons*, London: International Alert, 1998, p. 22.
26. Thomas Abraham, 'The Emergence of the LTTE and the Indo-Sri Lanka Agreement of 1987', in Kumar Rupesinghe, ed., *Negotiating Peace in Sri Lanka*, p. 22.
27. M.R. Narayan Swamy, *Tigers of Lanka*, p. 66.
28. Ibid., pp. 111-12.
29. For the various factors that have contributed to the proliferation of small arms in Pakistan, see Ayesha S. Agha, 'Light Weapons Manufacture in the Public and Private Sectors: A View from Pakistan', Project on Light Weapons (London: British American Security Information Council, 1996) Working Paper, British American Security Information Council; Ayesha S. Agha, 'Arresting Light Weapons Proliferation in Pakistan: Is there a way ahead[? Check whether there is a question mark at the end of this title]', in Abdel-Fatau Musah and Niobe Thomson, eds., *Over a Barrel: Light Weapons and Human Rights in the Commonwealth*, New Delhi: CHRI, 1999, pp. 109-10; and Chris Smith, 'Light Weapons and Ethnic Conflict in South Asia', in *Lethal Commerce: The Global Trade in Small Arms and Light Weapons*, Cambridge, Mass.: American Academy of Arts and Science, 1995, p. 537.
30. The Darra manufacturers initially produced only pistols and rifles. The influx of machine guns during the *jihad* against the Soviet troops in Afghanistan led them to manufacture all types of machine guns, including AK-47s. The AK-47s produced in Darra were relatively cheap when compared to the prices commanded by the original guns. For example, when the Afghan crisis was at its height, an AK-47 produced by the Darra markets cost between Rs. 4,000-5,000, whereas an assembled AK-47 cost between Rs. 18,000-20,000. Compare these prices with the cost of an original Soviet-made AK-47, which was then around Rs. 60,000-80,000.
31. Mahbub ul Haq, *Human Development in South Asia, 1997*, Delhi: Oxford University Press, 1997.
32. Cited in Imtiaz Ahmad, 'Refugees and Security: The Experience of Bangladesh', in Baral and Muni, eds., *Refugees and Regional Security in South Asia*, pp. 126-7.
33. Pervaiz Iqbal Cheema, 'The Afghan Refugees and Pakistan's Internal Security Problems', in Baral and Muni, eds., *Refugees and Regional Security in South Asia*, p. 192.
34. Afghan refugees have constituted the world's largest refugee group ever since the war in Afghanistan began in 1979. During the late 1980s, when the conflict was at it peak, more than 6.2 million Afghans lived as refugees, mainly in Iran and Pakistan. According to the UNHCR, before the start of the war against terrorism, there were around 1.2 million registered refugees in Pakistan, besides an unknown number of unregistered refugees living all over the country, particularly in the urban areas surrounding Peshawar, Rawalpindi, Lahore, and Karachi.
35. 'NWFP not to give land for new DPs camps', *Dawn*, 1 February 2001.
36. See 'Pakistan refuses new camp for Afghans', *Dawn*, 10 February 2001; 'Pakistan cannot afford to look after Afghan refugees', *Dawn*, 5 May 2001.
37. 'Why Jalozai camp drew world attention?', *Dawn*, 6 May 2001.

38. Ibid.
39. 'Talks on refugee status fail: UNHCR', *News*, 8 May 2001.
40. Ibid.
41. One of the main reasons for the decline of interest among the donor countries in providing assistance for Afghanistan in the pre-11 September 2001 period was the result of the policies pursued by the Taliban. For example, the chief of the 16-member Support Group for Afghanistan said, 'If the Taliban will continue to add one harassment to the other—whether it is bakeries in Kabul, or the most recent idea of having foreigners working in Afghanistan write a kind of letter of submission accepting all sorts of consequences, this could develop into not only a major obstacle but could bring to a grinding halt the entire programme.' See 'Afghan aid can be stopped, says donor group chief', *Dawn*, 7 June 2001.
42. 'Why Jalozai camp drew world attention?', *Dawn*, 6 May 2001.
43. For example, the US announced, on 4 October 2001, $ 320 million in humanitarian assistance out of which $295 was earmarked for Afghans suffering from drought, famine, and displacement. Japan, in October 2001, announced $ 120 million in additional aid for Afghan refugees. See 'Bush announces $ 320m aid for Afghans', *News*, 5 October 2001; 'Washington to give $ 320m assistance for Afghans', *Dawn*, 5 October 2001; 'Japan extends budgetary support, refugee aid', *News*, 6 October 2001.
44. Randolph Martin, 'Regional Dynamics and the Security of Afghan Refugees in Pakistan', *UNHCR Refugee Survey Quarterly*, vol. 19, no. 1, 2000, pp. 71-78.
45. For example, the cash doles given to Sri Lankan Tamil refugees every fortnight are as follows: Rs. 150 for one member, Rs. 270 for two members, Rs. 345 for three members, Rs. 382 for four members, and Rs. 502 for five members. In addition, the refugees also receive essentials such as rice, sugar, kerosene, *dhal*, etc., at highly subsidized rates. These facilities are not available to the local population. See Professor V. Suryanarayanan's Backgrounder, *Sri Lankan Refugees in Tamil Nadu: Humanitarian and Security Dimensions*, unpublished paper.
46. See Randolph Martin, 'Regional Dynamics and the Security of Afghan Refugees in Pakistan', *UNHCR Refugee Survey Quarterly*, vol. 19, no. 1, 2000, pp. 71-78.
47. Syed Shoib Hasan, 'Under the Spotlight', *Herald*, October 2001, p. 32b.
48. The Afghan settlers feel that since Pakistan has been receiving funds from all over the world in the name of the Afghan refugees, they 'have every right to take what (they) can in Pakistan'. See Syed Shoib Hasan, 'Under the Spotlight', *Herald*, October 2001, p. 32b.
49. Syed Shoaib Hasan, 'Crime and Punishment', *Herald*, December 2001, p. 28.
50. Ghulam Hasnain, 'Journey into the Unknown', *Newsline*, November 2001, p. 40.
51. Mahendra P. Lama, *Managing Refugees in South Asia*, p. 20.
52. Ibid.
53. Ibid.
54. Pervaiz Iqbal Cheema, 'The Afghan Refugees and Pakistan's Internal Security Problems,' in Baral and Muni, eds., *Refugees and Regional Security in South Asia*, p. 180.
55. After the Soviet troops invaded Afghanistan in 1979, Pakistan and the Central Intelligence Agency (CIA) of the US were involved, throughout the 1980s, in directly aiding the *mujahideen* groups against the Soviet-backed regime in Afghanistan. It has been estimated that both the US and Pakistan spent around

US $ 2 to 3 billion worth of assistance to the *mujahideen* in providing them with training and arms. See J. Bruce Amsutz, *Afghanistan: The First Five Years of Soviet Occupation*, Washington, D.C.: National Defence University Press, 1986; Abdul Samad Ghaus, *The Fall of Afghanistan: An Insider's Account*, Washington, D.C.: Pergamon Brassey's, 1988; Anthony Arnold, *Afghanistan: The Soviet Invasion in Perspective*, Stanford: Hoover Institute Press, 1981; Henry S. Bradsher, *Afghanistan and the Soviet Union*, Durham: Duke University Press, 1983; and Mohammad Yousaf and Mark Adkin, *The Bear Trap: Afghanistan's Untold Story*, London: Mark Cooper, 1992.

56. When the *mujahideen* failed to provide a stable government inside Afghanistan, Pakistan decided to create a new force altogether to achieve its objectives. This resulted in the creation of the Taliban by the ISI. Most of the Taliban cadres were recruited from among the Afghan refugee population living in the camps and those who were being educated in the various *madrassas* of Pakistan. For an excellent account of Pakistan's active role in creating and sustaining the Taliban, see Ahmed Rashid, *Taliban: Militant Islam, Oil and Fundamentalism in Central Asia*, New Haven: Yale University Press, 2000; William Maley, ed., *Fundamentalism Reborn? Afghanistan and the Taliban*, New York: New York University Press, 1998; Peter Marsden, *The Taliban: War and Religion in Afghanistan*, London: Zed Books, 1998; and Kamal Matinuddin, *The Taliban Phenomenon 1994-1997*, Karachi: Oxford University Press, 1997.
57. Most of the Afghan refugees who took refuge in Iran belonged to diverse ethnic groups, mainly comprising Tajiks, Uzbeks, and Hazaras, while the Afghan refugees who took refuge in Pakistan belonged to the Pashtun community.
58. The international assistance to Afghan refugees in Iran and Pakistan varied significantly. While the Afghan refugees in Pakistan received huge sums of money during the 1980s, the Afghan refugees in Iran received very little. See *The State of the World's Refugees 2000*, New Delhi: Oxford University Press, p. 117.
59. See Zahid Hussain, 'In the shadow of terrorism', *Newsline*, February 2000, pp. 17-22; Ismail Khan, 'Terrorists or Crusaders', *Newsline*, February 2000, pp. 23-5; 'Militancy and the State', *Herald*, May 2000, pp. 49-52.
60. For the linkages between the ISI and the Taliban and the other groups, see M. Illyas Khan, 'The ISI-Taliban Nexus', *Herald*, November 2001, pp. 21-6.
61. See Ghulam Hasnain, 'Karachi's Gang Wars', *Newsline*, September 2001, pp. 20-3; Zafar Abbas, 'The Karachi Connection', *Herald*, November 2001, pp. 36a-36c.
62. See Zafar Abbas, 'The Karachi Connection', *Herald*, November 2001, pp. 36a-36c.
63. The Sipah-i-Sahaba Pakistan, a sectarian Sunni group, was originally formed as the Anjuman Sipah-i-Sahaba Pakistan in September 1985 by Maulana Haq Nawaz Jhangvi of the Jamiat-ul-Islam (Fazlur). The main objective of the SSP is to declare the Shias as non-Muslims. The SSP has a presence all over Pakistan, especially in Punjab and Sind.
64. The Tehrik-i-Jafria Pakistan was founded in 1979 as the Tehrik Nifaz-i-Fiqah-i-Jafria (TNFJ) and is the major Shia sectarian group in Pakistan.
65. See the following for the sectarian madness in which these groups are involved: Mumtaz Ahmad, 'Revivalism, Islamization, Sectarianism and Violence in Pakistan', in Craig Baxter and Charles Kennedy, eds., *Pakistan 1997*, Boulder, Colorado: Westview Press, 1998 and Mukhtar Ahmad Ali, *Sectarian Conflict in Pakistan*, Colombo: Regional Centre for Strategic Studies, 2000.

66. According to the judgement of the Supreme Court of India: 'There is no doubt that the criminal conspiracy to murder Rajiv Gandhi was hatched by at least four persons comprising (LTTE chief) Veluppillai Prabhakaran, (intelligence chief) Pottu Amman, (hitman) Sivarasan and (women's wing chief) Akila.' See Praveen Swami, 'The Final Judgment', *Frontline*, 4 June 1999, p. 97.
67. The main objective of this trio was to provide shelter to Sivarasan and his aide Subha after the assassination had been executed. See Praveen Swami, 'The Final Judgment', *Frontline*, 4 June 1999, p. 98.
68. Hasan Aksari Rizvi, 'Afghan Refugees in Pakistan: Influx, Humanitarian Assistance and Implications', *Pakistan Horizon*, Ist Quarter, 1984, pp. 40-61.
69. Quoted in Pervaiz Iqbal Cheema, 'The Afghan Refugees and Pakistan's Internal Security Problems', p. 182.
70. See Bibhu Prasad Routray, 'The Healing Wounds of Migration in Assam', http://www.ipcs.org/issues/700/714-ne-bibhu-html
71. Shikha Bose, 'Victims of a Security Dilemma: Chakmas and Refugees from Bangladesh', in Baral and Muni, eds., *Refugees and Regional Security in South Asia*, p. 111.
72. Ibid.

9. *The Bihari Muslims of Bangladesh: In a State of Statelessness*

ZARIN AHMAD

Introduction

As issues of social identity are increasingly being addressed in the social sciences, international relations, legal studies, and human rights forums, the situation of the Bihari Muslims in Bangladesh comes to the fore. This group has so far remained on the periphery of research studies and policy making. Therefore, it becomes imperative to approach the issue both academically and legally.[1]

The Bihari Muslims, alternatively referred to as 'stranded Pakistanis', are the original residents of Bihar, West Bengal, Orissa, and Assam in India. But since the majority of them hail from Bihar they are commonly known as Bihari Muslims. They are Urdu-speaking Muslims who chose to migrate to East Pakistan at the time of the partition of the subcontinent in 1947. According to the United States Committee for Refugees (USCR), at the end of the year 2000, there were 300,000 Bihari Muslims living in camps in refugee-like situations.[2] They live in 66 camps located in Dhaka, Chittagong, Rangpur, Saidpur, Khulna, and other districts of Bangladesh.[3]

This paper is divided into four broad sections. The first section deals with the historical background. The second section addresses legal issues. The third section deals with the current situation of the refugees, and the fourth and last section suggests some steps to ameliorate their condition.

Background

The problem of the Bihari Muslims dates back to the partition of the subcontinent and the implementation of the two-nation theory based on religion. The Partition resulted in one of the biggest upheavals in human history, when 15 million people crossed the newly drawn international borders, accompanied by unprecedented violence. Amidst this exchange of population, 700,000 Bihari Muslims migrated to East Pakistan (now Bangladesh). As in all refugee situations, initially they were welcomed with much warmth and hospitality. But soon the euphoria died down and cracks began to appear between the Bengali Muslims and the Urdu-speaking migrants. The latter could not completely identify linguistically and socially with the predominantly Bengali milieu. They also had a sense of superiority because they spoke Urdu, which has traditionally been the language of the elite Muslims in the subcontinent. It needs to be mentioned in this context that the Bihari Muslims considered themselves to be the 'real architects' of the new state of Pakistan. But these were differences that could have been bridged between a host population and an immigrant population in the years to come. However, problems became more serious with the declaration of Urdu as the state language by the ruling elite of West Pakistan in 1948. This official step had serious political and economic implications. It obviously made government jobs more accessible for the Bihari Muslim Urdu-speaking people, and the rift between the two communities widened. The decades of the 1950s and the 1960s saw a gradual deterioration in the relations between the two linguistic groups and, more importantly, serious problems arose in the nation-building process in Pakistan. Among other problems, the linguistic divide and elite interests in preserving the status quo were some of the crucial factors contributing to the deteriorating social situation. Newer ethnic boundaries were created or recreated, and this time the people were divided primarily along linguistic lines.

Matters came to a head during the Bangladesh Liberation War of 1970-1. After a bitter conflict, East Pakistan split from West Pakistan and a new state, Bangladesh, was carved out on the basis of Bengali nationalism. The Bihari Muslims were greatly affected during and immediately after the Liberation War. There was large-scale violence unleashed against them as a response to the violence of the Pakistan Army against the Bengali nationalist leaders, in particular, and the population, in general. Although exact figures are not available, it is estimated that between 10,000 to 15,000 Bihari Muslims were killed during the period.[4] In the beginning, all of them wanted to and indeed were expected to be relocated to Pakistan. However, the reality was quite different. Pakistan accepted responsibility only for those non-Bengalis who were domiciles of the former West Pakistan, central government servants, their extended families, divided families, and another 25,000 people on humanitarian grounds.[5] The repatriation process was carried out between August 1973 and April 1974. According to the USCR, 160,000 people were repatriated to Pakistan but the rest remained 'stranded' in Bangladesh.

DEFINING STATELESSNESS

The Convention Relating to the Status of Stateless Persons, 1954, defines a stateless person as one 'who is not considered as a national by any State under the operation of its law'.[6] In the period immediately after World War I, the two groups, stateless persons and refugees were identified under a common umbrella, but gradually refugees began to be acknowledged as a distinct category based on the causes behind their flight.[7]

Refugees and stateless persons can be differentiated as distinct legal categories on the basis of the argument that refugees have a nationality but no national protection, whereas stateless persons are without nationality and also without protection. However, although legally they are differently situated, both refugees and stateless persons can be similarly located because both groups are without protection and are marginalized sections of the population.

The Bihari Muslims cannot be identified as refugees in the strict sense of the term. Going by the strict definition of the 1951 Convention, they did not face persecution in their home country nor did they flee due to 'persecution or fear of persecution' from their home country. Nor can they be categorized as internally displaced persons because once again they do not hold the nationality of a state nor are they displaced within it. They are, therefore, defined as stateless people because they do not have the privileges and benefits of citizenship of any state. They fled from India in 1947, but they were accepted and granted Pakistani citizenship thereafter. It is interesting to note that the citizenship laws of Bangladesh apparently do not debar them from being citizens of the country. Article 2 of the Bangladesh Citizenship (Temporary Provisions) Order, 1972 (President's Order 149 of 1972) provides:

(i) who or whose father or grandfather was born in the territories now comprised in Bangladesh and who was a permanent resident of the territories now comprised in Bangladesh on the 25th March, 1971, and continues to be so resident; or

(ii) who was a permanent resident of the territories now comprised in Bangladesh on the 25th day of March, 1971, and continues to be so resident and is not otherwise disqualified for being a citizen or under any law, for the time being in force;

Since all Bihari refugees migrated to East Pakistan or Bangladesh prior to the cut-off date, i.e. 25 March 1971, with the intention of settling there permanently, on the face of it they could be recognized as Bangladeshi citizens. But Article 2B of the Bangladesh Citizenship Temporary Provisions Amendment Ordinance, 1978 (Ordinance no. VII of 1978) categorically states that a person shall not qualify to be citizen if he or she 'owes, affirms or acknowledges, expressly or by conduct, allegiance to a foreign state. . .'. According to this definition, the Bihari Muslims would not qualify to be citizens because they chose to be citizens of Pakistan.[8]

Present Situation

The current circumstances of the Bihari Muslims are largely determined by the apathy shown towards them by the successive Pakistani governments and their exclusion from the process of nation building in the newly formed state of Bangladesh. Pakistan preferred not to acknowledge them and Bangladesh did not consider them 'our people'. This was primarily due to two reasons: (i) For the Bangladeshis, the Bihari Muslims brought forth memories of pre-Partition violence. It was also believed that some of the Bihari Muslims had overtly and covertly participated in perpetuating violence against Bengalis. (ii) Since Bangladesh was created primarily as a homeland for Bengali Muslims, the Urdu-speaking people obviously had no place in the system. Some of the policies adopted by the Government of Bangladesh are pertinent in this regard. The first Constitution of Bangladesh in 1972 declared Bengali as the state language (Article 3) and identified its citizens as Bengalis (Article 6). Bengali nationalism has been defined as: 'The unity and solidarity of the Bengali nation, which deriving its identity from its language and culture, attained [a] sovereign and independent Bangladesh through a united and determined struggle in the war of independence, shall be the basis of Bengali nationalism.' Further, the Government of Bangladesh passed a Presidential Order on 28 February 1972, declaring the properties owned by the Biharis as abandoned and giving the state custodial rights over them. The Bihari Muslims felt increasingly alienated and gradually left their homes to live in temporary refugee camps where they felt safe.[9] Though it was initially thought to be a temporary affair, they have remained stateless and homeless for three decades now. The camps are congested and squalid and the residents suffer from acute water and sanitation problems. In an interview with the researcher, an elderly Bihari Muslim respondent from a divided family originally from Patna explained his situation tragically yet poetically by saying: *Na Khuda hi mila nà wisaale sanam*, which literally means that they are twice deprived. By a quirk of fate, they belong nowhere, neither in their country of origin, i.e. India, nor in their 'chosen' country, i.e. Pakistan, and nor in their country of residence, i.e. Bangladesh.

It is ironical that almost three-fourths of the population was born after 1971, and hence the younger generation does not identify with Pakistan. A study conducted in 1997 by the Research and Migratory Movement Research Unit (RMMRU), Dhaka shows that 59 per cent of the people identified themselves as Bangladeshis rather than Pakistanis. According to the findings of the USCR, the traditional Bihari leadership prefers integration with Pakistan. Some felt confused about their roots and felt alienated. Others maintained that if they were granted Bangladeshi citizenship, they would get a chance to lead 'normal' lives. In fact, there is an effort on the part of the Bihari Muslims to integrate themselves into the local society.

THE WAY AHEAD . . .

The predicament of the Bihari Muslims living in Bangladesh is reminiscent of the bitter history of a forsaken people. Bangladesh wants them to be repatriated to Pakistan. In the Country Update of the Fourth Informal Consultation on Refugee and Migratory Movements in South Asia, held in Dhaka in 1997, the Bangladeshi representative Mr Fakhruddin Ahmed said:

> The present political climate has now become encouraging for the Bihari Muslims to be addressed. The present government of Pakistan headed by Nawaz Sharif has shown flexibility in the past. It is hoped that the Government of Bangladesh will vigorously pursue the issue and find an honourable solution. The number of stranded Pakistanis may not exceed 250,000 and would hardly create any imbalance that could lead to a serious ethnic crisis in Pakistan. The stranded Biharis have suffered for too long, and it is high time that the international community particularly UNHCR took advantage of the favourable

political climate to encourage both Pakistan and Bangladesh to find a lasting solution.[10]

Pakistan's official stand regarding the status of the Bihari Muslims is vacillating. Sometimes the state does not even acknowledge their existence. For instance, at the same forum, the Pakistani delegate, Justice Nasim Hassan Shah, did not mention the issue at all.[11] However, at other times successive governments of Pakistan have given assurances of their desire and efforts to repatriate the Bihari Muslims, but they have not taken any concrete steps towards achieving this goal. According to Loraine Mirza, in 1984, General Zia ul Huq had promised to take the Bihari Muslims to Pakistan, 'even if I have to carry them on my back'. Despite the fact that a Trust was set up with Saudi money, with a planned expenditure to the tune of $ 278 million, nothing much was done. Prime Minister Benazir Bhutto did not do anything either.[12] Pakistan has been avoiding the repatriation of the Bihari Muslims mainly due to two reasons. The first reason is due to the expense involved in transporting and resettling the refugees. As of now, the Bangladesh government has spent 160 crore taka on the maintenance and upkeep of the Bihari Muslims. The second and more pertinent reason is the apprehension that an additional three lakh refugees in Pakistan may change the demography of the country. This could add further strains on the conflict-ridden Pakistani society.

Any refugee situation is the joint responsibility of the host country, the country of origin, as well as the international community. The purpose of human security will be defeated if there are people suffering any where in the world. The issue of the Bihari Muslims needs to be addressed within this framework. Under normal circumstances, the repatriation of refugees to their home country is the desired solution. But in this case, the solution cannot be so simple.

- Pakistan and Bangladesh should jointly discuss the matter and try to resolve the issue keeping in mind the best interests of the people and should not use them to further their own narrow political interests. Pakistan should also acknowledge its accountability and responsibility towards the Bihari Muslim refugees and accept them with honour and dignity.
- Since empirical studies and research in the camps in Bangladesh have shown that the younger generation has expressed their willingness to integrate into Bangladeshi society, they should be granted citizenship. It is true that Bangladesh is a poor country

with a very high population density. However, it needs to be recognized that refugees are not always a liability to the host country but may also prove to be an asset, if given the chance to reach their full potential.

- The civil society and international humanitarian organizations can play a constructive role in this regard, by helping in the process of integration, relocation, and resettlement.
- The Model National Law on Refugees, which is currently being discussed by the academics under SAARC Law, should also address the issue of statelessness.
- The UNHCR should play a proactive role in addressing the issue of the Bihari Muslim refugees. Although this organization has not been involved in the matter so far, it can extend its mandate to address their plight.
- Some Islamic countries close to Pakistan and Bangladesh could play a role in resolving this problem. Although their proposed intervention may seem to the outside world to be inward looking, it could be acceptable if people believed that the ends were to justify the means.
- Till such time that a reasonable solution is reached, the Government of Bangladesh along with the international community could help to improve the living conditions in the camps and provide the residents with basic education and vocational training.

NOTES

1. Studies on the topic are few and far between. This has been a serious impediment faced by the author even in the present paper. For a full-length study, see Loraine Mirza, *Internment Camps of Bangladesh*, Markham, Ontario: Crescent International, 1998.
2. United States Committee for Refugees (USCR), *Country Report 2001*: *Bangladesh*, USCR, 2001. These annual reports could be assessed through http:\\www.refugees.org
3. Kazi Mahmudur Rahman, 'Bihari Refugees in Bangladesh: On Way to Integration', *South Asia Refugee Watch*, vol. 1, no.1, July 1999, pp. 28-31.
4. Shahdeen Malik, 'Overview of the Situation of Refugees, Stateless Persons and Internally Displaced Persons in Bangladesh', Country paper presented at the Regional Consultation on Refugee and Migratory Movements in South Asia, New Delhi, 14-15 November 1996.
5. Mohammad Tajuddin, 'Minorities in Bangladesh: A Conspectus', in Sumanta Banerjee, ed., *Shrinking Space: Minority Rights in South Asia*, Kathmandu: South Asia Forum for Human Rights (SAFHR), 1999, p. 99.
6. The Convention came into force in 1960. For the text of the Convention, see

Collection of International Instruments and Other Legal Texts Concerning Refugees and Displaced Persons, Geneva: UNHCR, 1995, p. 75.

7. Guy S. Goodwin Gill, 'The Rights of Refugees and Stateless Persons: Problems of Stateless Persons and the Need for International Measures for Protection', in K.P. Saksena (ed.), *Human Rights Perspectives and Challenges (In 1990 and Beyond)*, New Delhi: Lancer Books, 1994, pp. 389-90.
8. Shahdeen Malik, op. cit., pp. 30-1.
9. Hiram A. Ruiz, *Fifty Years in Exile: The Biharis Remain in India*, United States Committee for Refugees (USCR), Worldwide Refugee Information http://www.refugees.org/world/country india/bangladesh.ifm
10. *Report of the Fourth Informal Consultation on Refugee and Migratory Movements in South Asia*, Dhaka, 10-11 November 1997, *Country Report, Bangladesh*, pp. 33-5.
11. Ibid., pp. 39-41.
12. Loraine Mirza, op. cit., 148-9.

10. *Managing the Internally Displaced in Sri Lanka*

RENUKA SENANAYAKE

This paper examines the management of Internally Displaced Persons (IDPs) in Sri Lanka by the state and other key actors who are responsible for protecting persons from and during displacement and facilitating their return, resettlement, and reintegration. It includes a review of state policies concerning IDPs and the effectiveness of administrative structures set up to implement these policies. The paper also discusses the challenges that lie ahead in addressing issues related to IDPs in the context of fresh peace initiatives by the government and the LTTE. The main arguments are limited to the displacement arising out of the ethnic conflict and are based on recent research[1] carried out in Sri Lanka, using the UN Guiding Principles on Internal Displacement as a frame of reference.

This paper will adopt the definition of Internally Displaced Persons provided by the UN Guiding Principles on Internal Displacement, according to which IDPs are 'persons or groups of persons who have been forced/obliged to flee or to leave their homes or places of habitual residence in particular as a result of or in order to avoid the effects of armed conflict, situations of generalized violence, violations of human rights or natural or human made disasters and who have not crossed internationally recognized State borders'.[2]

Background of Population Displacement

The minority Tamils, who make up 18 per cent of the population, predominantly inhabit the north of the island of Sri Lanka. The majority Sinhalese, who constitute more than 70 per cent of the population, inhabit the south. The Muslims, a second minority, live scattered among the Tamils in the north and the Sinhalese in the south, with a fair concentration in the east. Since independence in 1948, the Sinhalese and the Tamils have been engaged in political disputes over power sharing. The Tamils accuse the majority Sinhalese of hegemonic rule. Initially, Tamil protests were limited to passive resistance with demands for equal power sharing but these took on a militant form in the late 1970s with the demand for self-determination.

In 1983, following the killing of 13 Sinhalese soldiers in the north by the Liberation Tigers of Tamil Eelam (LTTE), anti-Tamil riots broke out all over the country. Since then the Sri Lankan government and the LTTE have been engaged in armed conflict which today is the main cause of large-scale displacement in Sri Lanka.

The 1983 anti-Tamil riots displaced more than 200,000 Tamils living in the south and other parts of the country. At least half this number is believed to have sought refuge overseas, while the others fled to the north and the east. Tamils of Indian origin took refuge in the hill country and in the north.

In 1990, in an act of ethnic cleansing, the LTTE evicted the Muslim population in the north. The result was the displacement of over 80,000 Muslims and some Sinhalese. A majority of the Muslims sought refuge in Puttalam, in the North-Western Province, and have been unable to return in any large numbers to date.

In 1995, with the intention of driving the LTTE out of its northern Jaffna stronghold, the military launched Operation Rivirasa during which an estimated 300,000 Tamils were displaced from Jaffna.[3] Most of them fled or were forced by the LTTE to settle in the Vanni mainland, which lies south of the peninsula. Subsequent large-scale military offensives carried out in the same area forced hundreds of thousands of civilians to move further south, mainly to the garrison town of Vavuniya.

Apart from these main incidents, civilian displacement has also taken place because of direct or indiscriminate attacks on civilians either by the LTTE or the military. Routine harassment, child recruitment, fears of reprisals, and prolonged government-imposed economic embargoes have also caused displacement.

For many civilians displacement has been both long term and recurrent. Some IDPs such as the displaced Muslims from the north have been living in temporary settlements for over ten years. Others such as the inhabitants of the Kayts Islands off the Jaffna peninsula as well as residents of the districts of Jaffna, Mullaitivu, Mannar, and Trincomalee have been displaced repeatedly since the start of the war. Furthermore, the displaced are not homogenous, as they do not belong to the same community or the same strata of society.

The UNHCR estimates that at present some 1.2 million people are internally displaced from the north and the east. Of these, 200,000 live in 400 welfare centres maintained by the government. The agency also estimates that one in every 25 Sri Lankans is displaced, while in the Northern Province one in every three persons is an IDP. While all ethnic communities have been affected by displacement, it is estimated that 78 per cent of the displaced are Tamils, 13 per cent are Muslims, and 8 per cent are Sinhalese. The Tamils are the most affected due to their geographic concentration in the conflict-prone areas.

Protection from Displacement

The need to provide protection from displacement has received scant respect from the main parties to the conflict. Rather than work to prevent or avoid displacement, the two main parties to the conflict have caused displacement. A research document compiled for the UNHCR[4] states that 'the primary reason for displacement is the war waged around towns, villages and civilian settlements. People leave their houses for fear of being caught in the middle of fighting between the Sri Lankan Army and the LTTE.' A survey in 2001 carried out by the Medecins Sans Frontieres among the IDPs living in state-run welfare centres in the Vavuniya District confirms this view. The study states that aerial bombing and mortar fire have affected the villages and homes of a majority of the respondents.[5]

Direct attacks by the LTTE on Sinhalese and Muslim villages in the north and the east have also caused civilians to flee. The most glaring instance of collective punishment by the LTTE was the expulsion of the Muslims and the Sinhalese from areas under their control in the north during the decade long conflict. An estimated 100,000 people were given 48 hours to leave the province. The LTTE, had issued orders that no assistance should be provided to these civilians, not even the provision of water.

Human rights violations by the main parties to the conflict and the paramilitary groups and the threat of arbitrary arrest, detention, torture, sexual harassment, communal violence, forced recruitment of adults and children by the LTTE, and the launch of retaliatory attacks by both the LTTE and the military have also caused displacement.

Despite the prolonged nature of the conflict, measures have rarely been taken by the authorities to prepare for displacement. The only measures taken by the military have been last-minute deadlines for civilians to evacuate an area. The absence of emergency preparedness was evident during the government's offensive against the LTTE in 1995. The government had no plan to deal with the exodus of civilians from the rebel-held areas of Jaffna and the Vanni to the military-held town of Vavuniya. There was no mechanism in place to receive the thousands of civilians fleeing the biggest military offensive against the LTTE stronghold. Several months passed before they received food, shelter, and other essentials from the government and other humanitarian agencies.

Similarly, during the 1990 expulsion of the Muslims by the LTTE, the government did not have an emergency plan in place even though it had prior knowledge that the expulsion was imminent. Instead, the government deployed the military and the police to prevent the fleeing Muslims from proceeding south.[6] It took nearly four years for the government to provide these IDPs with basic humanitarian assistance.[7]

Neither have the UN agencies nor the INGOs and the NGOs assisting the government been able to respond effectively to emergencies with contingency plans. The World Food Programme (WFP) in some instances in the past had responded to the emergency needs of some of the displaced.[8] However, they have been unable to deal with all IDPs uniformly and respond to all emergencies due to lack of consistent funding for their programmes.[9] For instance, despite an agreement with the government to assist a certain number of the IDPs, the WFP has not provided assistance to these IDPs since December 2001 due to a shortage of funding.[10] The WFP also has not been allowed in the past to assist IDPs in the LTTE-controlled areas.[11]

Protection during Displacement

The Sri Lankan state assumes responsibility for a majority of the displaced, providing them with assistance. The state, however, does less to fulfil its role as protector. The provision of dry-food rations is the main form of assistance. In some instances, this is supplemented with shelter in the form of camps or material for construction of basic huts. Financial assistance for relocation and resettlement is also available, and in some instances the government has initiated the construction of relocation villages.

However, despite what might appear on paper as a framework for relief for the displaced, a view from the field points to glaring disparities in the treatment and coverage of the displaced. Further, the numerous policies and institutional obstacles stemming from poor coordination among the different institutions responsible for the displaced has resulted in a denial of even their most basic rights as citizens.

The state provides dry-food rations worth Rs.1,260 for a maximum of five members per family. This assistance, which is based on the cost of living estimates of 1993, has not been increased to reflect the changes in the cost of living since then. The displaced say that it covers their needs for 10 to 15 days at most. As this amount is a ceiling, larger families face particular difficulties as do vulnerable groups such as the IDPs confined to camps or restricted to particular areas as well as single-headed families. In Vavuniya most of the displaced have been totally dependent on the food assistance they receive because of the severe restrictions that have been placed on their movement.[12] Further, such assistance is notoriously delayed and is subject to arbitrary cuts.

The overriding concern in most matters relating to the displaced has been national security. The Defence Ministry and other related agencies play a role in making crucial decisions that affect the displaced. In the LTTE-controlled areas of the Vanni, despite requests for assistance for 3,794,000 displaced persons (a figure endorsed by the government officials), the state only provides assistance for 170,000.[13] Further, it was the policy of the state not to provide these displaced persons with material for housing. These factors combined with severe economic embargoes, including on medicine, placed on these areas have made IDPs living here extremely vulnerable to chronic malnutrition and disease.

The provision of assistance has been seriously undermined by the state's own policies of economic embargoes, restrictions on movement, and laws such as the Prevention of Terrorism Act and Emergency Regulations which granted wide powers of arrest and detention to the military. Thus, the IDPs, particularly those belonging to the Tamil community, have been subject to arbitrary arrests, detention, and torture. The displaced living in state-run welfare centres in the Vavuniya District used to be periodically rounded up in the middle of the night and put through identification parades.

According to the Human Rights Commission of Sri Lanka, approximately half the detainees in Vavuniya are IDPs.[14] Disappearances, extra-judicial killings, arbitrary arrests, abductions, detention, and torture of IDPs by the Sri Lankan army, the LTTE, and other Tamil militias have been frequent in the north and the east. Amnesty International states that torture is about the most common human rights abuse affecting IDPs and other non-combatants.[15] Rape of both women and men also takes place as a method of torture. Data from the Human Rights Commission confirms the prevalence of torture in custody, especially in areas which host a large number of IDPs such as Vavuniya and Trincomalee.

In an attempt to respond to increasing criticism of its human rights record, particularly concerning the Tamils, in 1996 the state set up a Human Rights Commission with a mandate to look into human rights violations. The Commission has been able to assist in individual complaints, including those of the displaced, particularly in locating the whereabouts of those arrested and providing access to those detained when state officials have admitted to such arrests. The Commission has been ineffective in making a substantial impact on the human rights condition of the displaced, particularly with regard to restrictions on movement, prevention of arbitrary arrests, detention, abduction, and torture, economic embargoes, extortion, and other methods of harassment by the state, the LTTE, and the paramilitary groups operating in government-controlled areas close to the battleground. The Commission has also been unable to challenge the denial of humanitarian assistance to those in need.

The Commission has also refused to entertain complaints of gender-based violence. In the past the Women and Children Police desks, with a special mandate to intervene in instances of violence against women and children, were not active in the areas of the north and the east, leaving such complainants with little access to redress.

Policy/Institutional Landscape

Policies relating to the displaced have not constituted an integrated and comprehensive set of rules, guidelines, or laws. This fact combined with the absence of a single coordinating body has led to wide disparity in the treatment and coverage of IDPs. In some instances what has passed for policy are *ad hoc* directives that were designed to provide emergency relief in the early 1990s.

During the tenure of the previous government there were more than 10 government institutions involved in relief, rehabilitation, and reconstruction.[16] Each of these ministries, departments, and institutions have had different areas of responsibility, geographical areas of coverage, and work at different administrative levels with little or no coordination. Consequently, the displaced are unaware of their rights, entitlements, and the department or body that they should approach to obtain redress.

The two ministries responsible for rehabilitation and reconstruction were the Ministry of Development and Resettlement and Rehabilitation of the North and Tamil Affairs of the North and East and the Ministry of Rehabilitation and Reconstruction of the East and Rural Housing Development. The former Ministry understood its mandate concerning resettlement and rehabilitation as applying to the IDPs living within the Northern Province at present and not to those displaced from the province, while the latter Ministry understood its mandate to cover the entire island, except the north. In practice, however, the latter Ministry focused on Muslims residing in the east.

There appears to be no rational explanation for such a division of ministerial responsibility. One can only conclude that it was based on political considerations such as providing these ministers with an opportunity to work with their vote base. The ministers in question represented minority communities whose support was crucial in the forming of the previous government. Needless to say, this meant that the IDPs belonging to particular communities and who were concentrated in certain areas were not provided for at the ministerial level.

Further, since the mandates of these ministries were reconstruction and rehabilitation, certain crucial issues such as exercising the right to vote, access to basic documents such as identity cards, birth certificates, etc., as well as humanitarian concerns prior to resettlement or relocation lay outside the ambit of these ministries. This has been confirmed by repeated appeals by the displaced Northern Muslims to these ministries to assist them in securing their right to vote.[17]

Moreover, there were few programmes aimed at displaced persons with special needs such as the disabled, unaccompanied minors, and single parents. There is also confusion concerning the nature and scope of the mandates of UN agencies and other INGOs working in Sri Lanka. As a consequence of this there is inefficiency in the management of the displaced. For instance, it is unclear as to which agency has the mandate for protection of the displaced island-wide. Both the ICRC and the UNHCR work in the uncleared areas. The UNHCR does not work in Puttalam in the north-west, nor in Batticaloa and Ampara in the east, two provinces which host large populations of IDPs.

INSTITUTIONAL LANDSCAPE SINCE NOVEMBER 2001

Following a general election in December 2001, new structures and coordinating arrangements were put in place to deal with the displaced. Under the new government, the three main ministries with a direct bearing on providing assistance to the displaced are the Ministry of Resettlement, Rehabilitation and Refugees (RRR), the Ministry of Eastern Development, and the Ministry for Assisting Vanni Rehabilitation.

Though the ministerial allocation was again determined on political grounds, there has been some improvement, particularly in relation to coverage and coordination. The Ministry of RRR is vested with the functions of coordinating certain tasks that include food assistance, compensation, and emergency relief.

The Ministry of Eastern Development considers itself responsible for the protection of displaced Muslims in the entire island. However, in relation to reconstruction and infrastructure development, the Ministry of RRR is vested with these tasks for the north, while the Ministry of Eastern Development is vested with these functions for the east.

The role of the Minister Assisting Vanni Rehabilitation is unclear. It is understood that he has been given the task of coordinating assistance to Northern Muslims and not, as his title suggests, assisting IDPs in the Vanni, who belong to the Tamil community.

Some departments continue not to extend their regular services to the displaced. For instance, the Social Services Department, which has programmes for the disabled, the elderly, and children, does not extend these services to the displaced population. Similarly, the Ministry of Women's Affairs in the past have had no programmes in the north and the east.

COORDINATION

In an attempt to improve the planning of humanitarian assistance, the previous government embarked on two processes: the Relief Rehabilitation and Reconstruction Framework using the UN Guiding Principles as a normative base and the Human Disaster Task Force entrusted with the task of drawing up a Human Disaster Management Plan. It was hoped that these two processes would result in a cohesive policy to address the needs of the internally displaced with a single authority overseeing relief, rehabilitation, and reconstruction. With the change of government, however, the future of these initiatives is unclear.

Recognizing the need for better coordination, the report of the UN Office for the Coordination of Humanitarian Affairs (OCHA) in April 2002 stated 'that much needs to be done by the Ministry of RRR to ensure better coordination within government . . . there often appears to be limited coordination between ministries. Yet the cross cutting nature of IDP issues requires close inter-ministerial cooperation.' The Ministry of RRR more recently set up a Policy Planning and Co-ordination Unit within the ministry.

In the past, UN agencies and INGOs have also come under criticism for their lack of a collaborative approach. At the suggestion of the UN office of OCHA, a UN working group on internal displacement was established under the aegis of the UN Resident Coordinator with the presence of the ICRC and the Ministry of RRR in order to facilitate the UN responses ranging from humanitarian support to rehabilitation and recovery.

Return, Resettlement, and Reintegration

Until recently, the government's policy with regard to return was to assist only those IDPs who were willing to return to their place of origin.[18] In 2001, the government, changing its own policy, embarked on a crash relocation programme to resettle all IDPs living in welfare centres in Vavuniya[19] to alternative locations in the same district, providing them with permanent shelters as opposed to the past practice of providing materials for construction.

While this move was a welcome change from the inhuman conditions under which these displaced persons were kept in camps, the displaced allege that they were not consulted and that the sites were close to the forward defence lines at the time.

The overarching consideration in selecting these sites appears to have been that ethnic demographies existent before the conflict be observed. For instance, since Vavuniya in the north was considered by the government to be an area where Tamils lived, they decided to settle the displaced there, despite the fact that these sites were dangerously close to the forward defence lines and that the location could well become a war zone, forcing these civilians to flee again. Concerns were also expressed as to the sustainability of these settlements.

CHALLENGES AHEAD

On 22 February 2002, the new government entered a ceasefire agreement with the LTTE.[20] While there is no direct reference to the displaced, the cessation of hostilities as agreed upon under the agreement and the resultant measures taken by the government to ease restrictions on movement and facilitate access to food and other supplies has brought some relief to the displaced. Most importantly, it has created a change in the atmosphere from what might be described as completely hopeless to a more hopeful situation.

The new government has also taken a number of steps to ease the living conditions of the conflict-affected people of the north, in particular, the uncleared Vanni. New initiatives include: the supply of power to Jaffna; the disarming of paramilitary groups such as the Eelam Peoples Democratic Party (EPDP), the Peoples Liberation Organization of Tamil Eelam (PLOTE), and the Tamil Eelam Liberation Organization (TELO) with plans to integrate them into the armed forces away from the conflict area; the opening of the A9 road to Jaffna for civilian travel; and the removal of restrictions on fishing.

However, a number of protection issues have emerged. The new government during a seven-month period has only provided food assistance once. The displaced have also been targets of harassment, abduction, forced recruitment, and extortion by the LTTE. According to the ceasefire agreement, the two parties shall not engage in hostilities. There is a provision for the establishment of a monitoring mission to oversee the implementation of the agreement. The agreement also states that parties shall, in accordance with international law, refrain from hostile acts against the civilian population.[21] However, there appears to be confusion regarding the extent to which the Sri Lanka Monitoring Mission, established in accordance with this agreement, would be open to receiving such complaints from individuals.[22]

Following the ceasefire, some IDPs have already gone back to their places of origin. However, for most IDPs returning home is not a viable option due to the uncertain political climate, the absence of basic infrastructure, and the lack of livelihood opportunities. For return to be a viable option a number of issues related to protection, assistance, and coordination need to be addressed. The most pressing problem under the issue of providing protection is the continuing distrust between ethnic groups, the proliferation of landmines, and the lack of mechanisms for monitoring human rights.

Also needed are durable solutions that address the problems of infrastructure development and provide for essential services, policies which lead to the integration of the IDPs into the local community, and mechanisms to resolve disputes arising from land ownership use and assistance

However, as this paper argues, policy and practice in Sri Lanka in relation to the IDPs are at variance with international humanitarian law and the obligations enshrined in the Sri Lanka Constitution itself.[23] As recognized by international law, national authorities have the primary duty to provide protection and humanitarian assistance to the internally displaced. To fulfil these obligations in the Sri Lankan context, a number of changes need to be made.

Perhaps the most important recommendation would be to abide by internationally accepted rules of war. In the context of ongoing conflict resolution, guarantees of basic human rights should be made part of the ongoing negotiation process. To improve service delivery of assistance to IDPs, a central body/authority overseeing all aspects of protection and assistance should be established. Such a body/authority should be suitably empowered to liaise with all levels of government.

Other recommendations include the establishment of an accessible rights-based legal framework for the displaced, the review of state policies and practices applicable to the displaced in accordance with internationally accepted guarantees of human rights, the guarantee of minimum standards/criteria such as informed consent, and the participation in the decision-making processes as well as livelihood possibilities when resettling/relocating the displaced.

Notes

1. *Human Rights Violations faced by the Internally Displaced Persons classified by reference to the UN Guiding Principles on Internal Displacement*, Colombo: Centre for Policy Alternatives, 2001.
2. *The Guiding Principles on Internal Displacement developed by the Representative of the United Nations Secretary General on Internally Displaced Persons*, Colombo: Centre for Policy Alternatives, 2001.
3. This incident is commonly referred to as the Jaffna Exodus.
4. Claudia Ibraguen, Review and Analysis of Secondary Literature on Internal Displacement in Sri Lanka, compiled for UNHCR, 2001.
5. Medécins Sans Frontières, Holland, Assessing Trauma in Sri Lanka, 2001. http://www.msf.org/countries/page.cfm
6. M. Fais, presentation on Northern Muslims at a Seminar on Human Rights of

Internally Displaced Persons – the Sri Lankan Challenge, organized by the Centre for Policy Alternatives on 12 January 2002, Colombo.

7. See n. 1.
8. The World Food Programme provided relief to the Northern Muslims in 1990.
9. See n. 1.
10. Frances Harrison, 'Food Ration Crises in Sri Lanka', BBC, February 2002.
11. See n. 1.
12. Since 1992, the military and the police have been curtailing the movements of residents and more severely the movements of the displaced through the imposition of a pass system. The pass system was withdrawn on 5 March 2002, following a ceasefire agreement signed by the government and the LTTE and a legal challenge sponsored by the Centre for Policy Alternatives, Colombo in December 2001.
13. See n. 1.
14. Interviews conducted by the author with the Human Rights Commission in Vavuniya, 2001.
15. Amnesty International, *Sri Lanka: Torture in Custody*, Colombo, 1999.
16. Ministry of Development, Rehabilitation and Reconstruction of the East and Rural Housing Development, Ministry of Development, Rehabilitation and Reconstruction of the North and Tamil Affairs North/East, Ministry of Defence, Ministry of Social Services Rehabilitation Reconstruction Authority of the North, Reconstruction EPPIA Commissioner General of Essential Services, Department of Social Services, Divisional Secretariat, Provincial Council and other administrative authorities of area of origin and area living at present.
17. Fundamental Rights Application filed with the Supreme Court in 2000, sponsored by the Centre for Policy Alternatives, Colombo, Sri Lanka.
18. The only documented exception to this practice was in the early 1990s when the late Mohamed HM Ashraff, Minister for Port Development, Rehabilitation and Reconstruction, assisted the Northern Muslims residing in the North-Western Province to relocate in this area.
19. Relocation ('relocation' in official parlance means opting for permanent settlement in a new area as opposed to the area from which one came) is seen by the Government of Sri Lanka as the main option for landless IDPs living in the welfare centres in Vavuniya. A majority of the displaced in these camps are Tamils of Indian origin.
20. Agreement on a ceasefire between the Government of the Democratic Socialist Republic of Sri Lanka and the Liberation Tigers of Tamil Eelam, 22 February 2002.
21. Agreement on a ceasefire between the Government of the Democratic Socialist Republic of Sri Lanka and the Liberation Tigers of Tamil Eelam, 22 February 2002.
22. Ian Martin, 'Human Rights in Sri Lanka after the Ceasefire', report of a visit on behalf of the International Working Group on Sri Lanka, 26 March–3 April 2002.
23. Chapter 3 of the Constitution of Sri Lanka of 1978 guarantees freedom of conscience; freedom from torture, cruel, inhuman, and degrading treatment; equality and non-discrimination; freedom from arbitrary arrest, freedom of movement, freedom of speech, and freedom of association.

11. *Managing Refugees: The Role of the UNHCR in South Asia*

SUMBUL RIZVI

INTRODUCTION

The problem of forced displacement has been one of the most pressing issues facing the United Nations throughout its existence. Among the most vulnerable groups of people in the world are those who are displaced, whether as a result of conflict, persecution, or other human rights violations. The United Nations High Commissioner for Refugees began as a small organization in 1950 with a three-year mandate to help resettle European refugees who were still homeless in the aftermath of World War II. Since that time the organization has continually expanded to meet the growing needs of refugees and other forcibly displaced people.[1]

Since 1950 the core mandate of the UNHCR has not changed. The protection of refugees and the search for solutions to the problems of refugees remain the central objectives of the organization. But the environment in which the UNHCR works and the types of activity undertaken by the organization have changed significantly over the past fifty years. The scale of UNHCR operations has greatly increased; the range of activities carried out by UNHCR has grown; the range of UNHCR's beneficiaries has steadily increased; the number of international actors involved in programmes aimed at protecting and assisting refugees and other displaced people has grown significantly. Lastly, the organization has become increasingly involved in volatile and unstable places, as well as in situations of ongoing armed conflict.

As the former High Commissioner for Refugees, Mrs Sadako Ogata has repeatedly said, the UNHCR's fiftieth anniversary in the year 2000 has not been a cause for celebration. 'The fact that the world still finds a need for UNHCR should serve as a sobering reminder of the international community's continuing failure to prevent prejudice, persecution, poverty and other root causes of conflict and displacement.'[2]

With the rapid growth in the number of people of concern to the UNHCR, the complexity of the problem of forced displacement too has grown by leaps and bounds. In current times, radical geopolitical shifts have resulted in drastic changes of policies by states. An added factor has been the enormous growth in the numbers of the internally displaced; the targeting of civilian populations in conflict where humanitarian workers too are not spared; the rise in human trafficking and declining opportunities for asylum have further gravely impacted the work of the UNHCR in the past decades.

Migration in South Asia

As this Conference [resulting in this book] is looking at migration, refugees, and IDPs in South Asia as part of its deliberations, I would like to reflect on migratory movements in South Asia and emphasize the imperative need to distinguish between those migrating and those being *forced* to migrate, the distinction being necessary to better appreciate the protection needs of refugees.

Migration trends are central to the environment in which refugee protection is to be realized. As far as protection is concerned, changes in migration patterns represent a serious complicating factor. Refugee problems are not only closely tied to the spread of inter-ethnic conflicts and the capacity of states to respond to and resolve them but also to globalization.[3] It is increasingly recognized that refugees are part of a global migratory phenomenon in which people are prompted to leave their own country by a complex combination of fears, hopes, and aspirations. We thus cannot overlook causes of migration while looking to address the causes of flight of refugees.

Migration in South Asia is more of an intra-regional phenomenon and is linked to historical developments as well as cultural and linguistic affiliations within the region. A major problem of the South Asian region is over-population, which has led hundreds of thousands of Bangladeshis to migrate illegally into Pakistan and into Bengal and Assam in India.[4] Social and political upheavals in one country invariably disturb the political stability of its neighbours and cross-border population movements are a reality in the South Asian region. The birth of modern nation states in this region in the mid-twentieth century has led to massive mass migration and the rejection of people with the process continuing till date.

Added to this is the fact that the countries of the South Asian region belong to a common ecological zone and ecological factors of flood, cyclones, and drought lead to further migratory flows. Given the geographical location of the region, the area also services rapidly increasing transiting movements at the global level. It is often said that countries in the South Asian region are essentially countries of emigration and that these forces of emigration are often attributed to the relatively weak economies of the region as well as social injustices existing in many of these countries. Illegal status leads to vulnerability and reduces the migrants to the status of pawns in the larger political arena of the region. Opportunist sections of political parties in the region have tried to use these 'illegal' people as captive 'vote banks' by trying to 'regularize' their stay.[5] The problem of illegal stay leads to further abuse of the economic migrants due also to the absence of the right to work. They find sustenance in low-paid jobs in the informal sector as cheap labour, which the local populations are often unwilling to provide; and hence the migrants continue to remain vulnerable to varied forms of exploitation.

Issues regarding the obligations of migrants have been raised often. A just balance has to be struck between the duty of immigrants to respect the religion, culture, and the way of life of the country whose hospitality they enjoy, and their own right to observe their religion, their claim to follow their own culture, and speak their own language. This is going to be a problem in many countries, especially in the Third World.[6]

Within the region itself, India has served as a natural magnet for migration largely due to the comparatively better economic opportunities available. It is noteworthy that none of the South Asian states share borders with each other, but all the South Asian states share borders with India.

While this article is not meant to cover migration issues in general, it may be pointed out that the illegal entry of migrants often deprives them of the right to return when the country of origin may deny the fact of migration of its citizens to a neighbouring state. However, *forced migration* in South Asia is a growing phenomenon, whereby people are compelled to flee from their places of habitual residence to save their lives, but such movements may not entail the crossing of an international border.

Refugee movements may comprise persons fleeing from individual persecution for any of the reasons as stated above or consist of mass influxes of people. Most of the refugee movements in South Asia involve mass movements for persecution reasons on the basis of ethnicity or race.

Decolonization and the emergence of the modern state system of South Asia saw forced movements on an unprecedented scale. The partition of the Indian subcontinent in 1947 created nearly 15 million refugees. After its independence Myanmar saw the outflow of about half a million people. In 1959, China's entry into Tibet forced over 130,000 people into Nepal and India. Pakistan's military crackdown in East Pakistan (later Bangladesh) in 1970-1 sent more than 10 million Bengali Muslims and Hindus into India in search of refuge. The three wars between India and Pakistan and the continuing violence in Kashmir displaced over 850,000 Kashmiris. State-sponsored ethnic cleansing in Bhutan has caused the eviction of more than 130,000 of its citizens. In Afghanistan, the takeover by the Soviet Union and later, by the Taliban, sent 3 million fleeing to Pakistan. The ongoing civil war in Sri Lanka has forced nearly a million Sri Lankan Tamils to leave their homes and hearths in search of safety.[7]

It is evident that the incidents of forced migration in South Asia have been on a large scale and have occurred with repeated regularity. Many of these movements have been absorbed within the concerned states, while some have spilled over international borders resulting in the creation of refugees.

The respective host governments have dealt with the problems of massive migrations in the South Asian region by way of *ad hoc policies*. Refuge to forced migrants from neighbouring countries has been provided largely on political and geo-strategic expediencies decided by the respective governments in power.

Internal Displacement

This brings us to internal displacement where, by contrast, *internally displaced persons,* who are also forced to leave their place of residence as a result of persecution, human rights violations, or civil and ethnic strife, but have not crossed an international border are examples of *forced migration*. Not being deemed refugees, they are denied international support and assistance in the absence of approval by the concerned state. This is in line with the principles of international law regarding state sovereignty and non-intervention, whereby the responsibility for the safety of these persons lies with their national governments, and any intervention would be considered interference in the internal affairs of the respective governments. In India, the internal displacement of Kashmiri Pandits fleeing persecution from Kashmir to safer parts of Jammu and Delhi can be cited as an example of internal displacement.

Another well-known example of internal displacement in South Asia is that of the Sri Lankan Tamils, who have fled for reasons of persecution from strife-torn areas into other safer parts of Sri Lanka. Those who crossed an international border and fled to India have been recognized as refugees, though both these movements originated from the same cause.

The responsibility for Internally Displaced Persons (IDPs) falls first and foremost on national governments and local authorities. However, in many countries, IDPs find themselves in a vacuum of responsibility within the state. Under such circumstances their only alternative source of protection may be the international community.[8] Some details of UNHCR operations in Sri Lanka are provided later in this chapter.

Historical Overview of the Role of the UNHCR in South Asia

South Asia has hosted refugee groups as diverse as the Tibetans, Chakmas, Sri Lankan Tamils, Bhutanese, Rohingyas, East Pakistanis, Myanmarese, Afghans, and Bihari Muslims. Cross-border movements for a variety of reasons are a reality in the region. South Asian states have often been termed as kin states since they share ethnicity, language, religion, culture, and traditions. Social and political upheavals within one country invariably disturb the social and political stability of its neighbours.[9] The resultant effects are migratory movements, which may also take place for reasons of economic expediency, environmental degradation, etc. The porous borders of the South Asian region pose no real deterrent to these movements.

The UNHCR's first intervention in the Indian subcontinent was during the Bangladesh refugee crisis. In 1971, the war which led to the independence of Bangladesh caused an estimated 10 million Bangladeshi refugees to flee to India in what became the largest single displacement of refugees in the second half of the twentieth century. This involved the UNHCR in its largest humanitarian emergency to date. During the crisis, the UN Secretary General called upon the UNHCR to act as the focal point for coordinating UN and other international humanitarian assistance. This was the precursor of the 'lead agency' concept used in later years. After hostilities ended, the UNHCR assisted in organizing a mass repatriation of refugees to Bangladesh. Most refugees returned by the end of February 1972. In 1973, the UNHCR was also instrumental in organizing the movement of large numbers of people between Bangladesh and Pakistan—one of the largest population exchanges in history. In South Asia, the UNHCR was also involved with the Tibetan refugees, the Rohingyas from Myanmar who fled to Bangladesh, and in assisting the Asians expelled from Uganda by President Idi Amin in 1972.[10]

During the 1980s, when the Cold War intensified and superpower involvement in civil wars in different parts of the world turned these into intractable proxy wars, new waves of refugees poured out, particularly in the Horn of Africa and in Central America. Asia was not unaffected. In fact, the largest numbers of refugees during this period were those fleeing Afghanistan following the Soviet invasion of the country in 1979, ultimately leading over six million Afghans to seek refuge in the neighbouring countries of Iran and Pakistan.

The 1980s was the decade of large refugee camps. States had a clear strategic interest in granting asylum, but showed little interest in finding long-term durable solutions to solve the refugee problem. On the contrary, refugees were used as pawns in geopolitical games to destabilize regimes and to encourage insurgency in their countries of origin. An immediate example of this was the Afghan Mujahedeen in Pakistan. During this period, the UNHCR also became involved in finding local solutions for the problems of internally displaced people; a notable example of this is that of Sri Lanka where the UNHCR has been engaged in protecting IDPs and returnees.

Through the early 1990s, mass influxes occurred in the South Asian region, largely due to grave human rights violations in the countries of origin. The Rohingyas from Myanmar flooded into Bangladesh, and the Lhotsampas from Bhutan fled to Nepal via north Bengal. The receiving states provided initial support to the refugees with the assistance of the international community.

The evolution of asylum policies in the industrialized world took on a new dimension when large numbers of asylum seekers began to arrive in these countries and suspicions about the motives of many of these led governments to adopt increasingly restrictive measures to deter new arrivals. Many of these asylum seekers originated from the South Asian region. Legislative changes which have been introduced in industrialized countries have seriously affected the ability of asylum seekers to gain access to asylum procedures and safety. Illegal trafficking and smuggling of people, including their prolonged detentions, became a serious concern. Policies to deter irregular migration have led to the already problematic distinction between refugees and economic migrants.

While acknowledging that states have legitimate interests in controlling access to their territory, it is important to note that states also have international and humanitarian obligations to provide protection to those fleeing persecution from their own countries and seeking refuge in asylum states. The UNHCR reaffirms the fundamental right to seek asylum as indicated in the first broad-based document created by the United Nations to further the UN Charter—Article 14 of the Universal Declaration of Human Rights.

Some of the recent mass refugee movements where the UNHCR has been involved in South Asia are provided below:

Bhutanese Refugees in Nepal and the Role of the UNHCR

The UNHCR has been engaged in protecting Bhutanese refugees of Nepali origin in Nepalese refugee camps since 1991-2. The cause of flight of Bhutanese refugees was based on human rights abuses, arbitrary denationalization of the Nepali-speaking southern Bhutanese citizens, the Lhotsampas, denial of their children's admissions to school, denial of cultural and linguistic rights, and forced imposition of the ruling community's culture and language on the rest of the population. The minority Lhotsampas launched a movement in 1990, demanding the rule of a democratic government, with constitutional guarantees of human rights and the rule of law. More than 125,000 Bhutanese people, forming a sixth of the total population of the country, have been forced to flee or have been forcibly evicted.

Those fleeing first arrived in the states of West Bengal and Assam in India in early 1991. They eventually entered into Nepal and established camps on the banks of the Mai river in Jhapa in eastern Nepal. On the request of the Nepalese government, the UNHCR office in Kathmandu became involved in the management of the Bhutanese refugee camps. Close collaboration and cooperation with the Government of Nepal has facilitated the work of the UNHCR. The Nepalese government has established a Refugee Coordination Unit (RCU) under the Home Ministry which looks after the administrative and law and order requirements of the camps. There are nearly 100,000 refugees in seven camps in eastern Nepal. The largest numbers are in the Beldangi I, II, and III camps, with the second largest in the Pathari camp. The other camps are the Khudunabari, Timai, and Goldap camps.

Currently, the governments of Nepal and Bhutan are engaged in talks to find a durable solution to the problem of the Bhutanese refugees by way of voluntary repatriation to Bhutan. The contentious issue of verification and the modalities of repatriation have been discussed. The Bhutanese refugees have been caught in the middle of stalled negotiations aimed at resolving their decade-long situation. The tenth round of bilateral talks in December 2000, promoted by international pressure by the US Government, the EU, and various European governments, UN Commission on Human Rights and the UNHCR, helped break the impasse between the two governments. The UNHCR is closely observing the verification process and is making efforts to ensure that it is carried out in accordance with international standards and that the human rights of the Bhutanese refugees are upheld.

It is pertinent to note that complex questions of nationality and statelessness that arise have led to fears among refugees that those who were arbitrarily stripped of their nationality prior to their expulsion may be denied their legitimate right to return to Bhutan. It has been felt that the UNHCR should be included as an independent third party to the process. Agencies like Human Rights Watch have encouraged the UNHCR presence in the camps for dissemination of information about the verification process and in order to counter prevalent rumours and fears.

In Nepal, the UNHCR is also engaged in providing protection to Tibetan asylum seekers and in liaising with the Government of Nepal on their protection and assistance.

Role of the UNHCR: The Rohingya Refugees in Bangladesh

The UNHCR in South Asia was also engaged in the protection and eventual repatriation of the Rohingya refugees, a Muslim minority from Arakan state in largely Buddhist Myanmar. These refugees fled Myanmar for Bangladesh in the late 1970s. The UNHCR became involved in a complex and controversial repatriation operation on the eastern border of Bangladesh. The conflict between the Rohingyas and the local

Rakhine population increased after Myanmar gained independence from the United Kingdom in 1948. When, in 1978, the Myanmarese authorities launched an operation to systematically scrutinize the status of individuals living in the border areas and sought 'to take action against foreigners who had filtered illegally', the effect was to target the Rohingyas, who were not regarded as citizens as the Myanmarese government alleged that these people were relatively recent migrants from the Indian subcontinent. Widespread arrests and expulsions followed, and by mid-1978 large numbers of the Rohingyas had fled to Bangladesh. It was estimated that more than 250,000 Rohingyas had sought refuge in Bangladesh.

The pressure caused by the presence of large numbers of refugees and the need to highlight the plight of the Rohingyas led the Bangladesh government to appeal to the United Nations for assistance. As a result, a large UN relief programme was launched and coordinated by the UNHCR from May 1978. Thirteen camps were established and as the crisis eased Bangladesh sought a permanent solution to the issues. Hence, in July 1978 a bilateral agreement was concluded between the two governments, to which the UNHCR was not a party. The agreement provided for the repatriation of the Rohingyas despite much opposition from among the refugees and serious clashes between refugees and Bangladeshi officials, resulting in the death of hundreds. Deteriorating conditions in the camps and the arrest of Rohingya leaders led more refugees to return and by the end of 1979 more than 180,000 had returned to Myanmar.

The UNHCR spent over US $ 7 million on projects to assist in the reintegration of the Rohingyas in Myanmar. With only a limited presence, the UNHCR could not, however, monitor the situation closely to ensure that the returning Rohingyas were treated fairly by the authorities. Continuing discrimination and the eventual creation of a citizenship law making it even more difficult for the Rohingyas to get Myanmarese citizenship led to another influx in 1991-2, whereby 250,000 people were registered in twenty refugee camps in Bangladesh. Returns in 1992-3 were again carried out bilaterally by a Bangladesh-Myanmar agreement, from which the UNHCR was again excluded. In 1993, the Myanmar government finally agreed to allow the UNHCR to have a presence in Rakhine state and in April 1994 when this was established, the UNHCR facilitated the voluntary repatriation of Rohingyas from Bangladesh. The UNHCR faced strong criticism from human rights organizations which argued that the situation had not improved sufficiently to allow for safe return. According to the UNHCR assessment, the Rohingyas were better off in their homes in Myanmar where the UNHCR had launched major reintegration schemes and had a presence. There was another influx of Rohingyas in 1996-7, when Bangladeshi forces forcibly repatriated large numbers; however, this ceased after interventions were made by the UNHCR.

Currently, the UNHCR is engaged in a dialogue with the government of Myanmar on the question of citizenship of the Rohingyas and to cease forced labour practices. Facilitation of reintegration is ongoing in Myanmar. Over 200,000 Rohingyas have returned to Myanmar, leaving around 20,000 in Bangladesh. In all, the situation of the Rohingyas in Myanmar is a matter of concern though the original cause of flight of many of these has somewhat diminished.[11]

Role of the UNHCR with IDPs in Sri Lanka

Since the early 1990s, the UNHCR has been assisting IDPs in Sri Lanka. The main objectives of the UNHCR in Sri Lanka are to improve access to national protection and humanitarian assistance for IDPs in the north and the north-east of Sri Lanka and to minimize internal population displacement and provide alternatives to flight from regions of instability. This is particularly relevant to India as UNHCR Colombo attempts to *prevent* more people from fleeing to India by providing them alternatives in their own country. Other objectives include facilitating the return and the re-integration of displaced populations and extending the capacity of the government, the NGOs, and the displaced communities to respond to displacement and bring about lasting solutions.[12]

At the end of 2001, official estimates are that at least 800,000 persons remain internally displaced within the country. According to the most recent statistics from the Commissioner General for Essential Services (CGES) for June 2001, there are 704,663 IDPs receiving food assistance from the government. Of this number, 528,736 persons are staying with friends and relatives. The remaining 175,897 IDPs are staying in 348 welfare centres, most of them located in the north and the east.

In Sri Lanka, the UNHCR is engaged in a number of activities relating to protection and provision of emergency relief to selected IDPs. These include advocating directly with the LTTE *against* recruiting children in armed conflict; advocating with all parties in the conflict to ensure civilian safety at times of armed conflict; and collaborating with UNDP and UNICEF on raising awareness regarding the dangers of landmines. Examples of the UNHCR's relief work in the year 2000 include rehabilitating an orphanage for girls, conducting training courses for counselling children traumatized by war, repairing wells and reservoirs and providing water pumps for irrigation, rehabilitating schools and providing mobile health clinics on a weekly basis for IDP communities, providing loans for income generation, and providing temporary shelter particularly during the monsoon season.

UNHCR Engagement in the 1971 Influx of East Pakistanis into India

Pakistan had two distinct halves: West Pakistan and East Pakistan, separated by more than a thousand km. of Indian territory. Politically and economically, Pakistan was dominated by the West which caused much resentment in the Bengali East. Relations between the two halves steadily worsened, beginning with the military regime of General Ayub Khan in 1958. Bengali demands for autonomy increased in the 1960s and culminated with unrest in West Pakistan as well. This resulted in the fall of Ayub Khan's government in 1969. Elections were held in December 1970. The East Pakistan-based Awami League won the most number of seats nationally, though its support was only in the East. In the West, the Pakistan People's Party (PPP) won a majority of the seats. Initially the Awami League demanded autonomy. Negotiations on a constitutional compromise with the PPP and the Army collapsed. In March 1971, Army rule was re-imposed, the Awami League was outlawed for having declared the 'independence' of Bangladesh, and the Pakistani Army launched a massive counter-insurgency operation. Wholesale attacks on those suspected of supporting the Awami League occurred, as did widespread repression, accompanied by a severe human rights violations. All this resulted in the deaths of thousands of civilians and soon led to a refugee exodus on a colossal scale.[13]

The UNHCR representative in India warned the High Commissioner of an impending refugee influx at the end of March. In April 1971, the government requested for international assistance to cope with the vast numbers of refugees. By the end of 1971, the government estimated that 10 million refugees had fled to India. The UNHCR was designated the 'focal point' for all UN assistance. At that time, the 'focal point' was an innovation. It required the mobilization of international support and funds, procurement and delivery of relief supplies to India, and working in tandem with the Indian government.

The Ministry of Labour and Rehabilitation coordinated the relief effort on the ground. The Indian authorities registered refugees on arrival, issued an entry document, and gave them food rations. By the beginning of December 1971, an estimated 6.8 million were living in 825 camps, while 3.1 million were living with host families and friends. Feeding such enormous numbers was a considerable burden on India and the government expected to be reimbursed by the international community for its efforts. The UNHCR played a key role in mobilizing pledges and support from international donors and by the middle of June 1971, a total of US $ 70 million had been pledged in aid. The UNHCR also liaised with other NGOs, such as the International Red Cross, in the relief effort.

As the year progressed, relations between India and Pakistan steadily worsened. India had initially expected that all the 'evacuees' (refugees) would return by September 1971. However, conditions for their return were not conducive. India continued to support the Mukti Bahini movement whose goal was an independent Bangladesh. War broke out in December. Within two weeks, Dhaka fell to the Indian forces, and Bangladesh was liberated.

The next challenge was that of repatriation. By the end of January 1972, six million refugees had returned home, and by the end of February, over nine million had returned to Bangladesh. Contributions pledged to the UNHCR in response to an appeal to help with repatriation amounted to US $ 14.2 million, of which US $ 6.2 million[14] was transferred to the Bangladesh government to help with the rehabilitation of returnees. Though transit camps were set up equipped with medical aid and food rations, the vast majority of refugees returned directly to their communities.

Residual populations in the thousands were, however, left in both countries—Bengalis in West Pakistan who wished to repatriate to Bangladesh and 'non-Bengalis' in Bangladesh. India and Bangladesh made a joint statement in April 1973 asking that stranded prisoners of war and civilian internees be repatriated. The High Commissioner visited the region to discuss mass repatriation.

In August 1973, the governments of Bangladesh, India, and Pakistan signed the New Delhi Agreement which stipulated that Pakistani prisoners of war and civilian internees in India, all Bengalis in Pakistan, and non-Bengalis in Bangladesh be repatriated to their destination of choice. The United Nations was formally requested to facilitate this repatriation and once again the UNHCR was asked to coordinate all activities related to this humanitarian effort. The UNHCR was to assist Bengalis in Pakistan and non-Bengalis in Bangladesh to repatriate to Bangladesh and Pakistan respectively. The High Commissioner launched another appeal to support one of the largest air lifts of civilians ever organized. By mid-February 1974, over 200,000 people had been repatriated. In effect, the UNHCR became the *de facto* implementing agency for the 1973 New Delhi Agreement. It has been argued that the successful implementation of the Agreement influenced Pakistan's decision to accept the independence of Bangladesh. By July 1974, the UNHCR began phasing out the repatriation process; by this time, 116,000 Bengalis had been airlifted to Bangladesh and 104,000 non-Bengalis to Pakistan. One of the most notable aspects of this entire relief operation was the highly politicized environment in which it was carried out. 'The crisis increased awareness within the United Nations that mass movement of refugees do not only result from conflict but can in themselves create serious threats to regional peace and security.'[15]

No operation is a hundred per cent successful. There remained some non-Bengalis (Biharis) in Bangladesh, who are best described as 'stateless' persons. In 1999, they numbered over 200,000. Most of them live in 66 camps with poor facilities.

UNHCR Operations with Regard to the Tibetan Refugees in India

Tibetans first fled in the thousands to India in 1959, after the Chinese suppressed a Tibetan uprising and the flight of their spiritual and temporal leader, the Dalai Lama, who made his home in the state of Himachal Pradesh. Although the Chinese border was sealed in 1960, Tibetans continued to arrive in India over the decades. At present, some 100,000 Tibetan refugees are resident in India.

When the Tibetan refugees first arrived in India, they were accommodated in makeshift camps in Assam and West Bengal. The UNHCR was not involved in the operation at this stage. After the 1962 India-China war, when it became apparent that the refugees would not return to Tibet, the Indian government requested international help to cope with the refugees. The UNHCR began providing some assistance in 1964, though the office was established a few years later, in 1969. The Indian government provided Tibetan refugees with ration cards, identity papers, residence permits, and travel documents. Over the decades, many have been granted Indian citizenship. The Dalai Lama's government in exile continues to be based in Himachal Pradesh. There are over 85 Tibetan schools in India, catering to some 25,000 students. The state governments in India have allocated refugee families land to build homes and allowed them access to water and other basic necessities. Tibetans are settled in different parts of India and they live in relatively good conditions.

Tibetan refugees do not fall under the mandate of the UNHCR. Apart from the initial assistance in the early 1960s, the UNHCR has not had much of a role with this group of refugees in India. Among refugee groups in India, they are seen as a privileged lot. The Indian government continues to play a fine balancing act between providing for the Tibetans in India, guaranteeing them certain rights without compromising on the country's bilateral relations with China.

Presence of the UNHCR in Chennai to Ascertain the Voluntary Repatriation of Sri Lankan Refugees

There are approximately 100,000 Sri Lankan Tamil refugees in India, of which some 64,000 live in 111 government-run camps in Tamil Nadu and some 35,000 live outside the camps in Tamil Nadu. The government takes care of their basic needs such as food and shelter and allows the refugees to seek employment. The recent beginnings of a peace process in Sri Lanka have led to some hundreds of refugees requesting repatriation. The UNHCR will soon facilitate some group repatriation on a pilot basis. In the past, the UNHCR, through its office in Chennai, had facilitated the mass repatriation of thousands of refugees as well as a small number of individual repatriations.

The UNHCR was invited by the Government of India in July 1992 to assist the government in ascertaining the voluntary nature and willingness of refugees who were being repatriated to Sri Lanka, their country of origin. In response to the request, the UNHCR opened its office in Chennai, in the Indian state of Tamil Nadu, on 4 August 1992.

Between 1992 and 1995, out of a total of 54,199 refugees, a total of 31,062 refugees returned to Sri Lanka with the assistance of the Government of India, after the UNHCR had verified the voluntary character of the repatriation. The repatriation operation was suspended in September 1995 due to the escalation of conflict in northern Sri

Lanka, which triggered a reverse flow of refugees into India in search of safety and security.

Voluntary Repatriation

Although the situation in Sri Lanka has not been conducive for repatriation after 1996, the UNHCR has been receiving a number of requests from refugees in the government-assisted camps seeking voluntary repatriation assistance, either for personal or family reasons. About 79 have returned with UNHCR support, from 1996 to date. After the government-assisted repatriation ended in 1995, the UNHCR received a communiqué from the government of Tamil Nadu. It suggested the following:

(a) Voluntary repatriation interviews should be conducted in the presence of government officials;
(b) Those found to be eligible for voluntary repatriation assistance from the UNHCR should be assisted to return in groups of ten or more persons; (c) Split families are not to be assisted for voluntary repatriation, as the government felt that there might be some returnees who would be inclined to come back to India and seek re-admission in those camps where their families were residing.

PROTECTION FOR CAMP REFUGEES

As the UNHCR has no access to the refugee camps, this does not preclude UNHCR Chennai from taking a measured yet proactive role through (a) contacts with NGOs, the media, and the refugees themselves; (b) encouraging the mass media and human rights advocacy groups to act as the 'eyes and ears' of the UNHCR for the protection of the refugees; (c) intervening, when appropriate, with the authorities regarding requests from refugees about their local problems, for instance, the restoration of camp registration and (d) facilitating resettlement for camp refugees who have the possibility of being accepted for family reunification by third countries.

Solutions

As none of the South Asian countries have a refugee protection regime and since they are not signatories to the UN Refugee Convention and Protocol, there is a vacuum in providing protection to refugees.

LEGAL DIMENSIONS OF THE REFUGEE SITUATION IN SOUTH ASIA

It is interesting to note that despite facing large-scale refugee movements, none of the South Asian states have developed refugee protection regimes on an individual or regional level. All refugee movements are dealt with by individual governments on an *ad hoc* basis, with shifting policies and standards of treatment in regard to different groups of refugees. Even refugees from the same country of origin and fleeing the same persecution causes may be treated differently in comparison to those who had arrived at a different point of time.

Refugees are often confused with economic migrants, and the absence of a local refugee determination system results in further complications. In such instances, the refugee is further marginalized and may be subject to grave human rights violations, including the imminent fear of *refoulement*, i.e. deportation to the country of origin.

Refugees in South Asia are treated as foreigners and thereby subject to the control provisions of the *Foreigners Laws* and related legislation governing passports, entry, stay, and exit of foreigners. Refugees who are not extended assistance directly by the government of the host South Asian state usually approach the office of the UNHCR to seek international protection and assistance. The UNHCR has a presence in the South Asian states. To this end, UNHCR, under its mandate,[16] conducts eligibility determination interviews and issues Refugee Certificates to those who qualify as refugees.[17] Although the UNHCR Refugee Certificates are not formally recognized by some of the South Asian states, in practice the authorities have taken cognizance of the UNHCR's role and extended stay is usually granted to UNHCR-recognized refugees. It can, therefore, be said that in the absence of *de jure* principles, the South Asian governments have extended *de facto* protection to refugees in their territory. While not having signed the Refugee Convention, Pakistan, India,and Bangladesh are members of the 56-state Executive Committee of the UNHCR, i.e. EXCOM, which meets annually to discuss UNHCR global operations.

In the Indian context, the application of the international human rights instruments which have been acceded to by South Asian states are not enforceable by the administrative authorities or the courts unless the specific provisions are incorporated into municipal law by the legislature. This process of passing 'enacting legislation' has been largely ignored.

The only provision in South Asia which may be applicable to refugees is on a regional level. The principles on the treatment of refugees adopted by the Asian-African Legal Consultative Organization (AALCO) in 1966, although non-binding in nature, has elaborated the definition of '*refugee*' and set forth particular rights and obligations of refugees and states. India has largely adhered to the principles laid down in the AALCO principles and has *de facto* applied the expanded definition of the term '*refugee*' as found in the *OAU Convention*.[18] The AALCO has revised the *1966 Bangkok Principles on the Status and Treatment of Refugees* with an expanded refugee definition. The revision was formally passed by a resolution of member states in 2001.

The lack of domestic legislation or the non-ratification of international instruments relating to refugees has not hampered the judiciary in South Asian states, such as in India, in its path to safeguarding the rights of refugees. Indeed, some court decisions have enshrined principles on: the right to seek asylum; *non-refoulement*; and voluntary repatriation. The courts have arrived at their decisions without specifically entering into a discussion of international refugee law. They have relied on applicable 'rights' provisions in the Indian Constitution. Notwithstanding the generally positive reactions of the judiciary in some cases, 'gaps' nevertheless remain. It may, therefore, be useful to consider the value of acceding to the international refugee instruments and/or adopt a national law on refugees.

Opinions have differed in South Asia as to the value of acceding to the *1951 Refugee Convention* as some commentators consider it Eurocentric and out of date as it was adopted in the specific context of a post-war Europe. It is also said that international refugee law is currently in a state of flux and some of the provisions of the *1951 Refugee Convention* have little applicability to developing countries. Commentators also say that signing the *Convention* would do little to change the protection which refugees already enjoy in most South Asian states.

The UNHCR has supported dialogue and debate on the establishment of a formal 'rule of law' in the context of refugee protection. This has been largely possible through the Eminent Persons Group (EPG), formally termed 'Regional Consultations for Refugees and Migratory Movements in South Asia', which has played a crucial role in developing a '*Model National Law on Refugees*' for the South Asian states. The Model Law has been handed over to the Ministers of Law and Justice.

This will enable the setting up of a mechanism on refugee determination, treatment, and search for solutions, further ensuring predictability, accountability, and due process. In the absence of a national legislation on refugees, the burden of ensuring refugee protection is *inter alia* shifted onto a number of actors, including the judiciary, in order to protect the rights and interests of the refugees in the respective states of South Asia. In the near future, South Asian countries may, nonetheless, consider acceding to the *1951 Refugee Convention* and the *1967 Protocol* and/or enacting a national refugee law that can be enforced in domestic courts. Adoption of a national law on refugees, in particular, may be more readily acceptable as it is more efficacious and could take account of the particular needs of the South Asian states in accordance with international principles of refugee protection.

The development of a regional mechanism may also be a useful forum for determining the causes of refugee flows and encourage the identification of remedial measures to stem such flows.

ADDRESS ROOT CAUSES OF CONFLICT

States have often shown great hospitality and generosity in hosting refugees and other displaced people. Likewise, UNHCR—together with its partners—has on many occasions played an important role in protecting and assisting these people and in helping them to restart their lives. But history has shown that humanitarian action is of limited value if it does not form part of a wider strategic and political framework aimed at addressing the root causes of conflict. Experience has shown that time and again humanitarian action alone cannot solve problems which are fundamentally political in nature. Unfortunately, the kind of international political commitment that states have shown in dealing with human displacement in some regions has been absent in other regions considered to be of lesser strategic importance.

POST-CONFLICT ENGAGEMENT

States have also demonstrated a lack of political commitment to solving problems during the post-conflict phase, when the spotlight of the international media has moved away. Refugees and other displaced people often return to places where a fragile peace needs to be consolidated through the processes of reconciliation, rehabilitation, and reconstruction.

NOTES

1. Kofi Annan, UN Secretary General in the Preface, *State of the World's Refugees, 2000* (henceforth cited as *SOWR, 2000*), New Delhi: Oxford University Press, 2000.
2. Sadako Ogata, former UN High Commissioner for Refugees, Foreword, *SOWR, 2000.*
3. Erika Feller, Director, Department of International Protection, UNHCR, in 'The Convention at 50: The Way Ahead for Refugee Protection', *Forced Migration Review*, Issue 10, April 2001, pp. 6-10. Published by the Refugee Studies Centre, Oxford University (UK).
4. Former Justice Dorab Patel, Islamabad, Pakistan in a paper presented at the Regional Consultations on Refugee and Migratory Movements held in Colombo, Sri Lanka, 25-27 September 1995.
5. Tapan K. Bose, 'Protection of Refugees in South Asia: Need for a Legal Framework', South Asian Forum for Human Rights (SAFHR), Paper Series 6, January 2000, Kathmandu.
6. Former Justice Dorab Patel, Islamabad, Pakistan in a paper presented at the Regional Consultations on Refugee and Migratory Movements held in Colombo, Sri Lanka, 25-27 September 1995.
7. Tapan K. Bose, 'Protection of Refugees in South Asia: Need for a Legal Framework', South Asian Forum for Human Rights (SAFHR), Paper Series 6, January 2000, Kathmandu.
8. Francis Deng and Dennis McNamara, 'International and National Responses to the Plight of IDPs', *Forced Migration Review*, Issue 10, April 2001, pp. 24-7.
9. Tapan K. Bose, 'Protection of Refugees in South Asia: Need for a Legal Framework', South Asian Forum for Human Rights (SAFHR), Paper Series 6, January 2000, Kathmandu.
10. *SOWR, 2000*, 'History of Forced Displacement', pp. 4-11.
11. *SOWR, 2000*, 'Rupture in South Asia', Box 3.3, The plight of the Rohingyas, p. 75.
12. *UNHCR Global Report, 2000.*
13. *SOWR, 2000*, p. 60.
14. *SOWR, 2000*, p. 71.
15. *SOWR, 2000*, p. 76.
16. Under its Statute, the Office of the UNHCR is authorized to provide international protection and assistance to refugees and to find durable solutions to their problems. See 'The Statute of the United Nations High Commissioner for Refugees as appended to UN General Assembly Resolution 428(V) of 14 December 1950'.
17. As such, the role of the UNHCR in India has been recognized by the courts. See *Zothansangpuii* vs *State of Manipur*, Civil Rule No. 981 of 1989, 20 September 1989, Gauhati–Imphal Bench: Petitioner not to be deported, but based on sureties may be allowed one month to go to Delhi to make representation to the UNHCR. Reason–if deported, petitioner's life could be in danger; also see *Bogyi* vs *Union of India*, Civil Rule No. 1847/89, 17 November 1989, Gauhati–Civil Appellate Side, Petitioner allowed to go to Delhi to make representation to the UNHCR, and if granted 'Refugee Status' he would be released forthwith and need not serve sentence.
18. B.S. Chimni, *Reader on International Refugee Law*, New Delhi: Sage Publications, 2000.

Contributors

P.R. CHARI, former member of the Indian Administrative Services, is currently Research Professor at the Institute of Peace and Conflict Studies, New Delhi. He has worked extensively on nuclear disarmament, non-proliferation and Indian defence issues and has authored many books on these subjects.

V. SURYANARAYANAN is a former Professor and Director of the Centre for South and Southeast Asian Studies, Madras University. He has worked extensively on Sri Lankan Tamil refugees and has published in reputed journals.

TAPAN KUMAR BOSE is Secretary General, South Asia Forum for Human Rights (SAFHR), Kathmandu, Nepal, and has authored many works on refugees including *Protection of Refugees in South Asia: Need for a Legal Framework.*

C.R. ABRAR is Professor in International Relations at the University of Dhaka and the Coordinator of the Refugee and Migratory Movements Research Unit (RMMRU). He is also the coauthor of *Aid, Development and Diplomacy: The Bangladesh Case* and *Displaced within Homelands: The Internally Displaced Persons of Bangladesh and the Region.*

T. ANANTHACHARI is a retired IPS Officer and a former Director General of Border Security Force. He has worked extensively on border issues relating to India including trafficking in drugs, arms and humans.

D.R. KAARTHIKEYAN is a former IPS officer and has held various positions in Central and State governments including Director, CBI; Special DG, CRPF; Director, Police Academy, Mysore, Chief of Intelligence, Karnataka and DG, National Human Rights Commission, India.

WASBIR HUSSAIN is Consulting Editor of *The Sentinel*, Guwahati, and Associate Fellow, Institute for Conflict Management, New Delhi. He has been covering insurgency, ethnic strife, and other major political and social developments in India's northeast for the past 18 years.

D. SUBA CHANDRAN is Assistant Director at the Institute of Peace and Conflict Studies, New Delhi, currently is working on the Ford Foundation study on *India's Security Problematique*. He has worked on Pakistan, Kashmir, Indo-Pak relations and suicide terrorism.

ZARIN AHMAD, is a research scholar at the South Asia Studies Division, Jawaharlal Nehru University, New Delhi, and has completed her doctoral thesis on internal displacement in Sri Lanka.

RENUKA SENANAYAKE is a researcher at the Legal and Constitutional Unit in Centre for Policy Alternatives, Colombo, Sri Lanka.

SUMBUL RIZVI is currently Associate Protection Officer with the UNHCR, New Delhi. She has been involved in refugee protection and human rights protection as a private litigation advocate from 1986 to 1997.

Index